Sandinistas

# Sandinistas

*The Party and the Revolution*

Dennis Gilbert

Basil Blackwell

Copyright © Dennis Gilbert 1988
First published 1988
First published in paperback 1990

Basil Blackwell, Inc.
3 Cambridge Center
Cambridge, Massachussets 02142, USA

Basil Blackwell Ltd
108 Cowley Road, Oxford, OX4 1JF, UK

*Library of Congress Cataloging in Publication Data*

Gilbert, Dennis.
    Sandinistas: the party and the revolution/Dennis Gilbert.
      p. cm.
    Bibliography: p.
    Includes index.
    ISBN 1–557–86006–8
    ISBN 1–557–86072–6
      1. Frente Sandinista de Liberación Nacional. 2. Nicaragua-
Politics and government—1979- 3. Nicaragua—Economic policy.
I. Title.
JL 1619.A52G55 1988
324.2725'075    de19

*British Library Cataloguing in Publication Data*

A CIP catalogue record for this book is available from the British Library.

Typeset in 10 on 12pt Sabon
by Gecko Limited, Bicester, Oxon.

Printed in the USA

# Contents

# Preface to the Paperback Edition

When I began writing *Sandinistas*, my intention was not to record events in Nicaragua, but to depict the political landscape where they were unfolding. For me, the defining feature of that landscape was and remains the Sandinista Front. I believe that understanding the Sandinistas and the way they relate to other political actors, domestic and external, is the key to deciphering Nicaragua's current circumstances and possible futures.

For this paperback edition, I have written an epilogue describing conditions in Nicaragua on the tenth anniversary of the Sandinista revolution. Some minor corrections have been made in the text, but none that would alter my conclusions, since neither the character of the Sandinista National Liberation Front nor the direction of its relations with the other interests I examined have changed in any fundamental way in the year since the original edition was published.

Ithaca, NY, August 1989            DG

# Preface

This is a book about the Nicaraguan revolution. Like events in Nicaragua, it revolves about the Sandinista National Liberation Front (FSLN). The early chapters look at the Sandinista Front directly. They explain what the party believes, how it is organized, how it selects and recruits members, and how it relates to its affiliated mass organizations and to the revolutionary state. The later chapters examine the party in action. They deal with the party's changing relations with peasants, businessmen, Christians, and Yankees.

Like many Third World revolutionary movements, the FSLN conceives of itself as a *vanguard* organization. This concept is crucial for understanding the Sandinistas and I will return to it repeatedly. In the Marxist-Leninist tradition a vanguard is a self-selected, disciplined, revolutionary elite, capable of leading a mass-based transformation of society. What distinguishes the vanguard idea from other elitist conceptions of leadership is its emphasis on mobilizing and transforming rather than neutralizing the masses. The people are to become the active "makers of their own history." But in a backward society such as Nicaragua, they cannot easily do so without the vision and leadership that a vanguard provides. Clearly this is a powerful but problematic idea. Leadership is needed to prepare the masses for an unaccustomed role. But how does the vanguard lead without dominating, teach without becoming dogmatic?

A second recurrent theme is the tension between the Marxist ideology of the FSLN and the pragmatic compromises the party has made as it confronted Nicaraguan realities. In the 1970s, the party accepted Catholic radicals into its ranks, despite the leadership's initial doubts that believers could be true revolutionaries. At the end of the decade, the party adopted a revolutionary strategy with little basis in orthodox Marxism. In power, the Sandinistas have developed policies by trial and error, often backtracking when national character or social structure prove resistant to their plans. The most dramatic example is Sandinista agrarian policy, where emphasis has gradually shifted away from state farms and toward family farms (chapter 4). Yet the Sandinista leadership still regards Marxism-Leninism as the party's guiding doctrine and conceives of the party as the vanguard linking the present with a distant, socialist Nicaragua. How can the tension between abstract theory and concrete policies be resolved? The future of the revolution is wrapped up in this question.

*Sandinistas* was written for the general reader. I have not assumed any knowledge of Nicaragua or of the Marxist background to Sandinista thought. This preface is followed by a brief history of the Sandinista revolution, and explanations of Marxist concepts are scattered through the book, where they are most needed, in what I hope are easily digestible morsels. At the same time, I have resisted the temptation to write the sort of wide-ranging account that might be attractive if the subject were Iceland or Indiana but is likely to seem superficial because it is Nicaragua, a focus of endless controversy. Instead, I treat a few key topics in depth: the FSLN, agrarian policy, the private sector, religion, and US-Nicaraguan relations.

Focusing on the FSLN was an easy choice. The Sandinistas run Nicaragua today but remarkably little is known about them by the journalists and academics who follow the country or, so far as I can tell, by those who manage American foreign policy. The other topics were chosen because each reveals something unique and important about the Nicaraguan experience, because each fills an arena of intense political conflict, and because, taken together, they provide a reasonable composite picture of the Sandinista revolution. Inevitably, significant topics have been slighted. Were more time available to fill more pages, I would certainly like to write about education, health care, economic policy, and the constitutional process. All of these topics are touched on at some point in the book and readers can follow the citations to relevant literature.

No one writes about Nicaragua today without revealing something about his or her values. I am certain that my own prejudices and ambivalences will be apparent to the attentive reader. But I have attempted to be as objective and honest as I know how. Above all, I have tried not to distort the truth by a selective telling of the facts. I have tried to give enough vital information so that those who may not share my opinions can form their own.

Perhaps I should add that this is not a work of political criticism, constructive or otherwise, aimed at Nicaraguan revolutionaries. I have written for my own compatriots. It is not for us to tell Nicaraguans how to run their affairs. If there is a lesson in the last century of Nicaraguan history, that's it.

## Sources and Acknowledgements

Material for this book was gathered during a series of visits to Nicaragua, totaling about ten months, from 1982 to 1986. I have interviewed Sandinistas, opposition politicians, businessmen, journalists, farmers, religious figures, shantytown residents, peasants, and diplomats. In 1984, I spent four months in Matagalpa, a provincial capital I knew from two previous visits, to get a sense of the revolution in a small town setting – an experience I have shared with the reader at various points in the book. Using material from my own interviews and a variety of published sources, I have, wherever possible, allowed Nicaraguans to speak for themselves.

My treatment of the FSLN is heavily dependent on analysis of Sandinista texts, ranging from published speeches to internal party documents. Interpreting these texts is complicated by the differences among them. I have attempted to find underlying consistencies in a mass of documentation without blurring conflicts that may exist between Sandinistas, ignoring shifts in party position, or disguising ambiguities in party doctrine. My interpretative strategy for Sandinista sources has been shaped by these assumptions:

1 *Audience.* What the party says to its own militants is more credible than what it says to other Nicaraguans. What it says to local audiences is generally more credible than what it says to foreign publics, especially the United States.
2 *Authority.* The members of the National Directorate of the FSLN are the most authoritative party voices, especially when they are addressing their own areas of concern. (For example, Directorate member Jaime Wheelock, who is also agriculture minister, speaks for the party on agrarian matters.) Any document issued in the collective name of the National Directorate becomes official party policy and is binding on all party members.
3 *Consistency.* What a party spokesman once said is less significant than what numerous party representatives have said on many occasions; long-held party positions carry more weight than those asserted for relatively brief periods.

In all but a few instances, I have employed original Spanish texts and done my own translations for quotation. An exception to this rule is the 1977 *General Political-Military Platform*, a key strategy document whose complete text I have been unable to locate in Spanish.* The available English translation is consistent with contemporaneous references to the Spanish original and a partial Spanish text later published in Havana.[1] A photocopy of the 1979 *Análisis de la coyuntura y tareas de la Revolución Sandinista* was obtained from the US State Department under a Freedom of Information Act request. This document is cited as the "72 hours

---

*As the paperback edition of this book is being prepared, I am editing a collection of Sandinista documents in Spanish. Among them will be the original text of the 1977 *Plataforma*. For information, write Dennis Gilbert, Hamilton College, Clinton, NY, 13323.

document," as it is widely known, but all page references are to the Spanish original. (For the convenience of interested readers, published translations of key texts are listed in the bibliography.)

It is impossible to write a work of this scope without a great deal of help. I have incurred a considerable debt to many friends and colleagues. Carmen Diana Deere and Tommie Sue Montgomery shared their knowledge of Nicaragua and materials they had collected for their own research on agrarian reform and religion respectively. Earlier drafts of the manuscript were read in whole or part by Carmen Diana, Tommie Sue, John Booth, Don Freebairn, John Gitlitz, Joe Kahl, Walter LaFeber, Bill LeoGrande (who has aided and abetted my interest in Nicaragua since 1982), Pat O'Neill, Laura O'Shaughnessy, Tom Quigley, Mark Selden, Ann Stanton, and Nadia Tongour. The final product owes a great deal to their insights and criticism, but it is only fair to stress – because the topic is Nicaragua – that they bear no responsibility for my judgements. In fact, I suspect that some would disagree with much of what I have written.

I am grateful to librarians at two institutions. At Cornell, I continually depended on Olin Library's able reference staff, especially Bob Kibbee and Nancy Skipper. The library's Latin America specialist, David Block, provided extensive help with my initial bibliographic search on the FSLN and subsequently located and acquired important material on the party. At Hamilton College's Burke Library, Lynn Mayo compiled a bibliography on religion in Nicaragua, around which chapter 6 was developed.

Thanks are also due to Keiko Yamanaka, who helped construct the tables in chapter 4, to Beverly Tobin and Jennifer Lange for proof-reading, and to Jan Pieroni, who typed 100 pages of the manuscript using an unfamiliar word-processing program. My talented and good-humoured research assistant, Amy Russ, saved me from numerous errors, large and small. Without her help the book would surely have taken much longer to complete.

Parts of chapters 5 and 7 are drawn from my contributions to two edited books: Thomas Walker, ed., *Nicaragua: The First Five Years* (New York, Praeger, 1985) and Morris Blackman, William LeoGrande and Kenneth Sharpe, eds, *Confronting Revolution: Security through Diplomacy in Central America* (New York, Pantheon, 1986). This material is protected by copyright and is used here with permission from the publishers.

Clinton, NY, June 1988                                                    DG

# A Brief Political Chronology of Nicaragua, 1855–1988

1855–7     Filibuster invasion of Nicaragua by WILLIAM WALKER

1909     US forces intervene in civil conflict to depose President JOSE SANTOS ZELAYA

1912–33     US Marines in Nicaragua

1927     Tipitapa Pact, brokered by US, ends conflict between Conservatives and Liberals; rejected by AUGUSTO CESAR SANDINO

1933     Marines leave Nicaragua; ANASTASIO SOMOZA GARCÍA appointed head of National Guard at US urging

1934     Assassination of SANDINO, ordered by SOMOZA GARCÍA

1936     SOMOZA GARCÍA seizes power and has himself "elected" president

1956     SOMOZA GARCÍA assassinated by young poet, RIGOBERTO LOPEZ

1957     LUIS SOMOZA DEBAYLE succeeds his father as president

1961     FSLN founded by CARLOS FONSECA, TOMÁS BORGE, and SILVIO MAYORGA

1960s     FSLN guerrilla fronts repeatedly destroyed

1967     ANASTASIO SOMOZA DEBAYLE "elected" president

1972     Most of Managua levelled by earthquake

1974     SOMOZA DEBAYLE begins second term; UDEL, new opposition coalition, formed by PEDRO JOAQIN CHAMORRO; Sandinista commandos seize guests at Somocista Christmas party

1976–7     FSLN splits into three factions; TERCERISTA faction, led by ORTEGA brothers, gains control of party directorate and abandons rural guerilla strategy for strategy of urban insurrection and broad political alliances

1978     Assassination of PEDRO JOAQUIN CHAMORRO followed by rioting and general strike organized by UDEL; TERCERISTA commandos seize National Palace; September insurrection in major cities defeated by National Guard; international mediation efforts, backed by US, fail

1979    Reunification of the FSLN and formation of nine-member NATIONAL DIRECTORATE; final offensive defeats Somocista forces; NATIONAL UNITY GOVERNMENT, headed by five-member junta, takes power on July 19

1980    National Literacy Crusade; rapid expansion of expenditures on social programs; national unity alliance between moderates and Sandinastas unravels as Sandinistas consolidate power; first contra attacks from Honduras; business leader JORGE SALAZAR, conspiring against government, dies in confrontation with State Security agents; Sandinistas supply Salvadoran guerrillas preparing "final offensive" for early 1981

1981    REAGAN administration cuts off all aid to Nicaragua; agrarian reform and decapitalization laws announced at second anniversary celebrations, along with confiscation of 13 private-sector firms; talks with US representative THOMAS ENDERS fail to produce agreement; US decides to back contras

1982–8  Contra War

1982    Government imposes state of emergency after contra attacks

1983    Visit of Pope John Paul II highlights conflict between official church and revolution; Archbishop MIGUEL OBANDO emerging as leader of opposition; Nicaragua aligns with Contadora peace initiative

1984    CIA-directed mining of Nicaraguan harbor; US Congress cuts off contra funding; US and Nicaragua begin high-level talks in Manzanillo, Mexico; national elections; opposition DEMOCRATIC COORDINATOR refuses to participate; DANIEL ORTEGA elected president of Nicaragua; Sandinistas win 63 percent majority in new National Assembly

1985    US unilaterally ends Manzanillo talks; new national government headed by Ortega inaugurated; contra funding for "humanitarian" purposes approved by US Congress

1986    New agrarian reform law; renewal of US military aid to contras.

1987    Central American presidents sign peace plan promoted by President OSCAR ARIAS; US Congress refuses to renew contra aid

1988    State of emergency lifted; Nicaraguan government signs truce with contras in March

# Historical Introduction

It felt, said one survivor, "like the end of the world."[1] Near midnight on December 23, 1972, the earth danced beneath Managua, reducing most of the Nicaraguan capital to instant rubble. After the tremors ceased, uncontrollable fires swept through the city completing their work of destruction. By official estimates 10,000 died – the real figure may be closer to 20,000 – more were injured, and 80 percent of Managua's structures were lost. The city was left without utilities or hospitals; most of its 400,000 people were homeless and many, as they would later discover, were jobless.[2]

## Portents

Nicaragua's strongman, Anastasio Somoza Debayle, was at his estate, El Retiro, just south of Managua when the quake struck. To the hard-drinking Somoza it seemed as if "we were pieces of ice in a cocktail shaker."[3] Somoza escaped harm and his estate's oversized ranch-style home required only modest repairs. But at La Loma de Tiscapa, an extinct volcano standing over central Managua – and for forty years, the nerve center of the Somoza family's power – the devastation was nearly total. The Presidential Palace, which had been occupied by Somoza and his brother and father before him, slid from its place at the summit into the crater of the volcano. On the northern slope, the headquarters of the National Guard crumbled and a wide fissure split La Curva Palace, Somoza's official residence as commander of the Guard – his only public position at that moment. The nearby US embassy, for years the only foreign legation on the hill, collapsed, killing the ambassador's secretary.

The embassy and National Guard headquarters were symbols of the twin bases of the Somozas' power. In the days after the earthquake the Guard momentarily failed them, but the Americans did not.

The National Guard, a police and military force, was created in the late 1920s and trained by US Marines. The Guard was intended as a replacement for the Marine force that occupied Nicaragua for most of the period 1912-32. When the Americans departed in 1932, they left the Guard under the command of the first Somoza, Anastasio Somoza García, who soon converted the force into a personal army. From the 1930s until its demise at the time of the Sandinista victory in 1979, the National Guard was always led by a member of the Somoza family.

When the earthquake struck Managua, National Guard discipline collapsed. Guardsmen, including Somoza's own security detail, deserted their posts to attend to their families or to devote themselves to looting, while ignoring victims' pleas for help. Guard vehicles were used by officers and their men to carry off merchandise from battered stores. In the weeks after the quake, Guardsmen conducted a lucrative trade in looted goods and pilfered relief supplies.[4]

Somoza's friend US Ambassador Turner B. Shelton helped him reestablish order and reimpose his own authority. In addition to disaster relief, Shelton called in an American force of 500 men from the Canal Zone. The troops camped at Somoza's estate, which became the effective seat of government. Shelton spent much of his time there at the dictator's side. During this period, Somoza ruled by decree, sweeping aside the interim governing triumvirate he and Shelton had invented in 1971 to get around a consititutional prohibition on Somoza's succeeding himself as president.[5]

The earthquake presented Somoza with limitless opportunities to feed an already bloated family fortune. (The first Somoza, a man of modest means at the time he assumed control of the National Guard, left his sons an estate valued at more than $100 million when he was gunned down by an idealistic young poet in 1956.[6]) In the first half of 1973, the official emergency relief committee, which Somoza ran, received funds totaling over $32 million from the US government, but the Nicaraguan Treasury inexplicably recorded only half that amount.[7] Somoza discovered that blood donated for quake victims could fetch a considerable price in the United States. This operation proved so successful that it resulted in a profitable new Somoza enterprise – "Operation Vampire," a Somoza critic called it – that purchased blood from poor Nicaraguans for export to the United States.

The most alluring investment opportunities in the post-quake period were in construction and real estate. Somoza's government directed all aspects of the reconstruction effort. Enterprises controlled by the Somozas and their associates had an uncanny way of knowing where a road was going to be built or a new barrio located and above-average success in their dealings with the government. They ultimately monopolized much of the reconstruction business.

The self-enrichment of the Somozas and their private army in the aftermath of the disaster did not escape the notice of Managuans who were struggling to rebuild their lives. The regime seemed to be giving them a condensed course in what it stood for. Nicaraguans, Somoza told a skeptical foreigner, "believe in me," but people on the street jeered when Somoza's black Cadillac sailed by.[8]

## Poverty and Progress

The rancid flavor of the Somoza regime was only the beginning of what was wrong with Nicaragua in the 1970s. Nicaragua was, even by regional standards, a wretched place. Statistics gathered toward the end of the decade show low per capita income, exceptionally high levels of malnutrition and the highest rate of infant mortality in Central America. Nicaraguans faced a life expectancy of 53 years compared with 70 in neighboring Costa Rica, a country with a slimmer resource base. They routinely died of maladies that could easily be controlled by appropriate public health measures. Half the population was illiterate, but the proportion of the national budget spent on education was the lowest in the region and most school-age children were not matriculated.[9]

Nicaragua's backward economy provided a limited basis for improving the lives of its people. Yet the majority of Nicaraguans were poor not only because their country was poor but also because the benefits of national production were inequitably distributed. The country was something of a maldistribution champion. Thirty percent of all income went to the richest 5 percent of income earners; just 15 percent went to the poorest 50 percent. The distribution of land was even more skewed. Among the rural population, 5 percent controlled 85 percent of the farmland, while nearly 40 percent held no land at all.[10]

True, the Nicaraguan economy, driven by farm exports, was growing in the 1970s. In fact, over the entire period from 1950 to 1977, the economy expanded at a remarkable 6 percent per year. But the country's pattern of development was fundamentally flawed. While the GNP climbed, distribution of land and income were becoming more unequal. By force, fraud, or economic might, the big producers of export crops were pushing peasant families off their land. These dispossessed families became seasonal farm workers and urban slum dwellers or fled to marginal lands on the agricultural frontier. Between 1965 and 1975, the GNP and the number of children under five suffering from malnutrition both doubled. Clearly, many Nicaraguans were getting poorer as their country grew richer.[11]

## Opposition

The Somozas had systematically closed off avenues of change to those unhappy with their rule. The traditional means of replacing governments in Nicaragua – raising an *ad hoc* army, typically of peasants pressed into temporary service – was inadequate from the moment a well-equipped professional army passed into the hands of the first Somoza. The modern equivalent of the *ad hoc* force, a conspiracy of professional army officers, was no more effective against the Somozas, who kept a tight rein on the National Guard. Both military methods were, in fact, repeatedly attempted but always thwarted.

Civic methods proved equally sterile. At critical junctures the Somozas were quite willing to use bloody force against political opponents. The 1967 election campaign reached a climax when the united opposition, 60,000 strong, held a rally in Managua to demand guarantees for a fair election. (The Somozas had their own way of counting ballots.) When demonstrators began to march on government offices, the National Guard, seldom coy about crowd control, opened fire, killing 40 and wounding 100 people.[12] A decade earlier, when Somoza García was assassinated, his sons had systematically rounded up and tortured his best-known opponents. This "investigation" revealed nothing – the assassin, who may have acted alone, was killed on the spot – but it crushed any thought of preventing the dictatorship from becoming a dynasty.

The rule of the Somozas did not rest wholly on guns. Somoza and his sons knew how to buy off their enemies. On occasion, they negotiated political pacts with their opponents that corrupted and factionalized the opposition. They were incongruously sensitive to constitutional formalities. Somoza-dominated congresses wrote and rewrote constitutions to allow the Somozas to perpetuate their power or to create the illusion that they intended to relinquish power at some future date. Sometimes the Somozas placed men they trusted to be loyal marionettes in the Presidential Palace.

From the beginning, the Sandinista National Liberation Front (FSLN) rejected all the traditional methods of resistance to the dynasty, in favor of a popularly based guerrilla struggle. The organization was founded in 1961 by Carlos Fonseca (its chief theorist and guiding spirit for many years), Silvio Mayorga, and Tomás Borge. Before their long war against Somoza was over, Fonseca and Mayorga died in combat. Borge survived to become one of the key figures in the new regime.

The FSLN took its name from Augusto César Sandino, a nationalist hero who led an army of peasant irregulars against US Marines and the National Guard in a six-year civil war (1927-33). Sandino, whose exploits won him admirers throughout Latin America, pioneered the use of guerrilla tactics against a modern conventional army. The war was indecisive on the ground and grew increasingly unpopular in the United States. Sandino won his primary objective when the Marines were withdrawn in 1933. But in the truce period that followed, Sandino was assassinated by Guardsmen on orders from Anastasio Somoza García, who was just beginning to turn his military position into political power. In Sandino, the FSLN found the perfect symbol for a movement employing his tactics against a regime headed by Somoza's son, defended by the National Guard, and backed by the United States.

Most of the original members of the FSLN were student activists from working-class or middle-class homes – highly nationalistic, morally repelled by Somoza, and troubled by the wretched social conditions in their country. They were, observed Fonseca, driven more by shame than by conscience.[13] Their nationalism was distinctly anti-Yankee. They regarded the Somoza regime, created and sustained by the United States, as the logical outcome of the century-old US intervention in their country's affairs.

In the beginning, their ideology was not so well defined as their tactics. Most had been exposed to Marxism in the university and some were ex-members of the stodgy, Moscow-line Nicaraguan Socialist Party (PSN). But their immediate inspiration was the young Cuban revolution and its guerrilla hero Ché Guevara. For these Nicaraguans the victory of the Cuban insurgency, was, in Borge's words, "the lifting of innumerable curtains, a flash of light."[14]

Few of the early Sandinistas survived the two decades that separated the foundation of the FSLN from the fall of Somoza. In the 1960s, two attempts to develop guerrilla fronts were crushed, with considerable loss of life. The second and more successful was in the mountains of Pancasan southeast of Matagalpa, where Sandinista columns operated for most of 1967, attracting a considerable following among local peasants. But the lightly armed Sandinistas were no match for the helicopter-supported National Guard troops who moved into the region once Sandinista activities were detected by local authorities. Many peasant families suspected of collaboration with the guerrillas were among the victims of the counter-insurgency campaign.

The FSLN, which always regarded itself as an armed political movement rather than simply a guerrilla force, was also active in the cities. The party attracted followers in the universities through a student front, developed a clandestine urban support network, and attempted, with less success, to organize workers and slum dwellers. Sandinistas painted the party's colors and slogans on the sides of buildings to remind the world of their existence, set off bombs on symbolic occasions, and robbed banks to raise money for arms. When Sandinistas assassinated (in the organization's language, "brought to justice") a National Guard torture artist in late 1967, the Somoza regime responded with a violent campaign against the party and its collaborators. In the months that followed, most of the Front's leaders were killed, captured, or driven into exile. By the end of the decade there was little left of the FSLN.

## After the Earthquake: The Regime on Shaky Ground

The 1972 earthquake set off a rolling political crisis that gathered momentum through the remainder of the decade. The disaster fed dissatisfaction at all levels of Nicaraguan society. The destruction of many Managua businesses resulted in heavy unemployment. Shortages contributed to inflation, which was exacerbated by the rising international price of oil. Wages did not keep pace and the consequent decline in living standards fed labor militancy. The regime, accustomed to controlling union activity with a heavy hand, could not contain the aggressive organizing and spreading strikes of the post-quake years.

Businessmen were disturbed by signs of growing popular discontent and resentful over the Somozas' unbridled monopolization of reconstruction opportunities. The Superior Council of Private Enterprise (COSEP), the country's leading business organization, became one of the regime's most tenacious critics. Catholic church authorities had clashed with Somoza over control of the distribution of relief supplies. Christian activists working in Managua shantytowns could not forget how Somoza had victimized the victims to satisfy his greed.

On the first anniversary of the quake, Somoza invited himself to a commemorative mass celebrated by the church hierarchy in Managua's main plaza. But the dictator departed in anger over anti-regime sentiments reflected in the bishops' comments and placards held up by the audience. Guardsmen loyally disconnected the sound system carrying the archbishop's remarks.[15] The church was changing under the influence of "liberation theology" and reaching out to the urban and rural poor through the work of progressive priests and nuns. Many of the people in the plaza whose placards so vexed Somoza were members of the Christian consciousness-raising groups ("Christian base communities") that were springing up in Managua's shantytowns and working-class barrios.

As the decade unfolded, the concerns of individual interest groups became less parochial and more political. The problem, they concluded, was not disaster relief or wages or unfair business competition, but Somoza and the regime he headed. In the long run, the FSLN would be the beneficiary of this process of politicization. One sign of the times was the formation in 1974 of UDEL (Democratic Liberation Union) a broad opposition coalition whose principal objective was Somoza's removal. UDEL's supporters ranged from conservative politicians to labor activists, though its leadership was drawn from the bourgeoisie. Its dominant personality was Pedro Joaquín Chamorro, a charismatic figure with a long history of resistance to the Somozas, member of a prominent upper-class family, descendant of presidents, and publisher of the influential Managua daily *La Prensa*.

The FSLN was barely noticeable in the agitated political atmosphere of the post-quake period. The party's membership (by its own strict standards) was down to several dozen people. After the defeats of the late 1960s, the Front adopted a cautious strategy. In the mountains of north-central Nicaragua, a few Sandinistas quietly cultivated peasant support and trained a small, ill-equipped guerrilla force. Sandinistas in the cities provided rear-guard support to the guerrillas and worked to develop a network of "intermediate organizations" – legal fronts through which the FSLN could attract collaborators and build a popular following. The party was able to forge strong ties to Christian activists who were organizing the urban poor and rural wage workers. Among university students, the FSLN remained a strong force.

In December 1974, the FSLN broke a virtual silence of five years with a spectacular operation designed to capture the popular imagination without exposing its growing rural forces. Thirteen Sandinista commandos invaded a Christmas party at the Managua home of José María Castillo, a wealthy and prominent Somocista. Castillo's guests, including some key national officials and close friends and relatives of the dictator, were taken hostage. (The guest of honor, US Ambassador Turner B. Shelton, had departed before the Sandinistas arrived.) After several days of tense negotiations mediated by Managua Archbishop Miguel Obando, Somoza agreed to release more than a dozen Sandinista prisoners (including future president Daniel Ortega), pay a $1 million ransom, allow broadcast of a Sandinista manifesto, and fly the released prisoners and the guerrillas to Cuba in exchange for the Castillo captives. The cheering crowd at the airport left little doubt that the departing Sandinistas had won a popular victory – especially among the young.

Somoza answered with a declaration of martial law and an ugly two-year campaign of repression in the cities and countryside. The FSLN again lost many of its militants and leaders, including founder Carlos Fonseca. The guerrilla force that the party had patiently built up since 1969 barely survived and was driven into a remote corner of the country, cut off from contact with its urban support base.

But the National Guard's counterinsurgency campaign in the mountains was largely directed against the peasantry. Some 2,000 people – many of whom had little or nothing to do with the FSLN – were killed, often after having been tortured and mutilated. In one well-documented case, a Guard battalion, accompanied by local officials, surrounded the village of Varilla, and murdered everyone they could find, including 29 children. The officials subsequently divided the villagers' land among themselves.

American priests of the Capuchin order working in rural Nicaragua and the Catholic bishops of Nicaragua denounced what the prelates called a "state of terror" in the mountains and the church subsequently released the names of hundreds of peasants who had perished.[16] Under prodding from congressional and State Department human rights advocates, US military and economic aid to the Somoza regime was halted in 1977. Somoza could claim a military victory of sorts over the FSLN, but he was simultaneously undermining his own political position at home and abroad.

Under the pressure of Somoza's counterattack, the FSLN came apart in a bitter, three-way factional dispute over how to fight the regime. The Prolonged Popular War (GPP) faction, led by Tomás Borge and Henry Ruíz, favored maintenance of the cautious, long-term, rural-based strategy that the FSLN had adopted in 1969. GPP stressed gradual accumulation of military forces and peasant support in remote mountain areas, where the guerrillas could most easily evade contact with Somoza's National Guard. The GPP leadership showed little interest in the cities, except as a source of support for the struggle in the countryside.

In 1975, GPP was challenged by the Proletarian tendency, under Jaime Wheelock, a young Sandinista intellectual who had just returned from studies abroad. In opposition to GPP analysts, Wheelock believed that Nicaraguan capitalism had developed to the point that the proletariat rather than the peasantry was the most promising social base for a revolutionary movement. Wheelock argued for a more orthodox Marxist strategy based on organizing urban and rural wage workers. In October, Wheelock and his followers were expelled from the party by the still dominant GPP tendency.

The Insurrectional tendency (popularly known as the Terceristas, "Third-Way faction") emerged after the GPP-Proletarian split. It was the most pragmatic of the Sandinista factions and the most sensitive to the shifting political winds blowing through Somoza's Nicaragua. Led by Daniel and Humberto Ortega, the Terceristas understood that Somoza had managed to unite most of the country against his rule, laying the groundwork for a popular insurrection. They even saw the opportunity to draw disaffected businessmen into a broad anti-Somoza alliance and were willing to soften their political rhetoric to gain upper-class support. The Ortegas and their companions were also convinced that, in Nicaragua's volatile political atmosphere, they could set off a national insurrection through bold military actions.

## Insurrection

By early 1977, with the principal GPP figures dead, in jail, or isolated in the mountains, the Terceristas had assumed control of the national party apparatus and begun to implement their strategy. In May, they circulated a key party document, *The General Political-Military Platform*, describing their plans in detail. Later that year, they formed the "Group of Twelve," a committee of prominent businessmen and cultural and religious figures. Several members of the committee were secret members of the FSLN or fathers of party members. The Twelve, because of their connections to respectable society and the Catholic church, created a political sensation in Managua by calling for Somoza's immediate resignation and the inclusion of the FSLN in a provisional government. They soon became, in effect, the legal political representatives of the FSLN. In mid-October, Tercerista forces launched a series of attacks on National Guard posts throughout the country, demonstrating that the FSLN was still alive and capable of challenging the regime militarily.

The year 1978 transformed the political landscape beyond recognition and gave the Terceristas the chance to test their theories. It opened with the assassination on January 10 of UDEL leader Pedro Joaquín Chamorro. Few hesitated to blame the murder of Nicaragua's most respected opposition leader on the Somozas.[17] Thousands accompanied Chamorro's casket to the cemetery. Angry rioters torched Somoza-owned businesses and a number of American firms. A few days later, UDEL called a national general strike to support demands for an investigation of Chamorro's death and force Somoza's resignation.

The strike, which was supported by the country's major business organizations, was widely observed in Managua and the main provincial cities. It produced daily demonstrations and violent confrontations between protesters and the National Guard, but failed to budge the dictator. In February, a spontaneous uprising broke out in Monimbó, a working-class barrio of Masaya, after Guardsmen tear-gassed a memorial mass for Chamorro. The Ortegas' younger brother Camilo, who entered Monimbó to help the rebels, died in the fighting along with some 200 barrio residents.[18] In the months that followed, strikes, demonstrations and riots were regular occurences in Nicaragua's cities.

On August 22, two dozen well-rehearsed Tercerista commandos, disguised as members of an elite National Guard Unit, seized control of the National Palace, in a colossal replay of the Castillo raid. The Palace, a large, blocky survivor of the 1972 quake on Managua's main plaza, housed a large part of Somoza's government. Among the hundreds of captives were the members of the Somoza-run National Congress, then in session, and its presiding officer, a Somoza first cousin. The agreement that ultimately freed them was quite similar to the Castillo settlement (Archbishop Obando was again the mediator, and Tomás Borge was among the 59 Sandinista prisoners released from prison). But the delirious enthusiasm of the crowds that lined the route to the airport far surpassed the 1974 reaction and demonstrated that the FSLN had captured the powerful popular emotions that had been building since the beginning of the year.

The weeks that followed brought a rush of events as if political pressures had suddenly overwhelmed the dam that had long contained them. The day after the National Palace was evacuated, FAO (the Broad Opposition Front, successor to UDEL) called an open-ended general strike, which produced violent rioting in many cities. Rioting turned to popular insurrection in the northern provincial city of Matagalpa. For a week the city was held by lightly armed youths, cheered on by the population and assisted by a few GPP guerrillas. A smaller rebellion broke out in Jinotepe, south of Managua.

Events had, in fact, escaped the control of the FSLN. Like Monimbó, these were spontaneous uprisings. The Terceristas, who had preached popular insurrection, knew that they still had neither the arms nor the organization to lead a national revolt. By the beginning of September, however, they had concluded that the revolt was coming with or without them and they had best put themselves at the head of the movement. On September 9, Tercerista fighters launched a national urban insurrection with simultaneous attacks on National Guard posts in five cities. Thousands of the same lightly armed young volunteers who had recently taken over Matagalpa quickly joined the uprising, as did GPP and Proletarian regulars, in spite of the fact that both factions had resisted the insurrection plan. The rebels took control of substantial portions of several cities, including Managua.

The regime concentrated its forces and retook the cities one by one. The process began with heavy shelling, bombing, and strafing attacks. Delivered without warning, the attacks left heavy civilian casualties. Then, well-armed National Guard troops moved in, accompanied by tanks. The insurgents had the advantages of popular support and familiarity with the urban battlefield, but they were outgunned and soon overcome.

By September 20, the Guard had retaken all the cities, but "clean-up" operations lasted well into October. Summary execution, rape, random destruction of property, and attacks on institutions such as schools, health centers, and Red Cross facilities were common features of the clean-up phase. From this period to Somoza's last days in power, young men were especially vulnerable, since the Guard assumed that any male from 13 to 30, especially in a working-class neighborhood, was an enemy of the regime. Teenage boys were commonly seized on the street and carried off to jail if they were lucky or to isolated execution sites.

The September insurrection sealed the fate of the dictatorship. For ten days the government was at war with the nation. Then it became an occupying power. Whatever political support or popular indifference the Somozas might have counted on evaporated as the Guard went about its business.

In the wake of the insurrection, Nicaraguan moderates, the United States, and other foreign powers promoted talks aimed at securing the dictator's voluntary departure. Somoza delayed, haggled, and maneuvered for weeks, but remained intransigent. Most Nicaraguans concluded with Archbishop Obando that Somoza

> will not go except by force. I know him well. His ambition for power is immense. He was born in power and he is wedded to it. Here political tactics count for nothing, only pride, vanity. He is like a child with a toy. The majority of us underestimated the capacity for horror and destruction of this man and his National Guard. We never thought that he was capable of leveling entire cities, as he has done and we have seen. We never thought that the beast was so beastly, one of my priests says.[19]

September's military defeat was a political victory for the FSLN. Convinced that Somoza would stop at nothing to retain power, Nicaraguans of all classes turned to the organization that had established itself as the armed political alternative. The Sandinistas immediately began to reorganize and rearm themselves. In March, representatives of the three Sandinista factions signed a formal reunification agreement.[20] Whatever reservations the other factions may have retained about the Tercerista tactics to which the document committed them, they were not willing to risk being left behind by history. The agreement established a nine-man National Directorate, with three representatives from each faction. The members, who would guide the FSLN for years to come, were the Ortegas and Victor Tirado for the Terceristas; Borge, Henry Ruíz, and Bayardo Arce for GPP; and Wheelock, Luis Carrión, and Carlos Núñez for the Proletarians. The Directorate functioned as a collegial body: the three factions did not trust each other sufficiently to appoint a single leader.

During the tense, often violent months between the September insurrection and the Final Offensive of May–July 1979, the FSLN was able to train and arm thousands of guerrilla fighters. The Sandinistas, who had barely been able to field 150 armed regulars in early September, benefited from a steady flow of munitions donated by Venezuela and Cuba or purchased on international markets and channeled through Panama and Costa Rica – their first substantial external aid.[21] The shipments included some heavy arms which would later allow the FSLN to conduct conventional warfare on some fronts. In urban barrios, the FSLN was creating a network of civil defense committees, to support the guerrillas and meet the emergency needs of the civilian population. Somoza was, at the same time, rearming and expanding the National Guard. In guns and numbers, the Guard remained superior to the FSLN but the odds had improved.

For five days in April 1979, a Sandinista column with strong local backing held the northern city of Estelí. Somoza responded with heavy bombing and shelling and finally a large-scale ground attack, leaving 1,000 dead, most of them civilians, and destroying much of the city.[22] The battle for Estelí was a fitting prologue to the bloody struggle about to begin.

At the end of May, the FSLN commenced its "Final Offensive." The business-led, moderate opposition, operating through FAO, backed the uprising with a general strike that closed down enterprises across the country. Volunteers rapidly expanded the ranks of the insurgents, and thousands of civilian collaborators provided rear-guard support. By early June, the Sandinistas controlled much of the north and were mounting a strong attack with a conventional army from the south. Thereafter, the National Guard fought to maintain control of the central-western part of the country including Managua. The Guard used artillery and aviation against the cities with the same deadly results they produced in September and April.

After weeks of brutal combat, the government managed to dislodge Sandinista forces from their stronghold in the militant, working-class neighborhoods of east Managua. But the rebels continued to advance from the north and south, so that by mid-July they controlled most of the country and were poised for a final drive on the capital.

On July 17, in the early morning, Somoza, his son Tachito and half-brother José (both Guard officers), and a few other ranking officials boarded a plane for Miami. The caretaker government they left in place endured for two days before its leaders followed the Somozas into exile on July 19, the official date of the revolutionary victory.

Somoza's legacy was a country destroyed, with 30,000 to 50,000 dead; several hundred thousand maimed or wounded; a quarter of the country's population homeless; heavy damage to the economy, including the destruction by bombing of a good part of Managua's modern industrial district; a foreign debt equal to nearly one year's GNP – much of it generated by irrecoverable loans to Somozas and their friends.[23]

The archbishop had been right. Somoza fought on long after he was repudiated by the entire population and reduced to bombing his own cities. Finally, he was forced to flee for his own safety. One result of Somoza's intransigence was the complete annihilation of his regime. In the final days of the war, the National Guard simply collapsed, as officers and men shucked their uniforms and fled in fear of popular retribution. Somoza's National Liberal Party vanished in much the same way. The regime's strength became, in the end, its weakness. Another Latin American army would have abandoned the dictator once his rule became untenable and found a new strongman. But after more than four decades, the Guard was so wedded to the Somozas that it could not exist without them. The revolutionary government would be able to write on a clean slate.

The circumstances of Somoza's departure also undermined the political authority of Nicaraguan moderates and of the United States. Neither had been able to move Somoza. Their loss was the FSLN's gain. Sandinista strategy, determination, and courage had achieved what demonstrations, prayers, and diplomatic pressures could not. An organization whose membership at the beginning of the decade could almost be counted on the dictator's toes and fingers had become the core of a mass movement without precedent in Nicaraguan history. Its military forces were about to become the national army. Its leaders would soon be the nation's top officials.

## Revolutionary Nicaragua

The political history of Nicaragua since the Sandinista victory in 1979 can be divided into two phases — before and after the coming of the American-sponsored contra war.

At the beginning of the first phase, the dictatorship was replaced by a national unity government (officially known as the "Government of National Reconstruction"), in which the varied political forces that had opposed Somoza were represented. Industrialist Alfonso Robelo and Violeta de Chamorro, widow of publisher Pedro Joaquín Chamorro, were appointed to the 5-person junta that headed the new government. Businessmen and leaders of moderate political parties were appointed to many cabinet and sub-cabinet positions. But it soon became apparent that the FSLN would be the dominant force in the new regime. Though Daniel Ortega was the only official representative of the FSLN on the junta, two others were party members and subject to party discipline. In December 1979, Sandinista leaders directly assumed the most important cabinet posts. The legislative Council of State was inaugurated in May with a Sandinista majority, after the FSLN had forced changes in its representational formula. (Council members were appointed by the organizations they represented.)

The key power center in the revolutionary Nicaragua was the nine-member National Directorate of the FSLN. While it was consolidating the party's control over the national unity government, the Directorate was also restructuring the Sandinista Front and creating a network of affiliated mass organizations out of the popular following the Front had attracted during the insurrection. The post-victory FLSN was a selective, committed, disciplined, hierarchical organization — a vanguard party — whose members provided political leadership in settings ranging from urban shantytowns to government ministries. The Sandinista mass organizations, including labor unions, neighborhood committees, and associations representing small farmers, women, and youth, were open to all Nicaraguans and attracted hundreds of thousands of members. Through them, the Sandinistas spread their political message and mobilized people for practical tasks from building latrines to harvesting coffee.

The Sandinistas' efforts to develop their popular following were aided by the social programs of the national unity government. In social policy the early years of the revolution were Sandinismo's finest hour. By 1982, the government had enacted a comprehensive agrarian reform law, increased primary school enrollments by over 50 percent, and was on the way to eliminating epidemic diseases such as polio through volunteer public health campaigns. The Health Ministry had set up a highly successful program to combat the major killer of infants in Latin America, diarrhea. Not surprisingly, infant mortality was falling. A literacy campaign conducted by thousands of young volunteers in 1980 had sliced adult illiteracy from 50 to 13 percent.[24] Sandinista social programs were able to achieve a great deal in a short time because Somoza had left so many basic things undone, but also because the FSLN was wholly committed to transforming the lives of the poor and knew how to appeal to the idealism of volunteers who would tutor illiterates or innoculate children.

While the Sandinistas were consolidating their political power and building a popular following, they were alienating their business allies. The national unity government had pledged itself to maintaining "political pluralism" and a "mixed economy" of private and state enterprises. Businessmen assumed that this meant that they would have a strong voice in the revolutionary government and that private enterprise would be able to operate in an environment relatively free of government control. Neither proved to be the case, and the Nicaraguan bourgeoisie began to doubt that capitalism or Western-style democracy had a future in Nicaragua. For its part, the Sandinista Front insisted that economic policy had to serve the poor rather than the rich and accused businessmen of trying to sabotage the revolution by refusing to invest and sending capital out of the country.

By the end of 1980, there was little unity left behind the national unity government. Outside the orbit of the FSLN and its large popular base in the affiliated mass organizations, the government's organized support was reduced to a few minor left and left-center parties. The middle and upper classes had largely abandoned the regime and a loose coalition of conservative anti-Sandinista interests was emerging with the business organization COSEP at its center. The new opposition coalition also included the editors of *La Prensa*, several conservative to moderate political parties, some non-Sandinista labor unions, and the Catholic bishops' conference.

The United States, which had initially offered the revolutionary regime cautious support, had also begun to pull away from it. The United States was disturbed by the political marginalization of the bourgeoisie, Nicaragua's developing ties with the Cubans and Soviets, and the country's support for the Salvadoran insurgency. In late 1981, the Reagan administration decided to back a small band of former National Guardsmen who were already conducting a private war against the Sandinista revolution. Within a few years this secret force, known as the *contras* (from *contra-revolucionarios*), had grown into a rebel army of 10,000 men that was the subject of public debate in the United States.

The brutal tactics of the contras, reminiscent of their National Guard roots, did not win them a significant popular following, but the war imposed heavy costs on Nicaragua and the FSLN. By 1983, the conflict had come to dominate national life and the second phase of the Sandinista revolution had begun.

The politics of the second phase was marked by the intensification of the FSLN's conflicts with the bourgeoisie and Catholic church. The strains imposed by the war and the accompanying economic crisis also cut into the party's popular following. "Survival" became the watchword of Sandinista policy. The national budget was reoriented toward defense. Civil liberties were sharply constricted. Economic and military dependence on the Soviet bloc deepened. Social programs suffered – with the notable exception of agrarian reform, which was accelerated to bolster flagging rural support.

In 1984, the Sandinistas staged national elections to institutionalize and, they hoped, legitimize their rule to publics at home and abroad. During the campaign, wartime restrictions on political expression were relaxed, but most of the domestic opposition boycotted the elections and the Western governments whom the Sandinistas had hoped to impress did not increase their support for the beleaguered revolution. The Sandinista president and vice-president (Daniel Ortega and Sergio Ramírez) and the National Assembly (with a 65 percent Sandinista majority) elected in 1984 superseded the national unity government. The new political structure was formalized by a democratic constitution approved by the legislature in 1986. But under conditions of continuing wartime emergency, the new constitutional order was more a promise than a reality.

The war doubled the problems of an economy that was already suffering from Sandinista policy errors and business hostility toward the revolution. Defense was expensive, even though arms were donated by the Soviets. The Sandinista army drew off manpower that was needed for such basic tasks as harvesting crops, while contra forces mounted a direct attack on the economy, destroying infrastructure and disrupting production. From 1980 to 1986, the value of Nicaraguan exports sank from $450 million to $230 million.[25] This was grim news for an economy that runs on imported machinery, replacement parts, and other essential materials that must be purchased with dollars. By 1984, there was a national shortage of corn and beans, the basic components of the popular diet. Shortages throughout the economy contributed to an annual inflation rate which exceeded 1,000 percent by 1987.[26] Wages did not keep up with price rises; skilled workers and professionals discovered that they could make more money speculating in scarce commodities than engaging in productive labor. The economy, in short, was coming unraveled.

Nearly a decade after Somoza's flight to Miami, times were hard. But, Sandinistas reminded themselves, both the FSLN and Nicaragua had survived worse moments.

# Part I
*Sandinistas*

# 1

# *The Ideology of the FSLN*

Sometime in the early 1950s, two Nicaraguan high-school students in the provincial town of Matagalpa came across a copy of Friedrich Engels's *Anti-Dühring*, an unbending Marxist polemic, written several years after Karl Marx's death. Though they barely understood what they were reading, Tomás Borge and Carlos Fonseca were intrigued. Marxism promised a coherent account of exploitative, oppressive societies such as their own. Later, Borge recalls, they discovered other works of Marx and Engels in the "dusty library" of a local poet. Lenin was still an "unlikely and distant bibliographic allusion."[1] His writings, never widely circulated in conservative Nicaragua, were unavailable in Matagalpa.

Borge and Fonseca probably read Lenin as students at the national university in León. There they enrolled in the youth organization of the Nicaraguan Socialist Party (PSN), Nicaragua's Moscow line Communist party. Fonseca later became a member of the PSN, visited the Soviet Union and wrote an idealized account of what he had seen. But the two Matagalpans and many of their friends chafed under the constraints of the PSN's Soviet-dictated orthodoxy and cautious political strategy. The Socialists taught that revolutionary action must wait for mature historical conditions to produce the militant proletariat prophesied by Marx. In the meantime, the Somozas remained, unchallenged, in power.

At some point, Fonseca became interested in Sandino, whose childhood experience and serious, studious nature he shared. Both were poor, illegitimate sons of prosperous fathers. Attracted to Sandino's unyielding nationalism and commitment to armed struggle, Fonseca devoted himself to studying his hero's short life and fragmentary writings. Ironically he found the texts of many of Sandino's lost manifestos in an anti-Sandino tract, putatively written by Anastasio Somoza, the man who had ordered Sandino's assassination in 1934.[2]

The party that Fonseca and Borge helped found in 1961 bore the imprints of their youthful encounters with Marx, Lenin, and Sandino. At Fonseca's suggestion, the organization was named after Sandino. Twenty-five years later a visiting American Marxist asked members of another generation of Sandinistas what writers they read in the party's education program. The answer was always the same: Marx, Lenin, Sandino, and Fonseca.[3]

## Sandino

Augusto César Sandino was more than a folk hero, though he was certainly that.[4] His patriotism, political rectitude, identification with the masses, ingenious guerrilla tactics, triumph over an elaborately equipped foreign army, and ultimate martyrdom at the hands of the first Somoza made him the subject of a powerful national myth. Somoza's own assassination in 1956 and his dynastic legacy nourished the myth. For Nicaraguans of diverse ideological inclinations, Sandino and the dynasty became historic poles of political good and evil, national pride and shame. Only the Marxist left, misled by its own orthodoxy and Sandino's apparent lack of ideological substance, seemed indifferent to him. Fonseca was an exception among Marxists and he spent hours convincing his fellow revolutionaries that their "National Liberation Front" should be "Sandinista."[5]

Because the leaders of the FSLN were Marxists before they became Sandinistas, they read Sandino through Marx. Victor Tirado, one of the few survivors of the movement's early years, later explained the relationship between Marx and Sandino in the evolution of Sandinista thought:

> Marxism for the Sandinistas was a complete revelation – the discovery of a new world. And the first thing we learned from it was to know ourselves, to look inside our country into our people's heritage – toward Sandino. Through Marxism, we came to know Sandino, our history, and our roots. This is, among other things, the teaching we received from Marx – reading him, as Fonseca said, with Nicaraguan eyes.[6]

Fonseca and other FSLN writers portray Sandino as a revolutionary and staunch anti-imperialist with social ideas verging on Marxism. He might more accurately be described as a Latin American patriot, a mystic, and a populist.

About Sandino's anti-imperialism there can be little doubt. He was profoundly offended by US manipulation of his country's affairs and contemptuous of Nicaraguans like Somoza, who staked their careers on US power. He preached Latin American solidarity in the face of Yankee domination of the hemisphere. Sandino is remembered throughout the region for pronouncements such as the following:

... they call [our forces] bandits. The real and legitimate bandits are in
the caves of the White House in Washington, from which they direct the
plunder and assassination of our Spanish America.

Wall Street knows the price of traitors.

... the sovereignty of a people is not to be debated but to be defended with
arms in hand.[7]

But the conception of Sandino as a proto-Marxist is forced and largely
based on selective quotation. In his own time, Sandino was unreceptive to
ideologues like the Salvadoran Communist Agustin Farabundo Martí, who,
in Sandino's words "have tried to twist this movement of national defense,
converting it into an essentially social struggle. I have opposed this with all
my might. This movement is national and anti-imperialist."[8] Contemporary
Sandinistas often cite Sandino's observation that the timid desert the cause
as the struggle becomes hard: "Only the workers and peasants will go
to the end, only their organized force will attain victory."[9] But they
fail to note that the victory Sandino sought was over the gringos, not
the bourgeoisie, and in the service of national independence, not socialism.

Sandino lent himself to such treatment. He was not a systematic thinker,
but a man who expressed himself epigrammatically in letters, interviews,
and short manifestos. He occasionally used terms like "proletariat"
and "capitalist," but with little apparent concern for their intellectual
or ideological content. Contemporaries consistently describe Augusto
César Sandino as a mystic, a passionate dreamer, a man driven by
messianic urges who took the title of Roman emperors as a middle
name and identified his mission with Bolivar's.

Sandino believed that little-recognized spiritual forces operate in human
affairs; he claimed presentiments of impending events and the capacity to
communicate telepathically with his men. In an interview, he expressed
skepticism of the capacity of the state to change society, since the state
cannot reform the interior character of men.[10] "Injustice," he wrote a
friend, "comes from ignorance of divine laws ... it is against the law
of LOVE, the only law that will reign on earth when human fraternity
comes and men are of LIGHT, as father the creator has ordained."[11]

Such mysticism did not keep Sandino from becoming a populist, who
consistently sided with the poor against the privileged. His views reflected
his own early experience of poverty and his conviction that the self-serving
rich (*vendepatrias*, "country-sellers," he called them) were responsible for
American domination of his country. He condemned both the foreign
company that abused its workers and the moneylender who coveted an
indebted family's land. His army seized the possessions of rich landowners
who cooperated with the enemy and distributed them to the poor. Sandino
favored a national program of agrarian cooperatives for landless peasants.

But he did not see the need to expropriate existing landholdings in land-rich Nicaragua for this purpose. There was plenty of unused land on the frontiers. Sandino had no systematic objection to capitalism: "Capital can play its part and grow; but the worker should not be humiliated or exploited."[12]

Sandino's anti-imperialism and his populist sympathy for the poor were more or less consistent with the thinking of the early Sandinistas. His insistence on defending his cause with "arms in hand" appealed to their impatience with the Moscow-line socialists. What was missing in Sandino, from their Marxist viewpoint, was a systematic understanding of class conflict or the role of the revolutionary party. But what Sandino thought was less important to the Sandinistas than what he represented.

"Sandino's fight," wrote Humberto Ortega in 1978, "gathers the anti-imperialist and anti-Yankee traditions of our people, which . . . fortify the moral factor and the national pride in the popular struggle . . ."[13] Through Sandino the Sandinistas were able to connect themselves with native traditions of popular rebellion and anti-imperialism. He allowed them to associate their movement with a charismatic figure without risking personalistic leadership.

The FSLN adopted Sandino's red-and-black flag and based its motto on his "fatherland and liberty."[14] Many of the party's slogans were drawn from his manifestos. By regularly using photographs and line drawings of Sandino in party propaganda, the FSLN made his broad-rimmed hat as recognizable to his compatriots as Lincoln's beard is in the United States.

The Sandinistas developed a strong emotional identification with Sandino, strengthened by some personal links to his movement (the Ortega brothers' father, for example, fought with Sandino). Sandino's example may have helped wean the early Sandinistas from a dogmatic Marxism they were already outgrowing. But there was little in Sandino's thought that they could incorporate into the party's emerging ideology. Instead of Sandino's ideas, the Sandinistas adopted their hero's symbols, his image, and his myth.

## Marxism

Sandinista leaders have often acknowledged their debt to Marxism. At a conference commemorating the centenary of Marx's death, Victor Tirado declared, "We, the founders and builders of the FSLN, prepared our strategy, our tactics and our program, on the basis of Marx's teachings." Neither the FSLN nor the revolutionary government has ever publicly labeled itself Marxist, Tomás Borge reminded an interviewer in 1984; "however, I believe that we are Marxists." Speaking before a Sandinista military audience Humberto Ortega was more forthright: "[We] are guided by the scientific doctrine of Revolution, by Marxism-Leninism."[15] Sometimes party spokes-men, responding defensively to attacks from the right, insist that Marxism is only one among many influences on the ideology of the FSLN.[16]

Bayardo Arce – like Tirado and Ortega a member of the FSLN's National Directorate – candidly addressed the problem of ideological labels in a 1984 interview with three European journalists:

> [Q.] *One of you once said that Sandinismo is the application of Marxism-Leninism to the reality of Nicaragua. Is that a definition?* [Arce:] I would say yes, as long as we leave the essential problem of the arbitrary connotations of language. . . . When you say Marxism or Marxism-Leninism, everyone grabs his mental register – meagerly supplied, of course, with facts – and click-click-click out comes the Kremlin. That's nonsense.[17]

The evidence examined in this chapter leaves little doubt that Marxism is the basic source of Sandinista thought. However, the Sandinistas have not treated Marxism as a fixed canon but as a body of insights that they can adapt to their own needs and Nicaraguan conditions. The iconoclasm of Sandinista Marxism is reinforced by an underlying suspicion of abstract theory. Fonseca warned the party of the dangers of "sterile dogmatism" and "pseudo-Marxist gobbledygook" and even suggested that Nicaraguan radicals were lucky to know so little about political theory. Their innocence, he believed, saved them from political paralysis and internecine conflict. (The debates that divided the FSLN in the mid-1970s were an obvious exception, which Fonseca concluded, were the result of "political tourism" and the consequent importation of foreign habits.)[18]

As generations of Marxist polemics demonstrate, Marx's intellectual legacy is subject to varied interpretations. Any Marxist attempt to under-stand the world must come to grips with the historical schema that Marx and his collaborator Engels first laid out in the 1848 *Communist Manifesto*. The *Manifesto* scenario forms the background against which the broad outlines of Sandinista theory developed.

In the *Manifesto* and much of his subsequent work, Marx was con-cerned with the transitional periods that separate three great historical epochs: feudalism, capitalism, and socialism. Marx analyzed the sweeping economic transformation that undermined feudal society and the political revolutions that substituted the rule of the bourgeoisie – the modernizing class of merchants and industrialists who promoted economic change – for that of the land-owning aristocracy. The capitalist order that arose out of feudalism freed the peasant masses from the hereditary obligations of serfdom and created unprecedented material abundance.

But capitalism, Marx concluded, was a flawed system. As it matured, capitalist society was itself moving inexorably toward self-destruction. The wrenching boom-and-bust cycle of the capitalist economy demonstrated the inability of the system to manage its own explosive productivity. The proletariat – the class of urban wage earners created by capitalist growth – threatened the political stability of the bourgeois order. Exploited by their employers and victimized by periodic depressions, the workers were developing a consciousness of their own interests and a capacity for political organization which would allow them to challenge the rule of the bourgeoisie and assume the lead in the creation of a new, just, and rational society: socialism.

The parallel which Marx draws between the two transitions depends on an implicit theory of progressive classes. At a critical moment in history, the progressive class, by pursuing its own objectives, moves the entire society forward. The bourgeoisie played this role in the first transformation. The proletariat would do so in the second.

Marx was convinced that human consciousness advanced in tandem with the material aspects of society. Historically, as people extended their control of nature and learned to cooperate for purposes of production, they freed themselves from superstition and developed a more progressive social consciousness. His view suggests a long-term optimism about the capacity of human beings to remake themselves. But it also carries a qualifying, short-run pessimism. If consciousness is linked to material progress, it cannot leap ahead of material development. Marx would not, for example, expect socialist ideas to prosper among feudal peasants or, for that matter, the peasants of contemporary Nicaragua: their backward material lives limit their political outlook.

Marx was a brilliant political sociologist. Much of what is known about the social bases of class consciousness depends on his insights. But he was obviously less successful as a prophet. The urban-based proletarian revolutions that he expected in the advanced capitalist societies never came. Instead, the revolutionary upheavals of the twentieth century occurred in backward, rural societies, like Russia, Mexico and China. As social theorists and revolutionaries surveyed the failure, they raised questions about Marx's work that would later be relevant to the development of Sandinismo.

One set of questions concerned the role of leadership. Do historical processes lead inevitably to revolution or do they require the efforts of radical intellectuals and professional revolutionaries like Marx and Lenin to unleash their potential? Another concerned the locus of revolution. If revolutions were not taking place in advanced capitalist societies, why not? Could a socialist revolution take place in a backward society? A third set of questions revolved around the post-revolutionary situation. If socialist revolutionaries came to power in a backward society, could they immediately initiate socialist policies or would they have to promote capitalist development to achieve the level of material abundance that Marx regarded as a precondition of socialism? In either case, what should be the character of the post-revolutionary state? Decades of Marxist debate have swirled about these questions.

No participant in the debate has been more influential than V. I. Lenin, whose ideas have dominated Latin American thinking about Marx since the 1920s. Lenin's contribution centers on the vanguard party, imperialism, and the revolutionary state.

Lenin's conception of a vanguard party probably did more than any other Marxist idea to shape the FSLN. Lenin contended that a vanguard organization of professional revolutionaries was a prerequisite to socialist revolution. Without the leadership of a vanguard party the workers, however militant, could never advance beyond what Lenin called "trade union consciousness," the viewpoint that focuses on narrow economic issues – hours and wages in a given firm or industry – while ignoring the character of the larger socio-economic system. Lenin proposed that membership in the vanguard party be selective. Only the most able, dedicated, and politically sophisticated would be asked to join. Since the vanguard's objective was the overthrow of the existing order, its operations must be clandestine, disciplined, and centralized. Security also favored an organization of modest size. But the vanguard could not succeed in isolation from the masses of workers. Members of the vanguard would have to immerse themselves in the lives of the workers and the activities of their unions and political organizations. The vanguard party exists to channel the "spontaneous" protests of the masses. "Unless the masses are organized, the proletariat is nothing," Lenin wrote in 1905. "Organized – it is everything."[19]

Lenin's vanguard, externally elitist and internally authoritarian, appears to contradict the democratic objectives of his socialism. When Lenin first attempted to impose the concept on his own party, Leon Trotsky warned of the dangers of "substitutionism": "Lenin's methods lead to this: the party organization at first substitutes itself for the party as a whole; then the Central Committee substitutes itself for the organization; and finally a single 'dictator' substitutes himself for the Central Committee."[20]

Lenin regarded the vanguard as a crucial but transitory expedient. He modified his initial conception of the vanguard's internal organization by adopting the notion of "democratic centralism." The party's actions must be governed by centralized authority, but leaders at successive levels in the party hierarchy should be elected by and accountable to those below.

Lenin's concern with imperialism grew out of his need to explain the continuing stability of the capitalist systems of Western Europe. He concluded that advanced capitalism had for the moment secured itself by extending its dominion over the underdeveloped areas of the world. In this manner the Western bourgeoisie was able to find profitable investment outlets for the large concentrations of capital that were characteristic of this "monopoly" stage of capitalist development and mollify some sectors of the proletariat by, in effect, sharing the spoils of colonial exploitation. Inevitably, these attractions extended capitalist competition into the underdeveloped world and even set off wars among capitalist powers over colonial possessions.

Under monopoly capitalism there were not only oppressed classes, but also oppressed nations. Lenin, who viewed revolution as a global process, urged socialists in backward societies dominated by the West to support national liberation movements, even when their participation required an alliance with the local bourgeoisie. In Marxist terms, such societies are at a precapitalist stage of development and their incipient national bourgeoisie might still play a progressive role. National liberation struggles can advance humanity on two fronts by simultaneously attacking monopoly capitalism in Europe and the remnants of feudalism in underdeveloped areas.

Lenin had no occasion to consider what might follow a successful national liberation struggle. He did urge that socialists maintain a separate identity within the liberation movement and regard their alliance with the national bourgeoisie as "temporary."[21] Lenin's own policies in backward Russia after 1917 suggest that he would favor rapid consolidation of socialist political power but only gradual implementation of socialist economic policies in a postcolonial society. The transition to socialism in an underdeveloped nation, he warned, must be a "prolonged, complex" process. Just how complex is suggested by the fact that by 1921 he found himself promoting capitalist development under state regulation in the Soviet Union. "We must," he declared in a speech that year, "first set to work in this small-peasant country to build solid gangways to socialism by way of state capitalism."[22]

Lenin's most detailed prescriptions for socialist rule in the transitional period occur in his writings on the state, especially the 1917 *State and Revolution*. In that work he characterizes all states as inherently class-based and coercive. "[T]he state," he declares, "is nothing but a machine for the oppression of one class by another . . ."[23] Only primitive societies, in which classes have not yet emerged, or future socialist societies, in which class distinctions have been eliminated, can escape the logic of this definition. Having no classes, they have no state. Lenin explicitly rejected the notion that Western democratic states, based on universal suffrage, stand above classes. He regarded parliamentary democracy as the form of class rule peculiar to capitalism, a convenient façade of abstract political equality to conceal the objective reality of economic oppression. Thus, he saw no prospect that socialism could evolve peacefully out of democracy.

If the state is inevitably coercive and class-bound, Lenin reasoned, the revolution must first smash the capitalist state and replace it with a proletarian state capable of constructing a socialist order over the resistance of the bourgeoisie – in Marx's words, "a dictatorship of the proletariat." The working class, writes Lenin, must develop "undivided power directly backed by the armed force of the people. The overthrow of the bourgeoisie can be achieved only by the proletariat becoming the *ruling class* capable of crushing the inevitable and desperate resistance of the bourgeoisie, and of organizing the working and exploited people for the new economic system."

Lenin conceived of the revolutionary movement as an alliance of urban workers and poor peasants organized by a vanguard party – the "teacher, the guide, the leader" of the people in their effort to "reorganize their social life without the bourgeoisie and against the bourgeoisie."[24]

As this account implies, Lenin conceives the dictatorship of the proletariat as a transitory historical phenomenon bridging capitalism and socialism. In the process of eliminating private ownership of the means of production – the economic basis of class differentiation – the revolutionary state abolishes social classes. By definition, there is no longer a role for the state. Lenin was convinced that the administration of common affairs, in the absence of class antagonisms, would be a simple matter.

## Class Conflict and History

Sandinista ideology starts from the Marxist premise that class conflict is inevitable in most societies and a source of progress in human history. In a pamphlet directed at students in 1968, the FSLN declared, "Historical experience . . . teaches that there can be no peace between millionaires and workers . . . that there can be no situations other than the following: either the rich exploit the poor or the poor free themselves, eliminating the privileges of the millionaires."[25] The text, written by Fonseca, goes on to attack the "demagogic" notion propagated by Christian Democrats that there can be "conciliation of classes." A popular glossary of political terms issued in 1980 by the Sandinista agricultural workers' union (ATC) and the Agriculture Ministry observes, "In the capitalist mode of production there are 2 fundamental classes, the bourgeoisie and the proletariat, which have opposed interests."[26]

In a 1982 May Day speech, Tomás Borge sketched the social evolution of humanity from prehistoric communities, through slave and feudal societies, to modern capitalist systems – stressing the productive forces and class struggles characteristic of each stage and emphasizing the contemporary role of "the working class, the most revolutionary class in history."[27]

The Sandinista Front has consistently described its own ideology, historical role, objectives, strategy, friends, and enemies in class terms. The party's leaders frequently observe that Sandinista thought is "classist."[28] The FSLN is the "leader of the class struggle" and seeks to change the "balance between classes in favor of the oppressed."[29] Formulations of the movement's friends and enemies have varied with political conditions but the workers and peasants are virtually always counted as revolutionary allies (with somewhat stronger emphasis on the former) and leading sectors of the bourgeoisie, in league with imperialism, are seen as opponents.[30]

## Imperialism and Peculiarities of Nicaraguan Development

The FSLN's *General Political-Military Platform* of 1977, an internal document issued by the dominant Tercerista leadership, declares that "the working class, represented and led by the Sandinista vanguard, the FSLN, will lead the revolution." The same text asserts, "The dialectical development of humanity leads to the transformation from capitalism to communism."[31] These statements, like the portions of Borge's May Day speech cited above, suggest faith in Marx's Marxism. But Sandinista thinkers from Carlos Fonseca to the current leadership have understood that the classical Marxist theory of history did not fit Nicaraguan conditions very well.

The economic and political system that the Sandinistas saw in their country was not the capitalism (or for that matter the feudalism) of the *Communist Manifesto*. Rather it was a distorted form of capitalist development that reflected the influence of "imperialism." Sandinista spokesman loosely use the term imperialism to refer to the economic and political power of the advanced capitalist countries, especially the United States. But the Sandinista glossary quoted earlier offers a more rigorous definition of imperialism along Leninist lines: "Imperialism is the most developed and final stage of capitalism," characterized by the international dominance of monopoly capital. In an imperialist world the capitalist powers "exercise a hegemonic power over other countries (their colonies), which they subjugate by strong links of political and economic dependency, and impede their economic growth."[32]

By Sandinista reckoning, imperialism was responsible for many peculiarities in Nicaraguan development. The growth of the national economy was distorted by an emphasis on the production of primary exports, such as coffee and cotton, needed by the developed capitalist economies. "Our function," Sandinista agriculture minister Jaime Wheelock once observed, "was to grow sugar, cocoa and coffee for the United States; we served dessert at the imperialist dinner table."[33] Wheelock and other Sandinista analysts concluded that the Nicaraguan economy, because of its derivative character, was incapable of self-sustaining growth and unable to meet the basic material needs of its own people.[34]

Imperialism had also stamped a "double nature" on the Nicaraguan state: "bourgeois state and intermediary of imperialist domination."[35] As could be expected in any bourgeois state, the Somoza dictatorship sustained the country's system of capitalist exploitation, but it also protected the interests of the United States. "American imperialism and the local oligarchy" were, for Fonseca, "two sides of the same coin."[36] The United States had installed the first Somoza when it discovered that it could not control Nicaragua through direct military intervention. The Nicaraguan bourgeoisie, including those sectors of the bourgeoisie that opposed the Somozas, also depended on the dictatorship to subjugate the country.[37]

The Sandinistas concluded that the dependent character of the Nicaraguan economy and the imperialist control of the state had misshaped the class system and ultimately stymied the historical development of Nicaraguan society. The national bourgeoisie had accepted its own subordination within a system of imperial domination, thereby losing the opportunity to play a progressive role in Nicaraguan history. Sandinista theorists dated the bourgeoisie's surrender of its historic responsibilities precisely from the day in 1927 that the Liberal oligarchy abandoned the fight against the American-backed Conservative regime, leaving Sandino to confront the American intervention on his own.[38] There would be no Nicaraguan replay of the bourgeois revolutions of Europe. In the inelegant language of the 1977 *Platform*,

> [O]ur country's bourgeoisie – which liquidated and castrated itself as a progressive political force when it totally surrendered to the interests of Yankee imperialism and allied itself with the most reactionary Nicaraguan forces on May 4, 1927 – will not be a vanguard in the struggle against tyranny or in the revolutionary process.[39]

If the bourgeoisie was unequal to its historic role, so was its counterpart, the proletariat. Nicaragua's backward capitalism had not created a substantial industrial working class. Most of the salaried labor force in export agriculture worked seasonally and depended on subsistence agriculture or marginal urban employment between harvests; there was little opportunity to develop a sense of class identity. Fonseca, according to Victor Tirado López (one of the party's oldest surviving leaders), held as basic premise that "'the working class is destined by history to lead a victorious revolution.'" But the working class was not a "myth" for Fonseca. "He always saw it as it was, as a class that developed in a backward capitalist country, and was the victim of the country's social, political, and cultural backwardness."[40]

From the Sandinistas' Marxist point of view, the panorama of Nicaraguan society with its dependent economy, imperialized state, subjugated bourgeoisie, and incipient proletariat was hardly promising. There seemed to be little room for either of the revolutions that Marx had promised. Yet the Sandinistas managed to cling to their revolutionary optimism and to adapt the theory of progressive classes to their needs.

Sandinista theory overcame the inadequacies of the proletariat by stretching the definition of the class base of the revolution and by emphasizing the vanguard role of the party. The FSLN came to conceive of itself as a leader of a "worker-peasant alliance," a notion drawn from Lenin.[41] During the early years of the party's history, under the inspiration of the Cubans, Chinese, and Vietnamese, the FSLN placed strong emphasis on the peasant half of this formulation as it pursued a rural-based military strategy. The failures of rural strategies in the 1960s and early 1970s provoked the factional debate of the late 1970s over the appropriate class basis for the revolutionary movement. Jaime Wheelock and his Proletarian faction were expelled from the party, in part for their return to a more circumscribed, orthodox Marxist social base. The Proletarians also spoke of the worker-peasant alliance, but left little doubt that the proletariat was "the fundamental class and . . . leader of the revolution."[42]

The triumphant Terceristas represented the opposite tendency, a call for broadening the revolutionary movement. In their 1977 *Platform*, the Tercerista leaders propose a "triple bloc made up of the proletariat, the peasantry, and the petite bourgeoisie" as the "moving force of the revolution." Adjacent passages suggest that this ordering was carefully calculated. The proletariat (defined to include both urban and rural wage workers) is the "fundamental force" of the revolution. Through "direct involvement in capitalist production" it has absorbed the "collective habits" and social consciousness which place it in the vanguard of the revolution. The proletariat will "determine the course of profound revolutionary changes in the present system of capitalist exploitation and oppression." On the other hand, the peasantry is less optimistically described as the "principal force of the revolutionary process" by virtue of its "numerical importance and because of its combative tradition." The FSLN must direct its efforts toward "the firm consolidation of the worker-peasant alliance, both to overthrow the dictatorship and to build a new society."[43]

This conception of the party's task would seem to place the petite bourgeoisie, third constituent of "the triple block", in a marginal role, at least in the long run. The petite bourgeoisie is defined to include "artisans, professionals, shop-keepers, people involved in service activities, and revolutionary students and intellectuals."[44]

The 1977 *Platform* also proposes the formation of a "Broad Anti-Somoza Front," including the bourgeois opposition to the dictatorship. This final enlargement of the movement, which proved to be a key element in Sandinista strategy, would seem to fully dissolve the class basis of the revolution. But the anti-Somoza bourgeoisie was clearly not regarded as part of the inner revolutionary "bloc," but as a partner in a Sandinista-dominated coalition. The *Platform* envisions the FSLN as "hegemonic" within this coalition, which it describes as a "*temporary and tactical*" alliance."[45] In an interview conducted a year later, Daniel Ortega refers to the platform and employs virtually the same language: the alliance with bourgeois progressives is "tactical and temporary."

The FSLN's revolutionary program is tied to the "proletarian, peasant, and middle classes."[46]

Since coming to power in 1979, the FSLN has often restated its commitment to the "worker-peasant alliance" as a central ideological tenet.[47] Sometimes less precise formulations of the party's social base are employed: the FSLN works for "the people" or the "exploited classes." In a 1981 speech, Borge included the "wide sectors of the middle strata of the population" in the "social base of the revolution," but in a separate speech delivered the same year he drew on Sandino's dictum, popular with contemporary Sandinistas: "'only the workers and peasants will go to the end, only with them can the final triumph be achieved.' That idea is being carried out by our revolution."[48] The ultimate role of the middle sectors and even of the bourgeoisie remains nebulous in Sandinista thinking.[49] But there can be little doubt that workers and peasants – whom the Sandinistas reasonably describe as the popular majority – are the classes the party especially hopes to mobilize and serve.

## Vanguard

Vanguard is the most common term in the Sandinista lexicon. It is difficult to find a party text where it does not occur. Some leaders, taking advantage of the flexibility of the Spanish language, have turned vanguard into a verb, something the organization does rather than is. The vanguard concept is without doubt Lenin's most important contribution to the ideology of the FSLN. Sandinista accounts of the vanguard portray a self-recruited, ideologically motivated, disciplined, self-abnegating, hierarchical, revolutionary elite. Above all, the Sandinistas emphasize their own conscious and heroic relationship to history. This sense is reflected in the comments of Dora María Téllez, one of the party's ranking leaders, in an interview conducted in the euphoric afterglow of the Sandinista victory. Téllez recalled the late 1970s when the Sandinista Front "was clearly emerging as the vanguard, the leader in the struggle against Somoza":

> There are a few men and women who at a given moment in history seem to contain within themselves the dignity of all the people. They are examples to all of us. And then, through the struggle, the people as a whole reclaim the strength and dignity shown by a few. That's what Sandinism is to the Nicaraguan people. It is our history, our heroes and heroines, and our people's struggle and victory.[50]

In less compelling language, the National Directorate made the same point, stressing the connection between vanguard leadership and revolutionary theory or strategy:

The revolutionary party, by taking a firm class position, a scientific ideology, correct strategy and tactics, united in political principles, places itself at the forefront of all society and gathers in its bosom the political and military leadership of the revolutionary forces which struggle and work to bring the revolution towards bigger achievements.[51]

The ATC-Agriculture Ministry glossary emphasizes the class element in the concept of vanguard, which it defines as an "organization that brings together the most representative part of a class, that expresses its interests and objectives, and fights to obtain them." The "exploited classes" require a vanguard to lead them to their "definitive liberation."[52]

The need for such a historically conscious elite was imposed by the same distorted pattern of national development that required broadening the social base of the revolution. The FSLN acts on behalf of an ideologically backward working class. As the "leader in the class struggle," the party must draw into itself the most "advanced" elements of the working class, while pursuing the long-range objective of raising the consciousness of the class as a whole. In the meantime, the organization acts as a substitute or stand-in for the proletariat. This notion is implicit in many party statements. "[The] FSLN exercises the control of power in the name of the workers and the other oppressed sectors," declared the National Directorate in a 1979 party document, "or, what would in effect be the same, . . . the workers control power through the FSLN."[53] In a 1984 speech, Wheelock asserted that the "working class is in power in Nicaragua." How? Through the Sandinista mass organizations. "But most important of all is the fact that the revolutionary leadership, the Sandinista Liberation Front, is the organization of the working people, the organization that returned power to the toilers after taking it away from *Somocismo*."[54]

Such statements appear to ´equate the party with those it serves, implying class representation not in the Western parliamentary sense but in the historic sense of Téllez's comment about "a few men and women." Sandinista social scientist Orlando Núñez, in a paper presented in 1980, provided a systematic theoretical account of this idea. Nuñez observes that the structural conditions existing in imperialized countries of the capitalist Third World obstruct the classical Marxist revolution. "The objective conditions are not at the same level as the projects we dream of; and in the beginning of the struggle, the proletariat does not present itself as the social force for transformation *par excellence*."[55] Under these conditions three distinctions become crucial for revolutionaries. One is between the "class content" of a revolution – its ultimate socio-political objectives – and the class composition of a revolutionary coalition; especially in the early phases of the struggle, the revolution may depend on a broad alliance such as Sandinismo's triple bloc. A second distinction is between the "national liberation" stage of the revolutionary process and the social revolution which follows; the latter, which implies not just economic reform but a transformation of the political consciousness of the oppressed, only becomes possible once power has been gained in the first stage. The third distinction is between the *historical subject* of revolution, the proletariat, and the *political subject*, the organization whose leadership enables the proletariat to come to power. The functions of the vanguard, under typical Third World conditions, are implicit in these distinctions. Because it understands history, the vanguard can steer a society through a complex revolutionary process, seizing power in the interests of an immature oppressed class and carrying through a social revolution as it brings the oppressed class to political maturity.

There is an enormous ideological tension latent in the vanguard concept. The vanguard wants to liberate and empower the oppressed and at the same time to control and transform them. The tension begins to manifest itself after the vanguard has deposed the unpopular old regime and assumed political power. It is then in a position to coerce those it purports to represent. What does the vanguard do if the masses resist its historical vision? The question is most likely to arise as a revolution traverses periods of domestic and external strain and the vanguard must demand current sacrifices in exchange for future (uncertain) benefits. This dilemma was briefly acknowledged in a speech by Jaime Wheelock, delivered in November 1980, when the government was being challenged by Alfonso Robelo's opposition National Democractic Movement (MDN):

> The other day an MDN dimwit told us that they even had the sympathy of the shoe-shine boys. And I told him that probably he was right, because what we had was *the sympathy of history*, the sympathy of our people, who know and recognize that we have asked them to sacrifice for a better future and he who asks for sacrifice evokes worries rather than smiles [emphasis added].[56]

Wheelock's remark is uncommonly candid. Even its self-contradictory character is revealing. The problematic nature of the vanguard is implicitly raised in discussions of building democracy and of the role of the FSLN militant. The FSLN instructs its members to learn from the masses, to cultivate modesty toward the masses, but also to educate and lead them. "We must ... banish any manifestation of paternalism, of elitism," Borge tells a party audience;

> comprehend that it is necessary to guide the masses, but also, to learn from the masses. Have sufficient humility to understand that the people are full of wisdom and that they can teach us, although this does not mean that we have to put ourselves on the level of the most primitive and backward sectors of our population, but rather to draw out this wisdom and learn from it in order to educate later. Learn from the masses in order to educate the masses, that should be the guide for our organization.[57]

Borge is wrong, of course. The vanguard is literally and inescapably paternalistic. It assumes the authority of a parent over an immature people. Like a parent, it can only be successful if it prepares its charges for an independent existence and relinquishes its power over them in the process – no easy matter to judge by the experience of the ruling vanguard parties in this century.

## Democracy

The FSLN's conception of democracy emphasizes democratic results over democratic process and popular "participation" over electoral institutions. Underlying these ideas is the party's vanguard notion of its own historic role. The FSLN never clarified the relationship between its concept of popular participatory democracy and the Western-style constitution formally adopted in 1987.

From the Sandinista point of view, a regime that serves the interests of the majority is democratic. One that does not is undemocratic, even if it honestly maintains formal democratic procedures. In an unequivocally worded communiqué issued in March 1980, the party attacked "democratism," the "liberal bourgeois ideology" that stresses abstract freedoms without regard to their real content in a class society. Under Somoza, the communiqué recalls, peasants were deprived of their land so that they would be free to sell their labor; capitalists were free to exploit the people however they wished; culture, information, and ideology were freely manipulated to preserve the existing order; and the dictator was free to crush any movement that defended the people. In order to disguise its "class connotation" the conception of freedom was presented to the Nicaraguan people as

> something pure and abstract which has always existed equally for all
> ... But with the Sandinista Popular Revolution, those stories were ended
> forever. The masses today understand that freedom is not something that
> exists simply because the word is used, but that it means two different
> things which in fact are completely opposed, depending on the class point
> of view with which it is considered. There is, therefore, no sacred abstract
> freedom for the masses; the only things that are indeed sacred are their
> own class interests and the principles of the Popular Revolution. Bourgeois
> freedom has nothing to do with popular freedom which reflects the objective
> interests of the people with respect to their right to organize and arm
> (politically, militarily, and ideologically) as a class to promote their historic
> plan of a society in keeping with their nature as a majority class.[58]

The Sandinistas accuse their conservative opponents of reducing the concept of democracy to elections. Somoza, they remind listeners, regularly held elections in Nicaragua and regularly won. Elsewhere candidates are merchandized like soap, with a slogan or a smile. To these corrupted models of democracy Sandinistas oppose the concept of popular participation. In an August 1980 declaration, explaining the Directorate's decision to postpone elections until 1985, the FSLN emphasized that "for a Sandinista, for a revolutionary," democracy means "PARTICIPATION of the people" in the entire range of the nation's affairs. The broader the participation, the greater the democracy. Further, democracy neither begins nor ends with elections. "True democracy" starts in the economic order, as social inequalities decline and the living standards of workers and peasants rise. From there, it extends to other realms.[59]

The concept of participation, regularly employed in Sandinista discourse, remains ill defined. The FSLN has created varied channels for citizen participation in the revolution, including the Sandinista mass organizations, political rallies, and "face the people" meetings, at which citizens are invited to question leaders about government policies. But Sandinismo does not clearly distinguish participation from political mobilization. If the two are equated, participation is reduced to a mechanism by which the party communicates its ideas to the people and the people manifest (or decline to manifest) their support of the FSLN. The conflation of participation and mobilization was suggested by the manner in which the August 1980 declaration was presented. After reading the text at a mass rally celebrating the triumphs of the national literacy campaign, Humberto Ortega challenged the audience of young literacy workers: "Are you in agreement that the Sandinista Front with this Directorate should continue conducting the revolutionary power of Sandino's working people? (Exclamations: Yes!!) . . . Then, this is a vote, a popular election, this is Sandinista democracy."[60] Such an assertion may be little more than a rhetorical flourish, but the notion of participation remains semantically and institutionally vague.

The Sandinista conception of democracy mirrors the FSLN's analysis of Nicaraguan society and the role of the vanguard. Underdevelopment has produced an underdeveloped people, who require the interim leadership of a conscious vanguard. Daniel Ortega implied as much in August 1980, when he commented, "The people have won the right to elections with their blood, but it is necessary for the people to go through a process of consolidation and transformation and popular democracy, which means that the workers will choose their representatives in democratic assemblies . . ."[61]

Sandinista leaders have repeatedly insisted that the revolution is "irreversible." Elections, therefore, should not be construed as an occasion to challenge the power of the revolution concentrated in the vanguard. Humberto Ortega told the literacy crusade audience that the planned elections were "elections to improve revolutionary power, but not to raffle who has power, because the people have power through their Vanguard, the Frente Sandinista de Liberación Nacional and its National Directorate."[62]

As the contra war expanded, a new element was added to the Sandinista conception of democracy: "the people armed [*el pueblo armado*]." To confront the war the government handed out tens of thousands of small arms to citizen militia in neighborhoods and villages throughout the country. Invoking this program in the midst of commenting on legislative preparations for projected national elections, Daniel Ortega told the Council of State, "Neither bullets nor votes will destroy the power of the armed people."[63] But when elections were held in 1984, the Sandinista leadership publicly portrayed them as a real contest for power. The party did not, however, offer a systematic redefinition of democracy to replace the official pronouncements of 1980. (The 1984 elections are examined in chapter 5.)

## A Two-Stage Revolution

The FSLN has long conceived of its task in terms of a two-stage revolution, typically denoted as national and social liberation. This conception of the revolutionary process is virtually implicit in the Sandinista analysis of Nicaraguan society and the organization's understanding of its vanguard role.

If an interrogation transcript found in the archives of Somoza's intelligence service can be trusted, the idea of a two-phase revolution is older than the party itself. In 1957, Carlos Fonseca was detained after a trip to several Soviet bloc countries and interrogated by a National Guard lieutenant who asked, "Are you a Communist?" Fonseca, who was characteristically stingy with concrete political information on such occasions but generous with abstract theory, launched into an analysis of Nicaragua's "semi-feudal, semi-colonial" society. Under existing conditions, he explained to the lieutenant, a communist society could not be constructed. First, a nationalist regime (with bourgeois participation) would have to come to power. Such a regime would free Nicaragua from imperialist domination and create the material bases for a new society, "in which man's exploitation of man has disappeared, nor does the state exist – in short, a society in which each individual, according to the formula of Marx . . . gives society what his capacities permit and receives what society can provide to satisfy his needs."[64]

The two-stage revolution is most explicitly described in the 1977 *Platform* and subsequently reaffirmed in many speeches and party documents. The *Platform* emphasizes the role of the vanguard in linking the two phases:

> Breaking the chains of imperialist rule determines our *national liberation* process. Breaking the yoke of oppression and exploitation of the reactionary Nicaraguan classes determines our *social revolution* process. The two historic undertakings will be inseparably linked with the existence of a solid vanguard and a Marxist-Leninist cause to guide the process . . . Our country's backwardness and its dependent capitalist system determine

the objective need to complete the *revolutionary democratic state* in order to assure the structural and superstructural [material and ideological] bases for the revolutionary process toward socialism.[65]

Sandinista texts do not suggest a sharp break between the two phases but something closer to a gradual rearrangement of tasks on the revolutionary agenda. The first phase would focus on liberating the country from "the dictatorship and imperialism . . . our immediate enemies" and otherwise laying the groundwork for the social revolution phase.[66]

Both before and after July 19, Sandinista leaders worried that the bourgeoisie, backed by the United States, might gain control of the revolutionary process and limit its action to the removal of Somoza.[67] Sandinista thinking emphasized the need to retain control of the anti-Somoza movement and consolidate the post-insurrection power of the FSLN. The key objective of the new government, the National Directorate agreed in March 1979, would be "the neutralization of potential internal and external enemies, while we accumulate the military and mass forces that guarantee the continuity of our [revolutionary] process."[68] Concretely, this meant the creation of a new, revolutionary army committed to the FSLN and the political mobilization of the population through a network of Sandinista mass organizations. While this was happening, the new government would carry out a social reform program to benefit the masses and win popular support. And it would begin to reorient the national economy, increasing state control, reducing foreign dependency, and encouraging growth.[69]

The mass organizations, the new education system, and even the army were to contribute to the development of a new political consciousness in the people, a critical prerequisite for the transformation of society. Days after Somoza fled Nicaragua, *Barricada*, the official party organ, was calling on Nicaraguans to join unions, neighborhood and other mass organizations: "MOBILIZE YOURSELVES POLITICALLY, EDUCATE YOURSELVES TO OVERCOME YOUR POLITICAL AND CULTURAL DEFICIENCIES, AND CULTIVATE REVOLUTIONARY VALUES."[70] One purpose of the new education system, *Barricada* explained some months later, was "to strip the system of exploitation naked before the eyes of the exploited and give them an instrument that will convert them into the active subjects [agents] of their own history."[71] In a 1981 speech before a Sandinista military audience, Defense Minister Humberto Ortega emphasized "political-ideological work." Both within the military and without, officers and soldiers should be "transmitters of consciousness."[72]

The political and economic range of the first phase program suggests that the FSLN expected to control the new regime. But Sandinista theory did not anticipate a Marxist-Leninist dictatorship of the proletariat; rather the new government would be a broad-based, "popular democratic" regime. The continuing economic and political participation of the progressive bourgeoisie was especially important if two critical goals of the first phase program were to be attained – successfully resisting imperialism and building the material bases for a new society. But the same party document that spoke of a popular-democratic government envisioned the regime operating under Sandinista "hegemony."[73] Since the party regarded itself as the vanguard representative of the exploited classes, Sandinista hegemony would imply a government with a definite class orientation. There was, then, from the beginning, a tension between the party's plans for a broadly based regime and its notions of its own role and class commitments. On occasion members of the National Directorate did, in fact, allude to the class orientation of the revolutionary government.[74]

"Socialism" is the goal of the second phase of the revolution, according to the repeated assertions of party documents and spokesman. "[O]ur great objective," wrote Fonseca in 1969, "is socialism . . ."[75] Two key internal documents, the 1977 *Platform* and the 1979 reunification accord among Sandinista factions, also take "socialism" as the final aim of the revolution. Although the *Platform* cautioned against open avowal of socialist intentions, the FSLN organized May Day observances in 1982 around the theme: "Defend the revolution, for the construction of socialism."[76] In speeches delivered from 1983 to 1986 before sympathetic audiences, National Directorate members Tirado, Wheelock, and Arce – representing all three of the party's factions – reaffirmed this article of Sandinista faith.[77]

The apparent socialist consensus among the leaders of the FSLN may hide more than it reveals. The Sandinistas have never clearly explained what they mean when they talk of socialism. Perhaps the following passage from a key party document published in 1980 was meant as a definition:

> The objectives of the Revolution are none other than to fight until it guarantees the well-being of all workers. Instead of the shack, decent and humane housing. Replace the floor with a bed to which the producer of social wealth has a right . . . This is the Sandinismo whose potential is contained in the economic and social project of the people, that today has its concentrated expression in the popular uses of the profits that the APP [People's Property Area, the state sector] is beginning to produce.[78]

Here, the state sector of the economy (most significantly, the large agro-export enterprises seized from Somoza and his associates) is seen as containing the germ of a new, socialist society, which will provide the worker a decent material standard of life.

Many Sandinistas are drawn to a vision of the future that promises more than material justice. Their socialism is built around the concept of a "new man," who has overcome the self-serving values promoted by capitalism (Sandinista spokesman seem entirely unself-conscious about applying the phrase *el hombre nuevo* collectively to men and women.) In a 1979 speech, party member Carlos Tunnermann, then Minister of Education, observed:

The new Nicaragua also needs a new man who has stripped himself of selfishness and egotism, who places social interests before individual interests. A new man who knows that the contribution that each individual can make to the community is very important and that the individual is most fulfilled when he works within the collectivity.[79]

This vision seems to appeal most to Sandinistas whose beliefs are rooted in a radicalized Christianity and to those who formed part of the GPP tendency within the party. Tunnermann himself is a Christian revolutionary.[80] For GPP alumni like Tomás Borge and Bayardo Arce, the archetype of the new man is the guerrilla fighter in the mountains, who is making the ultimate collective commitment.[81]

The most explicit Sandinista endorsement of this concept is a 1983 government document establishing national education policy. The document describes formation of the new man as *the* objective of Nicaraguan schools. The new man, product of a "new education" will be patriotic, committed to the interests of the masses, anti-imperialist, internationalist, the enemy of exploitation, racism, and oppression. He will be disciplined, creative, cooperative, hard-working, fraternal, modest, self-sacrificing, and persuaded that "individual interests should coincide with social interests." He will be ready to defend the nation and the revolution. The 1983 education document was issued in the name of the government, rather than the party, though it was published in *Barricada* and described as having the support (*respaldo*) of the FSLN's National Directorate.[82]

A new society built on a new, socially conscious humanity has been the goal of many Marxist revolutions. The example most familiar to the Sandinistas is, of course, Cuba. The concept of a new man has been associated with the most radical phases of that island's revolutionary history, when economic policy has attempted to substitute moral incentives for material incentives – by, for example, demanding increased revolutionary commitment from workers while reducing wage differences based on skill or responsibility. But the emphasis on moral incentives and egalitarian rewards – still prominent in Cuban thinking about socialism – is seldom echoed in the cautious Sandinista discussions of the new man.[83]

At least one important Sandinista appears to reject the notion of a new man altogether. Humberto Ortega offered his vision of the future in a 1981 speech to army officers. He stressed ham and television sets:

[We want to] escape underdevelopment and create wealth so that the people will be happy and not just further socialize our poverty. We want to see the day when all our people can eat ham and they can have television sets and take vacations. That's what we want. We're not going to promote a mentality that says that we should live like nuns or under socialism with a Christian character.[84]

There is, in fact, little indication that Sandinistas agree about what socialism means or how and when it might be achieved in Nicaragua. Victor Tirado concedes as much in a speech to Sandinista unionists:

> The Nicaraguan working class – we believe its big majority – sees socialism as the radical long-term solution (and some see it as the short-term solution) to its problems. Ideas about what socialism will be or should be in Nicaragua are still diffuse, not very clear, and it is natural that it be that way. At the right moment we will embark on the road to socialism.[85]

## The Ideology of the FSLN: A Glance Backward

The central argument of Sandinismo is this: The historical scenario of Marx's *Communist Manifesto* is essentially correct, but the historical development of Nicaraguan society has been derailed by imperialism. Imperialist domination of Nicaragua has meant a dependent economy, an underdeveloped state, an incipient proletariat and a bourgeoisie incapable of playing its historic role. Sandinista theory puts the historical train back on track by broadening the definition of the class basis of revolution and emphasizing the vanguard role of the revolutionary party.

The immaturity of Nicaraguan society requires a two-stage revolution. The gradualist character of this conception reinforces the need for a vanguard to guide the country through a complicated process of historical change. But the vanguard seems to be only one step ahead of the people it leads. Nearly a decade after coming to power, the FSLN is sure that it wants socialism but not quite sure what that means.

# 2
# The Party

"ORGANIZATION, ORGANIZATION AND MORE ORGANIZA-TION" demanded a front-page editorial in one of the first issues of *Barricada*.[1] Building organization was among the fundamental priorities of the FSLN during its first months in power, and strengthening organization remains a consuming preoccupation of the leadership. This emphasis grows directly out of Sandinista theory. The vanguard party and its affiliated mass organizations are central to the FSLN's conception of revolution. They provide the means to lift the people out of political backwardness and harness their energies to transform Nicaraguan society.

In the period immediately following the ouster of Somoza, organization had a preemptive significance: in order to consolidate its power the FSLN had to insure that the masses did not fall to the competing leaderships on the left or right. In the long run, organization would provide a channel for political education and a mechanism to support the implementation of Sandinista programs.

Given its commitment to a gradual, step-by-step transformation of Nicaragua, the FSLN inevitably found itself struggling to carry out policies over the recalcitrance of established institutions and traditional habits. Those who led the private sector, the church, certain labor unions, and the non-Sandinista media were soon openly hostile to the FSLN. Although Somocistas were quickly driven from top positions in the state bureaucracy, the new regime could not replace many middle and lower-ranking officials whose commitment to the goals of the revolution were uncertain. In the face of institutional inertia or resistance, the party needed a network of collaborators who could explain, promote, and monitor Sandinista policies.[2]

Within a year of the victory over Somoza, the FSLN had built a new system of power, based on the party, its affiliated mass organizations, and the Sandinista-dominated state. At the center of this system stood the National Directorate of the FSLN.

## The National Directorate

The first principle of Sandinista organization is the supremacy of the Directorate. When the structure of the party was formalized in late 1980, an official communiqué stated: "[O]ur National Directorate is the supreme leadership body and central authority of the FSLN and of the Sandinista People's Revolution."[3] The supremacy of the Directorate has been reaffirmed in varied contexts. In September 1980, the ruling junta of the national unity government officially recognized the vanguard status of the FSLN and its own subordination to the Directorate.[4] On the fourth anniversary of the revolution in 1983, Daniel Ortega, then coordinator of the junta, declared that "the Sandinista Front is here as the guide of the revolution, with the National Directorate as its highest leader."[5] The year after Ortega was elected president, an FSLN communiqué on party organization reiterated the language of the 1980 organization communiqué describing the authority of the Directorate.[6]

The composition of the National Directorate has not changed since it was formed in March 1979, completing the process of reintegrating the Sandinista movement. Each of the three factions was allowed three representatives, who received the title *Comandante de la Revolución*.[7]

They were nine young guerrilla fighters, most of them born in the 1940s and party members since the 1960s. Only Tomás Borge (b. 1930) was over 40 in 1979. Collectively they represented the second generation of Sandinista leaders. The long struggle against Somoza had destroyed most of the older first generation. Of the FSLN's founders, Borge was the sole survivor. They all speak frequently of their political and moral debt to the movement's "heroes and martyrs."

The comandantes were of more varied social backgrounds than those who ruled Nicaragua before them. Just two, Wheelock and Luis Carrión, were from upper-class families. Four came from middle-class homes and three from working-class households.[8] But none was the son of a peasant or farm worker – though the population was still half rural when they were born – and only one, Henry Ruiz, grew up with the poverty that remains the lot of most Nicaraguans. While young Carrión studied at a New England prep school, Ruiz sold tortillas in the street to help maintain his family.

Relative to their well-traveled, foreign-educated allies in the bourgeoisie, they were unschooled and had limited direct experience of the world outside of Nicaragua. Most had entered Nicaraguan universities, become active in student politics, and drifted away from their studies into the revolution. They had been to Cuba, typically for guerrilla training, but few had lived abroad for extended periods. Wheelock and Carrión, who could afford it, had the most cosmopolitan experience. Ruiz studied math and physics in the Soviet Union for a year, at the end of which he quit the communist party and returned home (without the Soviets' blessing) to devote himself to the armed struggle.

During the 1970s, the nine educated themselves as best they could. In exile, Jaime Wheelock, the one self-conscious intellectual among them, wrote well-researched books on Nicaraguan society and agriculture, good preparation for a future Minister of Agriculture. During long years in prison, Daniel Ortega read books on law, history, and geography and wrote poetry. Ruiz, who would hold economic portfolios in the government, tutored himself in political economy. Omar Cabezas's memoir of the guerrilla war captures Ruiz, at the end of a hard day's march – "[everyone] freezing cold, in the shittiest kind of shape, waiting for God knows what" – calmly reading a treatise on Marxist economics by Ernest Mandel.[9]

Of the nine, Borge, now Minister of the Interior, is without doubt the most intriguing.[10] A small, near-sighted man with thinning hair, he charms foreign visitors, moves easily among the common people of Nicaragua, and knows how to rouse an audience. He is the FSLN's most charismatic leader, and, if only for that reason, a threat to other members of the Directorate. He is regarded as the leader among them of the "ideologues," those most committed to radicalizing the revolution.

Borge's speeches look to a future free from greed, need, oppression, and exploitation. They often explain or apply some Marxist-Leninist principle, but Borge uses simple, unpretentious language and avoids invoking Marxist authors, preferring to cite the Bible. Borge, who once served as an altar boy but resisted his mother's efforts to turn him into a priest, has taken a special interest in liberation theology. He often speaks out on church issues but has avoided stating his own religious beliefs. Borge is also the revolution's spokesman on women's issues and human rights, though he makes passes at women who interview him and oversees a state-security apparatus (the DGSE) that is regarded with suspicion by human rights groups.[11]

Borge's opposite in most respects is President Daniel Ortega, who is recognized as the leader of the "pragmatists" on the National Directorate. Ortega is an uninspiring speaker, with a humorless public demeanor. On the record, he is something of a political mystery. In speeches and interviews he typically speaks *ex officio*, for the party and state. During the struggle against Somoza, he rarely published anything under his own name or spoke for attribution, allowing his younger brother and political ally Humberto to assume a more salient role. But in a party suspicious of personalistic leadership, Ortega's colorlessness and discretion were virtues and probably contributed to his emergence as first among equals on the Directorate and his nomination in 1984 as the FSLN's presidential candidate, a role Borge is said to have coveted.

Like Borge, Ortega is from a middle-class family. The Ortegas were a family of rebels. Daniel's father fought with Sandino and both his parents were jailed under the first Somoza. Later Somoza attempted to suborn the elder Ortega into political submission with an envelope full of cash, which Ortega promptly returned. His father liked to show Daniel the telegram containing Somoza's two-word response to his gesture: "Eat shit."[12]

A neighbor recalls that the Ortegas' radio was constantly tuned to Radio Havana. Daniel, Humberto, and a third brother, Camilo, who died in the insurrection, were politically active from their teen years. Daniel was jailed and tortured when he was 15, joined the FSLN at 18, and spent most of his twenties in prison, a period he recalled in a poem titled "I Never Saw Managua When Miniskirts were in Style."

As a youth, Ortega was also an altar boy and later taught Bible lessons in Managua slums. His religious convictions like Borge's remain a mystery, but according to a knowledgeable church source, he has quietly baptized his children – perhaps to satisfy his very Catholic mother. Ortega is a disciplined man, who led hunger strikes in prison and runs six miles a day. Those who have dealt with him characterize Ortega as flexible, tolerant, and unpretentious. A prominent opposition figure who knows Ortega well says, "He is the least self-righteous of them. He can see himself in someone else's shoes."[13]

Other prominent figures on the Directorate include Jaime Wheelock, Humberto Ortega, Henry Ruiz, and Bayardo Arce. Wheelock is described by two people who have worked with him as a vain man and a lover of beautiful things, ranging from well-cut uniforms to his comely wife. One of his university professors found him brilliant, intellectually arrogant, and possessed by a naive faith in the power of theory. But in office, Wheelock has undergone a political metamorphosis from the orthodox Marxist-Leninist who wrote dogmatic diatribes against his opponents in the internecine conflicts of the mid-1970s and anticipated rapid socialization of the economy after 1979, into an exponent of pragmatic, gradualist policies in the 1980s. Defense Minister Humberto Ortega is known for some hardline speeches, but he is also counted in the pragamatist camp, if only out of loyalty to his brother. Although he was the chief theorist among the Terceristas in the 1970s, since 1979 he has largely devoted himself to building up the Sandinista military and not played an important role in policy debates.

Ruiz is regarded as the purest Marxist-Leninist in the Directorate, strongly committed to a command economy and close relations with the Soviet Union. A former assistant remembers his response to suggestions that the Sandinistas should moderate their policies to attract more foreign aid from the West: "I'd rather go back to the mountains and eat monkeys [an unsavory source of protein for guerrilla fighters]. There are comandantes who have gotten used to living like bourgeois." Ruiz, who lives modestly, may be the most admired man in the party. "The best" of the nine, concedes a liberal politician who held high posts in the national unity government, "a gentleman, decent, respectful of the rights of others. He will always lose in a power struggle." (The same man had this description of Borge: "A Communist Somoza.") Bayardo Arce, by all accounts, shares Ruiz's politics, but not his personality. He is characterized as intelligent, abrasive, and intolerant. Arce, who worked as a reporter and university journalism instructor in the late 1970s, was given the responsibility of managing the party apparatus after the Sandinistas came to power.

The division of the Directorate into ideologues and pragmatists is rooted in, but does not duplicate, the factional splits of the 1970s. The clearly identified ideologues, Borge, Ruiz, and Arce, are the representatives of the Prolonged Popular War Tendency on the Directorate. The Tercerista representatives, the Ortegas and Victor Tirado López, are generally counted as pragmatists. Although Wheelock, the one-time leader of the Proletarian Tendency, is known as a pragmatist, the positions of the other two Proletarian members, Luis Carrión and Carlos Núñez, are unclear. The three ideologues are bound to each other by strong personal bonds forged in their shared experience of the guerrilla war. In contrast, the two leading pragmatists, Daniel Ortega and Wheelock, have no such shared history and are known to have cool personal relations.

The debate within the National Directorate revolves around such issues as the role of the private sector, support for revolutions in neighboring countries, and relations with the United States and the Soviet Union. Disagreement may also extend to the place of democratic institutions in the revolution. But it is by no means clear that pragmatists and ideologues have adopted consistent and coherent positions on these questions. Do the same two groupings appear on opposite sides on all issues? Is the nature of their disagreement tactical or fundamental? For example, if pragmatists and ideologues have different notions of how to treat the private sector, is that because they are divided over the nature of the future economy they hope to build or because they disagree over the character and timing of the transition phase?

If answers to these questions are unavailable, it is because the comandantes, keenly sensitive to the dangers of disunity, have carefully avoided airing their disagreements in public. The damaging factionalization of the movement in the 1970s taught the leaders of the FSLN a lesson, which was reinforced by the events surrounding the defeat of the Grenadan revolution in 1983: division is perilous; open conflict at the top is potentially catastrophic. Thus, the Directorate deliberates behind a high wall of public discretion.

The Directorate, say its members, operates as a collective leadership body, making decisions by consensus. While it is clearly not the case that all nine comandantes carry equal weight, there is little indication that one individual or faction has been able to impose policies on the others. Decisions on controversial issues must be supported by a six-vote majority. In an interview, Wheelock offered the following, possibly idealized version, of the decision-making process:

> We all give an opinion about the topic under discussion and this is very positive because it contributes greatly to the powers of analysis. By the same token, no judgement can impose itself because of external conditions, because of the weight that one leader's opinion might have, but rather a judgement imposes itself because of its absolute logic. We proceed perfecting and gathering the best judgements until we arrive at a collective judgement. Our opinions come together, really, like the opinions of a collective. In this way, it's harder to make a mistake ... The experience we have all these years is that, except for rare occasions, the National Directorate always

**Table 2.1**  Members of the National Directorate (DN)

|  | *Pre-1979 Faction* | *Positions and Responsibilities (1985—)* |
|---|---|---|
| Daniel Ortega | Tercerista | President of Nicaragua; Coordinator of DN Executive Committee |
| Humberto Ortega | Tercerista | Minister of Defense; Army Commander-in-Chief; member of DN Executive Committee; member of party Military Commission |
| Victor Tirado | Tercerista | Oversees Sandinista unions and farmers' association |
| Tomás Borge | Prolonged Popular War | Minister of the Interior; member of DN Executive Committee; member of party Military Commission |
| Bayardo Arce | Prolonged Popular War | Vice-Chairman of party Executive Committee; oversees daily workings of party apparatus; responsible for mass organizations; handles FSLN's relations with other political organizations, domestic and foreign; active in formulation of foreign policy |
| Henry Ruiz | Prolonged Popular War | Minister of Foreign Cooperation; major responsibility: Soviet bloc aid |
| Jaime Wheelock | Proletarian | Minister of Agriculture; member of party Executive Committee |
| Luis Carrión | Proletarian | Deputy Minister of the Interior; member of party Military Commission |
| Carlos Núñez | Proletarian | President of the National Assembly |

arrives at a consensus. The system of voting has been an exceptional procedure and on the rare occasions when we have a 5 to 4 vote, we have not taken that as a consensus and go back to discussing the problem.[14]

In keeping with their collegial style of leadership, the Directorate never named a party general secretary (the position from which Stalin consolidated his dictatorship). When they came to power, the members of the Directorate divided responsibilities in the state and party among themselves in a carefully calculated manner (see table 2.1 for the current division of labor). It was no accident that the comandantes – who had learned to respect guns – split the security forces between representatives of the two most powerful Sandinista factions. Humberto Ortega became Minister of Defense, with control of the military, and Tomás Borge became Interior Minister, presiding over the police and state security forces. Responsibility for the economy was also divided, by giving the key economic posts, agriculture and planning, to Wheelock and Ruiz. Daniel Ortega became the FSLN's official representative on the ruling junta, but he and the other Sandinistas on the junta let their colleagues know that they operated under the discipline of the National Directorate.[15]

The FSLN has evolved an organizational ideology that rejects the personalistic leadership of the *caudillo*, the traditional strongman of Latin American politics. The party has long been chary of vesting too much power in one person.[16] This was one of the reasons that the Directorate passed over Borge, its most compelling leader, when it selected a presidential candidate in 1984.

But the Directorate did not escape personalistic leadership by rejecting one-man rule. Instead of falling under the power of a single *caudillo*, the FSLN came to be ruled by a college of *caudillos*, each with his own minions. The term insiders used to describe them was "feudal lords," dominating their separate territories in party and state, always competing for turf. Observers noted that the comandantes in the government tended to surround themselves with members of their own pre-1979 party factions. For example, Wheelock's Agriculture Ministry was populated with veterans of his Proletarian Tendency and some Terceristas. "No one from [Borge's] GPP," a cabinet colleague later commented, "dared to walk into the building." Key posts in Humberto Ortega's Defense Ministry went to Terceristas.

Overcoming "divisiveness and feudalism" was part of the National Directorate's declared rationale for the alterations in party organization announced in an August 1985 communiqué. But the communiqué failed to reveal the source of these centrifugal tendencies in the party or to indicate how the changes could be expected to rectify them.[17]

In 1985, Daniel Ortega won new stature in both state and party, leading some to conclude that the collegial rule of the FSLN was breaking down. In addition to becoming president of Nicaragua, Ortega was named "coordinator" of a newly created "Executive Committee" of the National Directorate. But the powers of the Executive Committee – consisting, oddly enough, of a five-man majority of the Directorate – were limited. It was to be "an organ for implementing the [Directorate's] decisions," but having "none of the attributes" of the Directorate itself, which, the August 1985 communiqué emphasized, remained the supreme authority of the FSLN.[18] Moreover, Bayardo Arce, named "vice-coordinator" of the new committee, retained responsibility for supervising the daily activities of the party's central apparatus.

After 1985 as before, key government policy decisions were made by the full National Directorate. But Ortega's daily contact with state affairs enhanced his authority in policy discussions. The government reorganization which followed the 1984 elections increased his influence over domestic policy. Ruiz's planning ministry was abolished and replaced by an economic planning council headed by the president. The members of the council are the ministers with economic portfolios, including Wheelock and Ruiz, (now relegated to the diminished post of Foreign Cooperation Minister).[19] Major economic policy initiatives pass through this committee before they are referred to the National Directorate. This, for example, was the case of the 1986 agrarian reform law, initially formulated in Wheelock's ministry. The government's leading planner is now presidential advisor Dionisio Marenco, a Tercerista with private sector managerial experience.

Ortega's high visibility as a head of state and international representative of Nicaragua has greatly enhanced his influence in foreign affairs, but, like other Central American presidents, he cannot make independent decisions in security matters. Presidents in this region do not ordinarily tell generals what to do. With the exception of the Costa Rican president, all of Ortega's peers must contend with the veto power of the armed forces in foreign policy and military decisions. In Nicaragua the military is subject to the power of the ruling party. Ortega shares security policy-making with the rest of the Directorate, which is much more directly involved with security matters than it is with domestic affairs.

## The Party

Below the National Directorate there are four levels of party organization: (1) centrally, the Directorate staff and the Sandinista Assembly, a periodic meeting of about 100 party notables; (2) the regional and (3) the local ("zonal") party committees, whose organization parallels that of government institutions; and (4) the grassroots ("base") committees, consisting of party members in a particular workplace, neighborhood, or military unit.

The Directorate staff is a substantial bureaucratic operation consisting of some 600 "party functionaries" organized into seven "Auxiliary Departments."[20] Among the most important is the Department of International Relations, whose foreign policy experts overshadow the government's Ministry of External Affairs in the formulation of the country's international strategy. The responsibilities of the Department of Agitation and Propaganda include managing the political content of the national television network (Sandinista Television System) and the FSLN organ *Barricada*. The Department of Political Education, explains a party official, is concerned with "the ideological, cultural, and professional growth of party members." It offers formal instruction ranging from short courses on national problems to degree programs in economics and philosophy. The Department of Organization maintains the party's network of committees and mass organizations and oversees the placement of party cadres.

The Sandinista Assembly includes most of the key party and government leaders who are not in the Directorate, among them cabinet ministers, military officers, Auxiliary Department officials, regional party chiefs, and the national heads of the mass organizations. Although these leading Sandinistas are often influential in their own areas of responsibility, the authority of the Assembly is quite circumscribed. Officially defined as a "consultative body" that advises the Directorate on important issues, the Assembly meets a few days a year to consider matters put to it by the comandantes. Its members are appointed and removed by the National Directorate. The Assembly has no staff of its own and its committees are organized by the Directorate. It deliberates but does not vote.[21]

In 1986, the language of party communiqués elevated the Sandinista Assembly to the status of "*maximum* consultative body of the National Directorate."[22] But policy decisions were made that year in two critical areas with no substantive contribution from the Assembly, though both were discussed in Assembly sessions. Interviews with several Sandinista officials, including two Assembly members, revealed that the body's deliberations had no influence on the 1986 agrarian reform law or Sandinista positions on the national constitution. The FSLN's representatives to the multi-party commission charged with drafting a constitution worked on the basis of instructions from the National Directorate. Only after the commission had produced an initial draft was the matter submitted to the Sandinista Assembly, where the discussion served (in the words of one participant) to "clarify" the party's positions on the constitution rather than modify them. Constitutional issues on which party opinion was divided, such as the representation of the mass organizations in the national legislature, were not debated.

A cynical former central-staff aide describes the Sandinista Assembly as a forum where second-level Sandinistas demonstrate their ideological dependability. He recalls a 1982 paper on the economy prepared by Bayardo Arce that was referred to the Assembly's economic policy committee for discussion. One member of the committee suggested that there was no need to review anything that was written by a member of the Directorate. His committee colleagues agreed without hesitation.

Although the Sandinista Assembly includes key figures in the party hierarchy such as the head of the Organization Department and the "political secretaries" who lead the regional committees, the Assembly has no institutional authority over lower party organs. The regional secretaries are appointed by the Directorate and they, in turn, appoint heads of the zonal committees.[23]

Every member of the FSLN belongs to a grassroots "base committee" (or one of the higher-level party committees), in his or her workplace, neighborhood, or military unit. The committee is led by a political secretary chosen by the zonal committee. Base committees meet regularly to discuss ways to improve labor productivity at work, plan political activities, evaluate individuals proposed for party membership, and absorb the party's current political line.

One of the first items on the meeting agenda of any party committee, including the National Directorate, is "criticism/self-criticism," which Sandinistas describe as a shared effort to rectify inadequacies in the work or attitudes of the committee and its individual members. Members insist that they strive to be constructive in these exchanges, avoiding indiscriminate censure and emotional *mea culpas*. Speaking of the Directorate, Arce told an interviewer: "[W]e understand that we can only improve ourselves to the degree that we are able to recognize our own errors. We don't do it like someone who beats his chest to expiate his sins, but to socialize our experience and keep others from tripping over the same stone."[24] Criticism/self-criticism sometimes takes up an entire Directorate meeting, according to Arce, but the effort is worth making since it allows the members to "achieve a common viewpoint" (*unificar criterios*). The purpose of criticism/self-criticism, observes a party member, is "to make the collective function." References here to socialized experience, common viewpoint, and the collective reflect the party's determination to operate as a unified, consensual body.

Periodically, the political secretary calls a 15-minute "mini-meeting" of the base committee to deal with pressing news, such as an important decision of the Directorate. Once a month, the committee holds a study session. Topics range from the history of Sandinismo to the party's position on some key question such as a new diplomatic initiative. Speeches by members of the Directorate, which often appear in *Barricada*, are studied in these meetings as sources of the emerging party line. Individual committee members give presentations on assigned themes.

Such talks, says a party official, are considered part of the speaker's political education.

The members of a base committee function in their workplaces and neighborhoods as representatives of the vanguard. All party members are expected to play an active role in mass organizations such as unions and the neighborhood Sandinista Defense Committees (CDSs) to help mobilize people for political activities and to argue for the party's positions on crucial issues. Sandinista sympathizers who are not party members look to them for political guidance. "It's lovely to listen to them," says a middle-aged woman from a committed Sandinista household. "They understand so much that we don't."

Sometimes party members become involved in local political struggles, such as a fight for control of a labor union or a campaign to impose party policies on a reluctant state agency. In these conflicts – which have become less frequent as the party has consolidated its power – the FSLN gains a critical advantage by working through the disciplined minority of party members within the larger organization.

Some party members are professional cadres, devoting themselves to full-time political activity. To keep cadres from developing a parochial perspective on the revolution, they are rotated through varied jobs. Dora María Téllez, whose own posts have ranged from political chief of Managua to Minister of Health, explains:

> We have a policy in the Sandinista Front of rotating cadres from the national to the regional level and vice versa. We also rotate institutional [government], party-related and grassroots [mass organization] work so that each cadre gets a well-rounded background and a broad perspective. Because sometimes when you are always in the same place, you can become entrenched in a single point of view.[25]

The FSLN, according to its leaders, is governed by the Leninist principle of democratic centralism, which attempts to combine democratic accountability with hierarchical authority.[26] Sandinista organizational doctrine emphasizes collective leadership and "consultative" decision making, allowing varied opinions to be aired while the party line is being defined. "We try to develop collective forms of leadership at all levels," notes Arce, "to insure that decisions are not made on the basis of the wisdom of a single man but rather by a group discussion."[27]

But the democratic potential in these principles is undercut by the way leaders are chosen and the FSLN's insistence on party discipline. Party officials at all levels are appointed from above rather than being elected, and there is no formal mechanism for altering the membership of the National Directorate. The party's central organization is charged with protecting "the purity of the party line" from deviation.[28] Party members must, says Comandante Núñez, be prepared to "obey unhesitatingly the directions of the central and intermediate organizations," and must, according to Comandante Borge, be able to act with "a single will" once a policy has been discussed and settled.[29]

Arce acknowledges that the FSLN is currently less democratic than centralist.[30] This authoritarian tendency reflects the party's continuing fear of disunity. "The most serious internal danger facing the FSLN," warns the "72 hours document," "is the maintenance of divisionist, sectarian, or factional positions which . . . sabotage the internal cohesion of the organization . . ."[31] According to a ranking party intellectual, Sandinista centralism also reflects the guerrilla origins of the party and its contemporary military preoccupations: "You don't carry on a debate in the middle of a battle." But party leaders are aware of the dangers of centralism. The "72 Hours Document" warns: "An organization that does not stimulate collective discussion, the education of its militants, the participation of its members in the burning questions of the movement, is an organization that rapidly ages, loses its vigor and strength, and is politically liquidated."[32] Borge has called for the election of all party leaders at some future, unspecified date.[33]

## Militants: Recruitment

The FSLN is an elite party. Published estimates of its membership vary from 16,000 to 50,000, but even the latter figure does not exceed 3 percent of the adult population – low by international comparison with other governing vanguard parties.[34] (Of course, none of these estimates includes the hundreds of thousands of supporters of the FSLN who join the Sandinista mass organizations.) Lea Guido, then head of the party's Department of Organization, acknowledged in a 1986 interview that the party had lost track of the size of its membership. During 1985 the party purged itself of an unknown number of members, but at the same time the party was carrying on a recruitment drive, especially among the military.

Dependable information on the social composition of the party is hard to come by. Casual observation suggests that all classes are represented in the FSLN. Visits to a government office, a lower-class barrio, and an agrarian cooperative are all likely to turn up party members. But the middle and upper classes seem to be over-represented. Guido estimated that 30 percent of party members are professionals and technical experts, a figure that apparently does not include the many teachers and health workers in the party. In the top ranks of the FSLN there are more than a few sons and daughters of upper-class families. Guido herself – daughter of a Somocista Congressman, educated abroad – fits this description. The roll of the Sandinista Assembly is sprinkled with traditional uppper-class surnames like Cuadra, Chamorro, Cardenal, and Baltodano.

The Sandinista party has long taken the position that it will accept members of any class background as long as they are ready to defend the classes the party represents. Ricardo Morales, a ranking Sandinista leader who was killed by the National Guard in 1973, observed that Nicaragua needed a "proletarian vanguard," but its members need not be of the proletarian origins. "Those who assume the position of the proletariat, the thought and principles of the proletariat, who fight to carry out the historic mission of the proletariat – they are proletarians."[35] The first large group admitted to the party after the insurrection evoked these observations from a *Barricada* editorialist:

> [T]he majority of them, including government ministers and highly trained professionals, are of bourgeois extraction. Nonetheless, some years ago, they joined the [armed] struggle and [in the] Sandinista government they have shown themselves to be exemplary servants of the people. They have abandoned their bourgeois situation, abandoned the class viewpoint they held by inheritance, have renounced the present privileges of the social stratum from which they came to assume the defense of the historic project of the only revolutionary class, the working class. In synthesis, they have been granted membership for their class perspective [*conciencia clasista*].[36]

The majority of party members, Sandinista officials acknowledged in 1986, were soldiers or officers, both because of recruitment efforts within the army and because, in wartime, the FSLN was channeling many of its members into the armed forces (often, it appears, for political work).

Women, says the FSLN, comprise 24 percent of its membership. Their representation in leadership positions is on a similar scale: the Sandinista assembly is 20 percent female and the regional committees average 24 percent.[37] No woman serves on the National Directorate but, as the sizable minority in the Assembly suggests, women do hold some key leadership positions. One of them is Lea Guido, who has served as Minister of Health, chief of the FSLN's organizational department and most recently, head of AMNLAE, the Sandinista women's organization. Other prominent women in the party are Leticia Herrera, national head of the Sandinista Defense Committees, Monica Baltodano, secretary to the presidency for regional affairs (a cabinet position), Doris Tejerino, head of the national police, and Dora María Téllez, until recently Political Secretary of the crucial Managua regional committee. Herrera, Baltodano, and Téllez were military leaders in the insurrection and received the prestigious title of Guerrilla Commander (one step below the Commanders of the Revolution on the Directorate) at its conclusion.

Women are quite active in the Sandinista mass organizations, especially the neighborhood Sandinista Defense Committees (CDSs), whose leadership at all levels appears to be predominantly female. But the extreme demands that the party makes on members are inconsistent with the traditional family roles of Nicaraguan women. Aside from an extraordinary time commitment, the party requires that its members be willing to serve anywhere, in any capacity – including, of course, the military. While members agree that the party weighs personal situations when it makes assignments, the FSLN's overriding concerns are the military and political needs of a besieged revolution. Nicaraguan women are reluctant to risk lengthy separations from their families. Many complain that limited child care services and uncooperative male attitudes hobble their participation in the revolution. A young Sandinista militant attached to the staff of the National Assembly says that having a husband who belongs to the party makes little difference. "Our men are still very *machista*," she remarks. A young working-class mother, who has reluctantly passed up an invitation to join the party, expresses her own resentment with the same term.

The FSLN maintains a continuous search for new members through its committees in workplaces, neighborhoods, and military units. Says a party official, "We're looking for people who are outstanding in their work and in the tasks of the revolution, have a clear ideological conception of the Sandinista Popular Revolution and want to be members." Prospective members should be at least 25 (younger activists are expected to join Sandinista Youth). They may not be usurers, though there is apparently no explicit prohibition on owning property or receiving profit. Conscious that the arrogance or misbehavior of some members have affected the popular image of the FSLN, party committees are wary of candidates who might be overbearing, abusive, dishonest, less than model family members, or given to public inebriation. By 1986, past or current involvement in national defense had become an indispensable qualification for membership.

The typical sources of new members are Sandinista Youth, the army (which has its own Sandinista Youth structure), state agencies, and state-owned enterprises. Less frequently, candidates are recruited in their own neighborhoods by barrio party committees. There is an unintended bias against women in this recruitment pattern, which emphasizes workplace, army, and school (the traditional base of Sandinista Youth) over the neighborhood. Prospects generally receive invitations to join the FSLN from a party base committee. Those who accept become "aspirants," provisional members who must pass through a probationary period before they become full-status *militantes* (militants).

To win the militant's red-and-black pin bearing the image of Sandino candidates must demonstrate obedience to party authority, strong commitment to the party's political line and collective organizational values, and boundless capacity for work on the party's behalf. Several militants who were interviewed agreed that the party expects "ideological clarity" or "a clear Sandinista position." But, volunteers Lea Guido, "We do not ask people to be Marxist-Leninists." They must have an "anti-imperialist consciousness," she adds, and a "willingness to defend the [social and political] conquests of the revolution." Pressed, she concedes that, yes, the FSLN does expect its militants to identify with Nicaragua's workers and peasants. Party members told a visiting American Marxist that the FSLN educates its members with the writings of Marx, Lenin, Sandino, and Fonseca.[38]

For whatever reason, a high percentage of aspirants are found wanting. Rejected by the base committee or one of the higher-level party committees that must also pass on their candidacies for militancy, they are expelled from the party.[39] Successful candidates become militants within 12 to 18 months.

## Militants: Revolutionary Values

The FSLN strives to instill in its members a set of organizational values and a revolutionary mystique. In the catalogue of virtues that party spokespersons ascribe to the model Sandinista, modesty, discipline, self-sacrifice, and a collective spirit receive repeated emphasis.[40]

"Revolutionary modesty," suggested FSLN founder Carlos Fonseca, should be cultivated to counteract the personal vanity and rivalry that endangers the collective life of the vanguard. "Modesty and simplicity," urges a party propaganda manual, are "indispensable qualities" for the Sandinista doing ideological work among the masses.[41] It is symptomatic that the much-admired Henry Ruiz is known within the FSLN as "Modesto."

As employed by Sandinistas, "discipline" implies both dedication to duty and submission to party authority. A party member who failed to win advancement to militancy because of his drinking problem is described by a militant in his base committee as "undisciplined." According to a party militant in Matagalpa, "The party can send us wherever it wants and say 'be there tomorrow.' There must be discipline, a militant will, a Sandinista calling. Whoever can't meet these demands is out of the party. We can't have men who are vacillating, timid — not men of glass but men of steel."[42] In his memoir of the 1970s, Omar Cabezas recalls his effort to convince the owner of a funeral parlor to provide a hiding place for a Sandinista leader who was passing through León. "Look," he told the reluctant businessman, "in the daytime we put him in a casket and put another casket on top, and he can spend the day like that. The compañeros are very *disciplined.*"[43]

Being a Sandinista, Carlos Núñez explained to a university audience, means self-sacrifice: "daily work, systematic, arduous, difficult, one day here, another day in the most distant corners of the country."[44] A militant, says Borge (who was tortured in Somoza's jails) must be prepared "to suffer, to bear pain."[45] The organization's disposition to demand limitless sacrifice is suggested by the experience of a young pre-militant, who was thrown out of the party in 1983 after he refused to leave his job and his family for a third tour with the army on the northern front. He had returned from his second tour with malaria and an ulcer.

A collective spirit or consciousness, a sense of brotherhood, Sandinistas believe, is the glue that holds the vanguard together. This attitude reached its highest expression among the members of a guerrilla band. Omar Cabezas recalls, "a brotherhood among us; we treated each other gruffly, but actually we loved each other with a deep love, with a great male tenderness. We were a group of men bound by a single embrace, like brothers." Cabezas goes on to suggest that a "new man" was emerging from the brotherhood of the guerrillas, who contains within himself the germ of a new society: "an open, unegotistical man, no longer petty – a tender man who sacrifices himself for others, a man who gives everything for others, who suffers when others suffer and who also laughs when others laugh."[46] The communal values of this new man are, for Sandinistas, the antithesis of the selfishness and egotism they identify with bourgeois society.

From an organizational point of view, the collective spirit implies both an emotional bond among members and a willing subordination of the self to the needs of the organization. This latter sense is implicit in the other three virtues. Militants must be prepared to yield their lives (sacrifice), wills (discipline), and personalities (modesty) to the revolution. Fonseca made this total commitment explicit: "[O]ur obligation is to subordinate everything to the interests of the Sandinista cause, to the interests of the subjugated Nicaraguan people, to the interests of the exploited and oppressed of Nicaragua."[47]

The essence of the revolutionary mystique that the FSLN cultivates in its militants is the sense of immersion in a triumphant struggle for human progress. The oath required of each new member of the FSLN pledges the individual to "fight for the redemption of the oppressed and exploited of Nicaragua and of the World." Faith in ultimate victory is a recurrent theme in the personal accounts of party members such as Dora María Tellez, who tried to explain this "mystery" of the Revolution to a sympathetic interviewer shortly after the defeat of Somoza:

> What makes a man believe in his potential as a man? What makes a woman believe that she is capable of anything? That is one of the great mysteries about the Revolution. They don't teach it to you at school. You don't learn to believe in humanity on the streets. Religion doesn't teach it. It teaches us to believe in God, not in men and women. So it's difficult to awaken that belief in yourself and in others. It becomes an obsession – the people must rise up, they must. It begins with a vision, an imaginary idea. And holding onto that vision requires a constant process of nourishment. At first the Organization had very

little capacity to analyze our people's experiences. We had to understand that people are historically capable of making revolutions, that they must and will make them – that's a law. But I never understood it as a historical law. I think many people didn't. Of course there was the Cuban Revolution that showed us it could be done ... [But] all we knew was that we were going to make the Revolution, however long it took. Ten, 20, 30 even 40 years.[48]

Not all members are equal to the demands that the FSLN makes on its militants. As Arce acknowledged in July 1985, some "have been bad party members or have even betrayed the revolution." At the time, the party was in the midst of a purge of its membership. A few months earlier, the party had announced the expulsion and impending trial of a party member who, according to documents found in National Guard intelligence files, had fed the Guard information during the insurrection. But the cases mentioned earlier of members dismissed from the party for drunkenness and refusal to return to the war front were probably more typical.

The available evidence indicates that the separations were based on both personal inadequacies and ideological differences. Sandinista officials interviewed on the subject referred vaguely to "ideological diversionism," "liberalist tendencies," and "failure to uphold the positions of the National Directorate." A party intellectual observed that in the last stages of the insurrection, many of those who entered the FSLN "had little political education and did not know what the party stood for."

In their 1985 party reorganization communiqué the comandantes called for organizational mechanisms to guard against "lifestyles and working habits that alienate us from the masses."[49] This cryptic phrase suggests corruption and arrogance in the ranks of the party. By 1985, the FSLN was many times larger than it had been in 1979. Particularly during the peaceful interval between the insurrection and the expansion of the contra war, when the FSLN was transformed from a compact conspiracy into a ruling party, many people with limited commitments or self-serving motives must have been attracted to the party. The same communiqué indicated that the party was considering reforms of its base committees, hinting that the committees were failing, in many cases, to build strong relationships with the masses. This general line of self-criticism reveals a preoccupation with effectiveness of party members as grassroots representatives of the vanguard.

The 1985 purges were not accompanied by a public campaign calling for ideological purity or by an imposition of new ideological demands on the members of the Sandinista mass organizations, nor was there any indication of a political upheaval within the leadership. Rather the evidence points to a collective desire within the leadership to draw a boundary of discipline and ideology around the party. Arce described the purges as a process of "Sandinista reaffirmation" based on "what we expect from today's Sandinistas this year, in this war, in this economic crisis." Party members would be asked "to think about this" and those who were prepared to meet the organization's expectations "can stay with us, and those who feel they are not, then we will see how we can continue to be friends."[50]

# 3

# *The Party in the State and Mass Organizations*

"If you people want to live like goats on that hill, it's not my fault," the official told the leaders of a neighborhood Sandinista Defense Committee (CDS). He refused to connect their barrio on a rugged slope above Matagalpa to the city water system. The offended CDS leaders soon appealed to local party officials for support in their fight with the water bureaucracy. When members of the Sandinista farm workers' union (ATC), illegally occupied a private farm near Matagalpa, the agriculture ministry asked the party to pressure ATC to remove them. When a popular official of CST, the Sandinista urban union, was suddenly transferred to a CDS position, some union members were angry. They "didn't understand," the ex-unionist later explained, "that the Front has policies for placing people."

These three glimpses of everyday political life in Matagalpa, a provincial capital north of Managua, illustrate the centrality of the FSLN in the tripartite system of party, state, and mass organizations that has grown up in Nicaragua since 1979 (see figure 3.1). None of the larger questions about the character and future of the Sandinista political system can be answered without understanding the party's relationships with the state and the mass organizations, such as the CDS committees or the Sandinista unions.

## The Party and the Government

As he announced his cabinet in January 1985, President Daniel Ortega commented on the role of the party in the new constitutional order: "We cannot think that the FSLN is here and the structures of the state and the armed forces are somewhere else. The FSLN is the nervous system, the

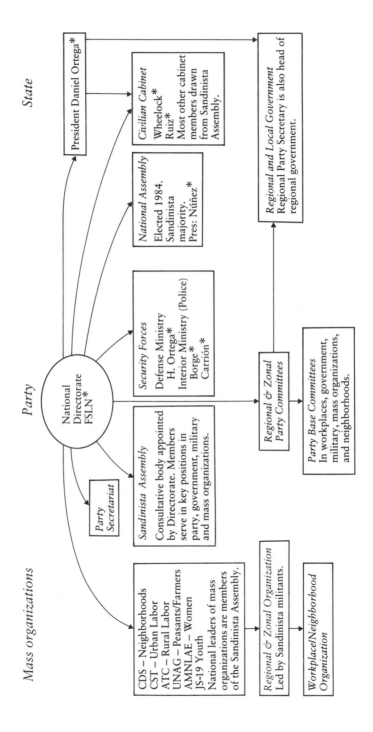

**Figure 3.1** The Sandinista system of power *
* Members of the National Directorate

State

Party

Mass organizations

President Daniel Ortega*

Civilian Cabinet
Wheelock*
Ruiz*
Most other cabinet members drawn from Sandinista Assembly.

National Assembly
Elected 1984. Sandinista majority.
Pres: Núñez *

Regional and Local Government
Regional Party Secretary is also head of regional government.

National Directorate FSLN*

Security Forces
Defense Ministry H. Ortega*
Interior Ministry (Police) Borge* Carrión *

Party Secretariat

Sandinista Assembly
Consultative body appointed by Directorate. Members serve in key positions in party, government, military and mass organizations.

Regional & Zonal Party Committees

Party Base Committees
In workplaces, government, military, mass organizations, and neighborhoods.

CDS – Neighborhoods
CST – Urban Labor
ATC – Rural Labor
UNAG – Peasants/Farmers
AMNLAE – Women
JS-19 Youth
National leaders of mass organizations are members of the Sandinista Assembly.

Regional & Zonal Organization
Led by Sandinista militants.

Workplace/Neighborhood Organization

motor force of everything and its cadres are present in all areas of revolutionary life. The National Directorate will be determining [policy] lines."[1]

By emphasizing the central place of the party and its Directorate, Ortega was reaffirming the position that the FSLN had publicly asserted since 1980 and privately held well before that.[2] In the minds of the party's top leaders, defining the relationship of party to the state means establishing a distinction between the vanguard role of the Sandinista Front and the executive responsibilities of the government.

In a 1981 speech, Wheelock described the state as "nothing more than the instrument of the people to make the revolution." But Wheelock implied that the FSLN would compromise itself politically and undercut the effectiveness of government administration if it interfered with the daily operations of the state: "[The Party] confer[s] on the state a political line, give[s] it eyes by which to orient itself, without tying its hands and feet because that could deprive the state of its executive character and complicate the party's leadership mission." The party, Wheelock emphasized, "does not substitute itself for the state."[3]

In 1984, Arce took a similar stance. "I can't give orders to the most recently recruited soldier," asserted Bayardo Arce in a 1984 interview. "The army has its own command and the government its administration." The Directorate limits itself to developing "general lines of policy." But this division of responsibilities was only gradually institutionalized, as Arce recognized in the following carefully formulated response:

> In the beginning, we were involved in everything because in the absence of institutions someone had to decide. The only visible authority recognized for revolutionary practice was the National Directorate. But one of the first things that we did was define a functional framework. Thus, we created a government, a military structure, and a security organization. The National Directorate has reserved for itself the definition of *major lines of political economy, military doctrine, agrarian reform, and foreign policy.*[4]

Note that Arce reserves the principal decisions in domestic policy and security affairs for the Directorate. He also distinguishes the military and the police from the government, implying a direct relationship between the Directorate and the security forces, rather than one mediated through the government.

Since late 1979, members of the National Directorate have occupied the key ministerial positions. The cabinet that Ortega announced in January 1985 included five members of the Directorate, nine members of the Sandinista Assembly, and four others, two of whom could be identified as Sandinista militants.[5] The party also held over 60 percent of the seats in the newly elected National Assembly, allowing it to control legislation and the drafting of a national constitution.

The party reorganization announced later that year strengthened party-state ties, especially on the regional level. The position of regional party secretary was merged with that of the president's regional "delegate" (a ministerial rank position). Thus, in each of nine regions and special zones the same person is the ranking representative of both party and state. All of the people appointed to this position were members of the Sandinista Assembly.[6] The Directorate presented the change as a direct response to the war emergency, requiring firmer leadership and better coordination of military, political, and economic administration.

The influence of the FSLN reaches deep into the state through committees of the Sandinista militants in each government office and public enterprise. In the early years of the revolution, these party committees helped the FSLN gain control over a bureaucracy whose loyalty to the goals of the revolution – even after the elimination of Somocistas from leadership positions – was uncertain. The committees explain party positions to their fellow employees (via personal contacts, assemblies, and political bulletin boards), mobilize people for Sandinista political activities, recruit new party members, and promote the implementation of Sandinista programs within their agencies. The National Employees Union (UNE), the party-run union that represents most public employees, is an important vehicle for these efforts.

## The Party and the Military

Since 1979, the FSLN has maintained a special relationship with one sector of the revolutionary state, the security forces. The Sandinistas were determined to avoid the fatal mistake of left-wing governments from Guatemala (1954) to Chile (1973) that were overthrown by their own right-wing military. They were also unwilling to accept the military veto over national policy that has constrained the policies of many reformist governments in Latin America.

As early as the party's 1969 "Historic Program," the FSLN made public its intention to replace the National Guard with a "patriotic, revolutionary, people's army" motivated by "revolutionary ideals" and capable of defending "the rights won against the inevitable assault by the reactionary forces of the country and Yankee imperialism."[7] This goal was reaffirmed in 1979 by the "72 hours document," which outlined plans for transforming the guerrilla movement into a national army loyal "to the revolution and to the leadership of its historic vanguard: the FSLN." The document stresses the need to develop a "permanent political education program" and a strong party organization within the armed forces.[8]

The new Sandinista Popular Army (EPS) was created along the lines described in the document. The EPS and the forces of the Interior Ministry, including the Sandinista Police and State Security, were placed under the direct control of the National Directorate, by-passing authority of the junta and the Council of State.[9] (Their special status was implied by the label Sandinista, a designation otherwise reserved for party organizations.) A Defense and Security Committee, led by Borge, Carrión, and Humberto Ortega, was created by the Directorate to coordinate security policy and oversee the party network within the armed forces.[10]

The Nicaraguan security forces are led by members of the National Directorate and the Sandinista Assembly. One-third of the Directorate and 30 percent of the Assembly members hold leadership positions in the EPS or the Interior Ministry. Within the EPS they are the commander-in-chief, chief of staff, and both deputy chiefs, five out of seven regional commanders, and 11 other ranking officers. A similar situation exists in the Interior Ministry, whose leaders include two members of the Directorate and 13 members of the Sandinista Assembly.[11] Of course, thousands of other Sandinista militants serve in the security forces. It is hardly surprising that Sandinistas continue to describe their party as "a political-military organization."

As the programmatic documents of 1969 and 1979 indicate, the FSLN intended to create an ideologically committed military. The two security forces have political sections led by Sandinista Assembly members, in addition to internal FSLN and Sandinista Youth structures. Guerrilla Commander Omar Cabezas, who heads both the Sandinista party apparatus and the political section of the Interior Ministry, views the ministry as "one of the fundamental instruments of revolutionary power." The leader of Sandinista Youth in the Interior Ministry describes his organization as "an auxiliary force to the FSLN in pushing forward the political and ideological tasks which the Interior Ministry requires to consolidate itself as a revolutionary power structure."[12]

Military conscription, which began in late 1983, gave the FSLN the opportunity to carry its message to tens of thousands of Nicaraguan youth. The draft challenged the military, writes an army officer in an EPS publication, "to convert the army into a great school for the formation of patriotic and revolutionary values." The combatant must have "ideological conviction and consciousness of what he is fighting for . . . must be able to go into combat ready to give everything, even his blood if need be." He should return to civilian society, "with firmer ideological conviction, more patriotic, more Sandinista."[13]

Casual conversations with soldiers suggest that the FSLN has made effective use of the opportunity to win support for the revolution. Most are drawn from lower-class families,[14] and are open to the ideals of the revolution. The army's political message is simple and undogmatic, emphasizing the revolution's commitment to the poor and the identification of the EPS with Sandino's earlier anti-imperialist crusade.[15] Many conscripts return to civilian life with membership in Sandinista Youth or even the FSLN.

Their very survival is undercutting earlier resistance to the draft and their enthusiasm for the revolution is likely to bolster sagging civilian support.

## The Mass Organizations

The Sandinista mass organizations (also called popular organizations) link the party vanguard with the general population. In contrast to the FSLN, the mass organizations are typically open to anyone within a broad demographic category (neighborhood, workplace, occupation, gender, or age cohort) who is not overtly opposed to the revolution (see table 3.1). According to their national leader, the neighborhood CDSs (Sandinista Defense Committees), accept "anyone who desires to work ... We do not require anyone to be a Sandinista militant ... CDS members can belong to any political party. They can be Catholics, Evangelists, or any other religion."[16] Only Sandinista Youth, consisting largely of students and soldiers, deviates significantly from this loose standard. Functioning as a gateway to party membership, Sandinista Youth distinguishes between ordinary members and militants. From the latter the organization expects a level of ideological conformity and revolutionary discipline that is more characteristic of the party than the mass organizations.

The popular organizations have three broad purposes: to draw people into the activities of the revolution, to expose them to the ideology of the

**Table 3.1** The principal Sandinista mass organizations and their memberships, 1984

| Organization | Constituency | Membership |
| --- | --- | --- |
| CDS (Sandinista Defense Committees) | Neighborhoods | 520,000–600,000 |
| CST (Sandinista Workers Central) | Urban Labor | 111,500 |
| UNAG (National Union of Farmers and Cattlemen) | Peasants, Cooperatives, Small Farmers | 75,000 |
| AMNLAE (Luisa Amanda Espinosa Nicaraguan Women's Association) | Women | 60,000 |
| ATC (Association of Rural Workers) | Rural Wage Workers | 40,000 (full-time) 110,000 (part-time) |
| JS–19 (July 19 – Sandinista Youth) | Youth | 30,000 |

*Sources:*  Luis Serra, "The Grassroots Organizations," in T. Walker (ed.), *The First Five Years* and Gary Ruchwarger, "The Sandinista Mass Organizations," in Richard Harris and Carlos Vilas (eds), *Nicaragua: A Revolution Under Siege.*

revolution, and to represent the viewpoint of their members within the revolution. Sandinistas portray the popular organizations as the germ of the popular democracy they are creating in Nicaragua. Formal mechanisms have been created to provide the mass organizations with a voice in the formulation of public policy. For example, representatives of mass organizations participate in national and local councils that advise government agencies whose work is relevant to their membership. The popular organizations perform some para-statal functions. CDS committees, for instance, are the neighborhood administrators of the rationing system. Until the 1984 election, the mass organizations were represented in the national legislature.

The concerns of the mass organizations range from neighborhood improvement (CDS) and the legal status of women (AMNLAE) to the maintenance of production (CST) and farm commodity pricing (UNAG). All attempt to involve their members in party-sponsored demonstrations, in volunteer work, and in defense activities such as the militia. And all preach the FSLN's political message to their members, adjusted in each case to the audience and the concerns of the moment. The peasants and farmers of UNAG, for example, are likely to hear less talk about class conflict and socialism than the members of Sandinista Youth or the urban workers in CST.

## A Case Study: Sandinista Defense Committees in Matagalpa

The national network of Sandinista Defense Committees is the largest and most pervasive of the mass organizations. In Matagalpa, a town of about 60,000 inhabitants in mountainous coffee country, committees have been organized in all the barrios of the old core city and the growing ring of shantytowns in the surrounding hills.[17] Participation in the committees, support for the revolution, and class composition all vary in rough proportion to distance from the central business district. Matagalpa's more affluent merchants and farmers live in or near the business district. Moving up and out from the center, the population mix becomes increasingly working class and, then, under class. The housing standard gradually declines from ample, stucco-finished, elegantly appointed establishments to wretched one-room, dirt-floor huts, built of scrap materials and protected against the weather by sheets of garbage-bag quality plastic.

Every neighborhood includes friends and enemies of the revolution, but enemies are much more common in the center of town. There, most people have little or nothing to do with the CDSs. For a CDS leader and Sandinista militant in one of the outlying barrios the attitude of affluent Matagalpans is easy to understand: "They have reasons to be opposed. They lived from the exploitation of the people. They can't do that now." The committees have their strongest support in the hills, where bitter memories of the old regime linger, the redistributive goals of the revolution are popular, and basic urban services, which a CDS can help provide, are often lacking.

In Matagalpa, as elsewhere in Nicaragua, the CDSs have multifarious responsibilities. Especially in the less developed areas of the city, the committees combine volunteer labor with government-provided materials to build or improve streets, schools, health posts, and water and lighting systems. The CDSs participate in the allocation of land in new barrios. They also collaborate with the Health Ministry's immunization and sanitation campaigns, support the Education Ministry's adult education program (Popular Education Cooperatives), and help administer the food rationing system. As their title implies, the committees participate in the defense of the revolution. They recruit volunteers for local defense forces (the territorial militia) and maintain a neighborhood night watch known as "revolutionary vigilance," designed to control crime and spot counterrevolutionary activity. Finally, the committees are a mechanism through which the FSLN politically instructs and mobilizes the population of Matagalpa.

Barrio Sandino, two facing rows of tin-roof shacks ascending a steep hill just north of the city, provides an example of what a CDS can achieve as a voluntary neighborhood improvement organization. Prior to 1979, the barrio, then known as El Chorizo (The Sausage), had no light, water, or sanitation facilities. (A prominent Somocista, who lived down the hill, made money by selling the people water at 10 centavos a can.) El Chorizo was built along a narrow, rocky cow-path that became a muddy morass in the winter and the scene of robberies and assaults at night. According to the residents, the barrio was infested with criminals, many of whom were known to the population but protected by the National Guard. (Some probably served the Guard as political spies in the neighborhood.)

From childhood, the people of El Chorizo kept themselves alive by working at low-wage jobs, taking in laundry or selling firewood and other low-value items door to door. Their biographies are full of hunger, long, expensive illnesses, and abuse by the authorities and the rich. Before 1979, their rights to the small patches of land they lived on was a continual preoccupation. One woman with five children recalls having her shack and small garden leveled three times by a rich landowner whose property adjoined the barrio. He was backed on each occasion by Guardsmen, whose leader calmly tore up the "paper" she offered to attest her claim to the land.[18]

In 1977, "muchachos" from the FSLN began to work in the barrio. They helped some of the poorest people organize a land seizure. "The Guard came," remembers one resident. "They threatened the people. They accused them of communism. They took shots at some houses. But the people said: you can kill us, but we're not leaving." The authorities were unable to dislodge the invaders and the matter was apparently lost in the confusion of the larger struggle then developing in the country.

Life is still hard in Barrio Sandino. Most families are probably no more economically secure than they were a decade ago and the war has imposed new burdens on many of them. But the CDS and supporting government programs have transformed the neighborhood and improved the everyday experience of its residents. The committee has turned Barrio Sandino's cow-path into an all-weather street, brought light and water to the neighborhood, constructed latrines, and built a one-room school house/community hall. It actively supports public health and adult education programs. The CDS night watch has not spotted any counterrevolutionaries, but it has made the street safe at night, and El Chorizo's criminal element, uncomfortable with the new atmosphere, has departed. Families are no longer in danger of losing their homes because a sympathetic government controls urban land allocation in collaboration with the city-wide CDS and the rich are now reluctant to call attention to themselves by infringing the rights of the poor.[19]

The Barrio Sandino committee and the other neighborhood CDSs are linked to state agencies and the FSLN by a city-wide ("zonal") CDS committee. The five zonal committee members are full-time organizers, who prepared for their positions with a three-month course in community work at a school which trains leaders for the Cuban CDRs (neighborhood committees equivalent to the CDSs). They work extraordinarily long hours for modest pay. The job, acknowledges one, makes an ordinary family life impossible. All are young, competent, and committed to the revolution. They often wear their militia uniforms on the job, but their bearing is far from martial – sometimes they wear only half the uniform, top or bottom, and their interactions with barrio residents are generally friendly and informal. The uniforms are a show of solidity and readiness in wartime, but they also reflect the Front's conception of itself as a political-military organization.

Although the zonal committee is formally elected by the city-wide assembly of barrio CDS leaders, the hand of the party is evident in the selection process. The two women and three men on the committee are all members of the FSLN who moved into their current jobs from positions in the Sandinista labor movement. One recalls,

> I was working for the regional CST when the Frente decided to move me to the CDS. There was a fight over this decision because some of my compañeros at the union did not understand that the Front has policies for placing people. I was happy working for the CST, but I saw the importance of political work with the masses.

Prospective zonal committee members are presented unopposed to the assembly, for an up or down vote expressed by a show of hands or a round of applause. The official candidate is, of course, unlikely to be rejected by this method.

One of the principal duties of members of the zonal committee is organizing barrio committees. Until recently, the barrio election process in Matagalpa was similar to the zonal pattern. Elections were held when deemed necessary by the zonal committee. Typically, a member of the zonal committee would meet with a small group of barrio residents identified with the revolution to select candidates for positions on the barrio committee. The candidates, generally unopposed, would be presented at an open meeting for confirmation. In 1985, however, the national Sandinista leadership dictated a series of reforms in barrio CDS elections, including a more open nominating process, multiple candidacies for barrio offices, and secret balloting.

"The CDS," says a barrio committee member, "is 60 percent politics." Zonal committee members refer to their responsibility for the "political education" and "conscientization" of the city population. The committees are used to mobilize people for political demonstrations. Zonal committee members regularly attend barrio CDS meetings to discuss neighborhood projects, but also to deliver short political talks. Their remarks typically present the FSLN'S interpretation of *cuestiones coyunturales*, problems of the current political situation. In mid-1984, topics included the significance of Arturo Cruz's opposition presidential candidacy (or non-condidacy), American aggression, food shortages and government measures to deal with them, and the 50th anniversary of Sandino's death. Although the tone of these talks is generally quiet and reasoned, they sometimes reflect the passions of the political moment. For example, two days after Cruz supporters attacked Sandinista demonstrators (including mothers of soldiers fallen in the contra war) outside a political meeting in Matagalpa, a zonal committee member told residents of a working-class neighborhood,

> Yesterday we mobilized people for an act of repudiation of the criminal Arturo Cruz. Some of Cruz's people from Managua and people we know here, National Guardsmen, bourgeois cowards, attacked the mothers of martyrs. These people are enemies of the revolution ... We will not be fooled. We know who they are. We are watching them. And we will be glad to match forces with them. We have to defend the streets. ... The workers must reflect. ... There is a contradiction between the bourgeois bastards who want to destroy popular power and the workers.

The political messages barrio residents received through CDS channels are reinforced by party members who live in the neighborhood. Even if they are not CDS officers, they are regarded by the committees as "important political guides," who can help "orient us" because they have more advanced political knowledge. According to the regional head of the FSLN, one of the basic responsibilities of barrio party committees is "to educate CDS members, especially the leaders."

The members of Matagalpa's zonal committee, who often find themselves rationalizing government actions or mediating between public authorities and the barrio committees, insist that their organization is independent of the state. "We are not an appendage of the state but a bridge," comments one leader. In fact, the zonal leadership is quite willing to confront public authorities over issues that are important to barrio residents, as long as they can do so without opposing fundamental positions of the party. The FSLN actively encourages the mass organizations and its own members to fight "bureaucratism" – arrogance and inefficiency – in the state. For their part, barrio leaders are not passive in their relations with the party and state. Many have learned how to use CDS and party officials to get what they want out of public officials. A conflict between the CDSs and the local director of INAA, the national water agency, illustrates this pattern.

When representatives of Barrio Sandino visited INAA to request help with the water system they hoped to build, the official turned them down with the comment, "If you people want to live like goats on that hill, it's not my fault." Some bureaucrats, the coordinator of the barrio committee later commented, "acted as if we were still living in the times of Somoza." Barrio Sandino soon learned that other barrios were dissatisfied with the same official. One issue was INAA charges for water that was not being provided. CDS coordinators collected water bills in their barrios and met with the director to demand that the bills be reduced. According to the Barrio Sandino representative, the man's replies were "indecent, totally indecent." After this incident, the city-wide CDS leaders' assembly formally voted to ask INAA for the official's removal. They were apparently supported in this by the party and the man lost his job.

No single revolutionary institution has evoked more disparate reactions than the CDS. Sandinistas characterize the committees as grassroots popular democracy, an institution designed to empower the masses and allow them to participate actively in reshaping their communities. Enemies of the revolution, especially those outside the country, see the CDS as an instrument of totalitarianism, a national network of spies and political enforcers. Contra gunmen have made CDS activists and their families a favored target when they invade small communities.

The leaders of the revolution themselves have repeatedly criticized "abuses of authority" by CDS committees, such as withholding ration cards from families that refuse to participate in the neighborhood night watch or harassment of neighbors who are ideologically opposed to the revolution. "[A]ll CDS activities are voluntary," the National Directorate warned in a sternly worded letter to CDS coordinators. The commit-tees, counseled National CDS secretary Leticia Herrera, must employ "persuasion" rather than "repressive measures" to win support.[20]

Interviews with Matagalpans of different social classes and varied ideologies in 1984 turned up little evidence of the overt abuses criticized by national leaders (abuses may be more common in the militant working-class barrios of Managua). A resident of an older working-class barrio said that the organizer of the night watch in his neighborhood had threatened to withhold ration cards from people who refused to participate. The threat was resented, but apparently not very effective (few participated in the watch), and never carried out. Two informants, one from a prosperous central city barrio and the other from an outlying shantytown, indicated that they had initially attended CDS meetings just to avoid problems with organized Sandinistas in the barrio. But both had stopped going without suffering consequences. In the past, according to a member of the zonal committee, there were abuses of the rationing system by barrio coordinators who were frustrated at the lack of participation in CDS activities, but such misuse of CDS powers has been eliminated.

It is difficult to find people in Matagalpa who have been victimized by the CDSs or who can even cite concrete cases of mistreatment, but some respondents indicate that they fear the committees or feel pressured by them. For example, a young man who is probably cool toward the revolution, but quiet about his opinions, acknowledges that he has had no direct problems with the CDS: "The only thing is that they have you marked [*señalado*]. They invite you to a meeting and after I refused several times with various excuses, people tell me, 'they're watching you, someone up there is watching.' Those were the words they used. There is a pressure." The extent of such pressures appears to vary from barrio to barrio, suggesting that the problem is not central policy, but the attitudes of leaders in certain neighborhoods, whom CDS critics describe as "fanatics." On the other hand, the feeling of being watched is not groundless. Nationally the CDS organization describes itself as the "Eyes and Ears of the Revolution." The night watch keeps track of comings and goings in each neighborhood. Barrio committees record attendance at meetings. Some CDS leaders clearly know who is friendly to the revolution and who is not. There is no indication that people are being persecuted for their opinions, but in the conflictive political atmosphere of contemporary Nicaragua, fears flourish.

Do the CDSs empower people at the grassroots, as Sandinistas claim? The question is simply irrelevant to affluent Matagalpans, who have little need for the committees and little to do with them. The poorest Matagalpans, those who live in the shantytowns, have been empowered by the CDSs with regard to the state and the rich. As the experience of Barrio Sandino demonstrates, the people of the shantytowns are better able to defend themselves against avaricious landowners and hostile or indifferent bureaucrats than they were under the old regime.

It is less likely the CDSs can empower the people of Matagalpa vis-à-vis the FSLN. There is a top-down quality to the CDS organization, whose leaders from the zonal committee members to the national secretary are Sandinista militants, in effect, appointed by the party and subject to its discipline.

The 1985 barrio election reforms, announced during a period of critical self-examination by the national Sandinista leadership, reflected the party's awareness that the undemocratic character of the CDSs was costing the committees popular support. Matagalpa zonal CDS leaders, interviewed in 1986, echoed the stern conclusions of the party leadership. "Participation had declined . . . we had been a little coercive . . . [in the barrio elections] we imposed a given compañero . . . we had lost the confidence of the people."

In late 1985, CDS elections were held in barrios throughout the country. According to a Matagalpa zonal leader, over half of the coordinators of barrio committees in the city were replaced. Residents of five outlying barrios, interviewed in 1986, confirmed that secret ballots were employed in the elections. In one barrio, however, a coordinator whom residents accused of stealing materials that the community had obtained to build a school was reelected, apparently by fraudulent counting of ballots. At least two of the barrios had strongly contested elections which produced victories for candidates closely identified with the FSLN. In Barrio Sandino, the incumbent coordinator, a Sandinista militant, was reelected without serious opposition. But across the highway, in a larger, more middle-class barrio, 28 people ran for CDS offices; a new coordinator was elected who is a Sandinista militant and a city engineer. The deposed coordinator (a Sandinista activist but not a party militant) later suggested that the victor was attractive to voters because they thought his municipal connections would be useful to the barrio.

These results do not suggest that election reforms are making the Matagalpa committees more independent of the FSLN. In fact, the party's continuing domination of the CDS apparatus above the barrio level, the committees' historic identification with the FSLN reaching back to the insurrection period, and the organized strength of Sandinista activists in each neighborhood may limit the extent to which the committees can ever become independent of the party. It is hardly in the interests of any barrio that needs the cooperation of the zonal CDS and government agencies to elect an anti-Sandinista committee. Nor is it likely that the reforms were intended by the FSLN to produce greater political independence. The party has, for example, steadfastly refused to remove "Sandinista" from the committees' name and continues to insist that their first purpose is, in fact, defense of the revolution. What the party apparently wanted was a neighborhood Sandinista leadership that was less abusive of its powers and enjoyed greater popular support. That sort of leadership will not necessarily empower the people vis-à-vis the party, though it may be more aggressive in registering popular complaints and representing neighborhood interests.

## The Party, the State, and the Mass Organizations

The concept of a mass organization is implicit in the notion of a revolutionary vanguard. What distinguishes the vanguard idea from other elitist concepts of leadership is precisely its emphasis on *mobilizing* and *transforming*, rather than *neutralizing*, the mass.[21] These ends assume mass organization under vanguard guidance. Inevitably, the tensions inherent in the vanguard idea are reflected in the mass organizations. Carlos Núñez, speaking for the National Directorate, expressed their dual nature in a 1980 speech:

> Under the guidance of the Frente Sandinista de Liberación Nacional, the mass organizations direct themselves, we can say, along two important lines. In the first place, our mass organizations should concern themselves with and work to strengthen the political project of the Revolution. And in the second place, they should be real instruments to express, channel, and receive the most pressing demands of the masses.[22]

Núñez leaves little doubt that he expects the mass organizations to be vigorous defenders of their constituencies, pressing "the demands of their members, of the social sectors they represent." If their needs are not met through established channels, if they "knock and no one listens," they should turn to "other forms of political persuasion . . . internal criticism, public criticism, utilization of all the communications media, even mobilization" to gain a hearing for their concerns. But Núñez weaves countervailing observations into this advice: the mass organizations operate "under the guidance" of the FSLN, within "the general line of the Revolution"; they mobilize their members "to fight positions adverse to the Revolution."[23]

Núñez seems to be suggesting a kind of revolutionary pluralism under Sandinista hegemony. The different sectors of the revolution have the right to press their concerns, to criticize, even to resort to open protest to command official attention. But policy must ultimately conform to the long-term goals of the revolution as defined by the vanguard. For example, the unions may present the workers' wage demands, but settlements should contribute to the economic stability and growth essential to the health of the revolution.

The FSLN's hegemony over the mass organizations is based, in part, on the popular support that the party continues to enjoy, but also on a series of formal mechanisms. One is the mass organizations' explicit recognition of the vanguard status of the FSLN. CST, the Sandinista labor confederation, declares in its "Regulations" that it is not a party organization and accepts members from all parties, but "the CST recognizes the Frente Sandinista de Liberación as the indisputable Vanguard of the revolutionary process." Basic documents issued by the Sandinista women's organization (AMNLAE), rural workers' union (ATC), and farmers' association (UNAG) employ very similar language. However, a set of revised "Statutes" presented to UNAG's 1986 congress (during a period when UNAG was striving to project a more independent image) refers only to the organization's participation in the "Sandinista People's Revolution" without ever mentioning the party.[24]

The leadership of the mass organizations is closely associated with the FSLN. The national heads of the six principal groups are all members of the Sandinista Assembly.[25] It also appears that mid-level mass organization leaders are typically Sandinista cadres.[26] Frequently leaders are moved laterally into their positions from other posts in the revolution, rather than moving up through the organization they serve.[27] Moreover, the FSLN has drawn many of the mass organizations' grassroots activists into the party. Like Sandinista militants serving at higher levels, they are subject to party discipline and expected to represent the party line within the organization.

These patterns of leadership recruitment undercut claims that leaders of the affiliated groups are democratically chosen. Formally, all mass organization officials are elected to their posts. But as the Matagalpa CDS organization demonstrates, election can be a polite form of imposition. Serra describes a UNAG assembly that "ratified" the regional committee "by applause."[28] At this point, it is impossible to say how common this pattern may be.

The mass organizations regularly receive "orientations" from the FSLN, setting out broad policies for Sandinista organizations, suggesting propaganda lines, and assigning specific revolutionary tasks. A regional FSLN committee, for example, may ask the regional CDS to recruit a certain number of people for a demonstration or for the militia. Mass organization leaders submit periodic reports on their activities to party counterparts, with whom they hold regular face-to-face meetings.[29]

Despite these formidible party controls over Sandinista affiliates, mass organization leaders insist that their groups are independent and that orientations are not orders. "We are an autonomous organization," asserts a CDS leader in Estelí. "We don't have a vertical relation with [the Front]."[30] His claim gains some support from periodic clashes between the FSLN and its mass affiliates.

Two early confrontations grew out of the determination of some labor leaders to push the revolution forward, in the face of the National Directorate's conviction that unbridled radicalism would produce economic chaos and political dissolution that could compromise the long-term security of the revolution. In 1980, the rural workers' union, ATC, launched a successful campaign to pursuade the leadership to confirm the status of rural property that had been seized by land-hungry peasants in the aftermath of the victory. The following year saw a struggle between the Sandinista unions and the revolutionary government over owners' decapitalization of private sector enterprises. The unions, which were demanding strengthened protective legislation and confiscation of guilty firms, organized protests and seized enterprises they accused of decapitalization. When the Labor Ministry issued a communiqué declaring such seizures illegal, the decision was attacked by the CST but publicly supported by the governing junta. Later that year, the government acceded to union demands by confiscating several major firms and supporting stringent new legislation. The government's concessions did not prevent union representatives in the Council of State from voting against provisions in the legislation supported by FSLN representatives that prohibited further seizures.[31]

In 1983, representatives of the women's group AMNLAE unsuccessfully fought a military conscription bill that exempted women. The AMNLAE delegates voted against the compromise provision incorporated into the final legislation that allowed women to volunteer for active service.[32] More recently, UNAG publicly challenged the Sandinista leadership on a key constitutional issue – direct representation of the mass organizations in the legislature – but apparently backed down when the party failed to alter its position against such representation.[33]

Some of the mass organizations are more independent than others. The least autonomous, after the early period of the revolution, have been the Sandinista unions.[34] The purpose of the unions, from the Sandinista perspective, is to represent the interests of the workers – not by pursuing immediate economic demands, but by defending the revolutionary process. "[T]he objectives we are defending," explains Lucio Jimenez, head of the CST and a member of the Sandinista Assembly, "are the revolution and its conquests – in short, socialism."[35]

Since 1979, Sandinista spokesmen have called on workers to form a unified labor movement under party leadership and to contribute to production by maintaining labor discipline, improving work efficiency and guarding against decapitalization by owners anxious to move their resources out of the country. Strikes are no longer appropriate: "The strike," declares a national assembly of Sandinista labor leaders, "is a form of struggle utilized by the workers against the class enemy, the capitalist exploiters. This form of struggle has no place in Nicaragua because power is in the hands of the workers."[36] Increases in wages and other individual economic benefits receive only qualified endorsement from Sandinistas, who believe that such gains would only contribute to politically destabilizing inflation. Instead, the party has emphasized expansion of the "social wage," collective benefits such as improved educational opportunity, health care, and work conditions.[37]

Convincing workers to subordinate their traditional economic demands to the long-term interests of the revolution proved difficult, especially given the expectation of immediate benefits that the revolutionary victory encouraged. Sandinistas played on the prestige the party had won among workers by defeating Somoza, appealed to their patriotism and to their sense of class solidarity. Members of the National Directorate appeared at union meetings to plead for cooperation. But where such mild tactics fail, more intimidating measures are employed. Defiant workers may lose their jobs in state enterprises. Labor activists are repeatedly called in by State Security for questioning. Union leaders are subject to arbitrary arrest and on occasion to long jail sentences. The harshest treatment has been reserved for the opposition labor confederations that compete with the FSLN unions for support, often by encouraging high wage demands and fomenting strikes. But uncooperative officers of Sandinista unions have not been immune. Subjected to such treatment, the opposition unions have barely managed to survive. Sandinista unions have won most of the organized labor force, but (like official labor movements elsewhere in Latin America) they appear to have little autonomy and cannot be sure of the loyalty of their own members.[38]

Although Sandinista theory describes the workers as "the main protagonists in the construction of the New Nicaragua,"[39] by the mid-1980s, the most autonomous of the mass organizations was not a representative of the working class but of small and medium-sized farmers. Until 1984, UNAG was a generally tame organization which devoted its efforts to smaller peasant farmers and cooperatives. But after 1984, under new leadership, UNAG broadened its rural social base and became an increasingly aggressive defender of its constituency. UNAG has sought better crop prices, credit concessions, improved supply of inputs, and stepped-up distribution of land under the agrarian reform. It has also defended members whose land, the organization believes, has been taken unjustly. As a result of its independent policies UNAG has frequently clashed with local government and party authorities, and occasionally with the national leaders. But even UNAG is not a fully autonomous organization. The post-1984 transformation of the organization was apparently the result of a conscious decision of the FSLN reflecting a broader Sandinista response to flagging rural support in the mid-1980s. All the members of UNAG's national board are still Sandinista militants and National Directorate member Victor Tirado still plays an important role in guiding the organization's policies and selecting its leaders.[40]

The evidence of open conflict between Sandinista authorities and the mass organizations has led some writers to attribute "relative autonomy" to the Sandinista affiliates.[41] As the experiences of the Sandinista unions and UNAG demonstrate, there is considerable variation in autonomy from organization to organization and from one period to the next. Sandinista ideology may play a role here. The very centrality of the working class in the party's revolutionary theory tempts the party to impose itself on the unions.

The Sandinista affiliates clearly have more autonomy vis-à-vis the state than they do in relation to the party. The Matagalpa CDS groups are much freer to confront government agencies – as they did with the water board – than they are to defy the FSLN. Leading party spokesmen urge the mass organizations to become more aggressive defenders of their respective social sectors. But they seldom suggest that the mass organizations should challenge the party. By directing popular dissatisfaction toward the state and placing the vanguard at a distance from both the state and the mass organizations, the party preserves the ability to make graceful concessions under pressure.

The relative autonomy of the mass organizations is constantly threatened by the powerfully centralized and disciplined organization of the FSLN. Two recent developments may have further weakened their position. One is the war, which has compelled the party to tighten its control over many aspects of national life. The other is the abandonment of the corporatist system of representation that gave the mass organizations a place in the national legislature.

On the other hand, by creating the mass organizations and preaching the gospel of democratic participation in a society with traditionally low levels of political mobilization, the FSLN has evoked new expectations and trained a grassroots leadership where none existed before. The 1985 reform of the CDS elections and the new latitude permitted UNAG are encouraging signs. They suggest that the FSLN is beginning to understand that its affiliates will not be able to maintain a mass following unless the groups are at least as responsive to their members as they are to the party. In other words, people can vote with their feet. By withholding participation in the popular organizations, they can pressure the party to turn the popular democracy it preaches into a political reality.

## The Vanguard and the Sandinista System of Power

The vanguard is the concept that bridges Sandinista ideology and organization. Their analysis of the old regime led the Sandinistas to Lenin's notion of a elite party of professional revolutionaries – capable of guiding a backward people through a complex social revolution. The gradualist (two-phase) character of the revolution foreseen by Sandinista theory reinforces the need for the vanguard. By developing an organizational network that extends throughout society, the vanguard party is able to implement revolutionary policies over the recalcitrance of established institutions while gradually transforming society.

Since 1979, the Sandinistas have developed a tripartite political system, consisting of the FSLN, the affiliated mass organizations and the party-dominated state. Power within this system radiates from the National Directorate, which is, in effect, the vanguard within the vanguard.

Party leaders characterize the FSLN as guided by democratic centralism, but concede that it is more centralist than democratic. There is no institutional mechanism for changing the membership of the Directorate and no formal check on its authority. All other party leaders are appointed from above, rather than elected. Members are expected to adhere to the party line and "obey unhesitatingly" the orders of party authorities.

Mass organizations are implicit in the idea of a revolutionary vanguard: they are the vanguard's necessary link with those it would instruct and lead. The FSLN's relationship with its own mass organizations reflects all the tensions inherent in the vanguard concept. The vanguard wants to liberate and empower the oppressed and, at the same time, to control and transform them. The Sandinista popular organizations were created to represent their constituencies, but also to mobilize them behind a program prescribed from above.

The mass organizations are an important test of the participatory democracy the Sandinistas believe they are building in Nicaragua. Unfortunately, these organizations have received little systematic study.[42] The following generalizations about them can only be regarded as tentative: (1) The mass organizations receive broad policy guidance from the FSLN and are led by Sandinista cadres, subject to party discipline. (2) In practice, the autonomy of the mass organizaitons varies considerably, from UNAG's aggressive defense of its constituency to the captive status of the Sandinista unions. (3) In settings such as Barrio Sandino the mass organizations mobilize popular energies for popular ends (e.g., building a school, vaccinating children). (4) The mass organizations are more likely to empower their members vis-à-vis the rich or the state than the party. (5) The mass organizations provide organized sectors a channel to voice their concerns within the revolution, rather than an instrument to challenge the leadership of the revolution. They hold out the possibility of a revolutionary pluralism under Sandinista hegemony.

It is appropriate that the red-and-black flag of the FSLN flies over many government offices. The party draws a distinction between executive responsibilities of the state and its own vanguard role. But by reserving for itself the formulation of national policy in crucial areas, by staffing government offices with its own cadres, by creating parallel partisan structures within public bureaucracies, and by assuming direct control of the security forces, the FSLN has carefully institutionalized its power over the state.

The Sandinistas preside over what looks like a monolithic system of power. Yet, there is more play in this system than its formal outlines suggest. Within the party there is an emphasis on collective leadership – epitomized by the National Directorate – and consultative decision-making that run counter to the concentration of power. The separation of party, state, and mass organizations is a significant source of political flexibility. It allows the mass organizations to challenge the state without seeming to resist the party. And it permits the party to back away from unpopular policies without appearing to do so. The conflict over water board policies in Matagalpa illustrates the possibilities of this system in miniature. The long struggle over agrarian policy discussed in the next chapter demonstrates its potential on a grand scale.

The new constitutional order, officially inaugurated in January 1987, lies wholly outside the Sandinista system of power. The Western-style constitution does not address the vanguard status of the party, nor does it recognize the popular democracy the Sandinistas hoped to create in the mass organizations. Inaugurated in wartime, unrecognized by much of the opposition, and stifled by its own emergency provisions, the constitution has had little effect on the way Nicaragua is ruled. In peacetime, however, it may prove to be more than a dead letter.

# Part II
*The Party and the Revolution*

# 4
# Peasants: Sandinista Agrarian Policy

Not long after the Sandinistas came to power, a visitor asked several young peasant-students at a government tractor school if they had known hunger as children. All answered affirmatively. Their experience was hardly extraordinary, though somewhat paradoxical. During the decades they were growing up, the Nicaraguan economy – led by agriculture – was flourishing, but hunger was spreading. The number of small children suffering malnutrition doubled between 1965 and 1975. By the early 1970s, 57 percent of children under the age of five were found to be malnourished. A 1971 survey found that the average daily diet of people in the poorest 50 percent of the population provided 1,761 calories, well below the UN nutritional standard of 2,600 calories.[1]

In Nicaragua prosperity was being achieved at the cost of hunger. The key to this sheer divergence between human welfare and the economic growth is the model of capitalist economic development based on farm exports which has dominated the Central American economies since the late nineteenth century.

## The Contradictions of Agro-Export Development

Prior to the rise of export agriculture, the people of the Nicaraguan countryside were predominantly peasant cultivators, producing corn, beans, and other subsistence crops for family consumption.[2] Low population density permitted most families sufficient land for their own maintenance. Some farmland was held in large private estates and available to peasant families under sharecropping arrangements. Other land was communally owned under surviving pre-Hispanic and Spanish-colonial legal traditions. While communal land was typically parceled out among households to be farmed individually, it did not become private property and could not be sold.

These traditional arrangements were swept away by two waves of agro-export growth. The first, in the late nineteenth century, was based on coffee cultivation. The second, in the decades following World War II, was built on cotton, beef, and expanded coffee production. During these periods of expansion, land controlled by peasant cultivators was concentrated in the hands of export entrepreneurs, typically men from the city. Fields long devoted to traditional subsistence crops began to serve the needs of affluent (by Nicaraguan standards) foreign consumers. Dispossessed peasants became rural wage workers, dependent on seasonal employment on the cotton and coffee estates; cultivators of marginal land on the agricultural frontier; and residents of urban shantytowns.

Both export booms were set off by expanding international markets. For example, beef production rose in response to the growing fast-food market in the United States. But, from the beginning, agro-export development was also promoted by conscious public policy. Legislation passed in the late nineteenth century permitted the dissolution of communal landholdings, a crucial step toward private land concentration. For more than a century, Nicaraguan governments provided special credit and tax incentives, built roads and other needed infrastructure, and helped exporters gain control of land and labor. In Nicaragua as elsewhere in Central America security forces were expanded to help impose agro-export development on a reluctant rural population.

The Somocista governments were especially anxious to promote farm exports since the Somozas were by far the largest producers in the export sector.[3] After 1960, agro-export development received added encouragement from US aid programs which took export diversification as a basic development strategy.

Agro-export development produced sharp contrasts in Nicaraguan agriculture between the large, modern estates devoted to export production and the smaller, peasant-operated farms that produce grains for the domestic market. The country's best land, technical expertise, financial resources, and rural infrastructure were increasingly devoted to the export sector.[4] The most visible evidence of this tendency came in the 1950s and 1960s, with the transformation of the fertile León and Chinandega region from the country's principal granary into its main cotton-producing area. The consequences were evident in crop statistics: between 1950 and the late 1970s, the harvest of domestic food crops grew more slowly than the population, while the production of major exports grew much faster.[5]

Agro-export development created poles of affluence and misery in Nicaragua: at one extreme, export producers and other capitalists associated with them; at the other, landless peasants and the swelling population of the urban shantytowns. A rough approximation of the rural class structure that emerged from a century of export growth is presented in table 4.1, based on

**Table 4.1** Rural Labor and Land Distribution, 1978

| Social group | Percent of Farm Labor Force | Percent of Farmland |
|---|---|---|
| 1 Large Bourgeoisie (over 900 acres) | 0.5 | 41 |
| 2 Small & Medium Bourgeoisie (90–900 acres) | 4.5 | 44 |
| 3 Rich & Medium Peasants (20–90 acres) | 21.5 | 15 |
| 4 Poor Peasants (under 20 acres) | 36.5 | |
| 5 Permanent Wage Workers (Landless) | 20.0 | 0 |
| 6 Seasonal Workers (Landless) | 17.0 | 0 |
| Total | 100 | 100 |

*Source:* Carmen Diana Deere et al., "The Peasantry and the Development of Sandinista Agrarian Policy," *Latin American Research Review*, 20 (1985), pp. 78–9.

land-holding and employment data from the 1970s.[6] The top two categories constituted a rural bourgeoisie, a tiny percent of the rural population, that controlled 85 percent of agricultural land. At the bottom of the rural class structure was the semi-proletariat of the landless or land-poor (categories 5,6, and part of 4), whose survival depended on low-wage employment in agriculture. This class grew in size as the population and the proportion of land devoted to agro-export production expanded. The middle of the rural class structure (3 and part of 4) consisted of peasant smallholders who constituted around half the rural population, though they controlled a rather small proportion of the land. The rich peasants in the upper reaches of this sector were affluent enough to hire others to work for them and often produced a substantial marketable surplus. The less affluent smallholders ate most of what they produced and did some agriculture wage labor.

The rural semi-proletariat is export agriculture's most characteristic social product. It is a *semi*-proletariat because most of its members can only expect to find steady wage-labor employment during the three- or four-month harvest period. In recent decades, the seasonal swing in agricultural labor demand has intensified. The gap between harvest and off-season labor needs is increased by modern cultivation practices and is considerably greater in cotton than coffee. A large cotton plantation which requires a few dozen permanent workers uses close to a thousand people at harvest time.[7] Cattle raising requires a steady but very small labor force.

Between harvests, members of the semi-proletariat must piece together a living as best they can. Those with modest plots of land cultivate food crops and raise small animals. Many become peddlers, selling handicraft items, food prepared at home, firewood, and other low-priced goods. Women may work as domestics. Although households in this class typically depend on more than one source of income, their earnings are marginal and erratic. The instability of economic life and the migratory requirements of harvest employment undermine the family life of the semi-proletariat. Over a third of Nicaraguan families are headed by females.[8] It is probable that the decline of the smallholding peasantry and the corresponding rise of the semi-proletariat have contributed to this high statistic.

There are obviously multiple links between agro-export growth and the spreading malnutrition of recent decades. Devoting the most important farm resources to exports undermines national self-sufficiency in basic foods. Although exports yield dollars that can be used to import food, agro-export development concentrates income, like land, in the hands of a small class of exporters. Nicaragua has been forced to import grain since the 1950s,[9] but the poor are unable to purchase sufficient food – imported or otherwise – to feed their families. The landless, seasonally employed rural workers who harvest cotton and coffee are especially vulnerable.

The Somoza regime might have repaired some of the human damage done by agro-export development by distributing land or creating permanent employment for the semi-proletariat. But to have done either on a significant scale would have risked depriving exporters of the cheap seasonal labor on which their enterprises depended. A small agrarian reform program, begun under the impetus of the Alliance for Progress, shielded export interests, while doing little for the rural poor.

Agro-export development inevitably engendered popular resistance. Over the last century, government security forces have repeatedly battled peasants who opposed the (typically fraudulent) process by which they were deprived of their land, blocked efforts to organize unions for rural wageworkers, and opposed peasant land seizures. As early as 1881, an Indian uprising over land and labor policies left 5,000 dead.[10] Dispossessed peasants and impoverished rural workers joined Sandino's army in the 1930s and supported the FSLN struggle in the 1960s and 1970s.[11]

## Agrarian Politics and the Ideological Heritage of the FSLN

The Sandinistas' early rural policies were shaped by their party's ideological heritage and their own studies of the agro-export system.

Sandino, his latter-day followers knew, had expressed faith in a joint struggle of peasants and workers and was interested in forming peasant cooperatives. But he never elaborated these notions and his experiment in cooperative farming was terminated the moment it began, by his assassination and the bloody campaign against his disarmed followers.[12]

Marx was puzzled by peasants. From the viewpoint of his central theory, the peasant in post-feudal society could only be regarded as a remnant of a lost world. Yet, two generations after the French Revolution, Marx observed that the peasantry remained a decisive force in French politics. In his famous essay, *The Eighteenth Brumaire*, Marx examined the 1848–51 upheaval that brought Louis Bonaparte to power in France. He concluded that a radical revolution backed by the proletariat had been defeated by a reactionary peasantry. Why? Peasant smallholders, Marx thought, had plenty to rebel against. They were exploited by both the bourgeoisie and the state.

But peasants were also victims of what Marx called "the idiocy of rural life." Superstitious, isolated from one another by a backward, family-scale technology and tiny communities, they were unable to recognize their own class interests or unite with others to defend them. (To Marx, the peasants were like a sack of potatoes: all similar but separate.) Nonetheless, Marx concluded – with little apparent justification in his own analysis – that the peasants would ultimately recognize the bourgeoisie as their class enemy and "find their natural ally and leader in the *urban proletariat*, whose task is the overthrow of the bourgeois order."[13]

Largely concerned with the contradictions in capitalist society that could bring socialist revolutionaries to power, Marx did not leave detailed pre-scriptions for post-revolutionary policy makers. But, according to economist Carmen Diana Deere, four basic elements for a new agriculture can be deduced from his work: (1) nationalization of the land, (2) the development of large-scale, scientific agriculture, (3) the socialization of agricultural production, through collective control of the work process and profits from rural enterprises, and (4) the maintenance of a worker–peasant alliance.[14]

With the first three points, Marx was assuming that in agriculture, as in industry, capitalism would pave the way for socialism. Capitalism would create the large, modern farms whose benefits could be socialized by a revolutionary government. The fourth point, Marx knew, was more problematic. Was the peasant's farm – small, backward, untouched by capitalist modernization – to be nationalized? If so, how could a worker–peasant alliance be sustained?

Lenin assimilated Marx's agrarian program. The worker–peasant alli-ance, something of an afterthought for Marx, became central to Lenin's revolutionary strategy.[15] Like Marx, he placed the proletariat, with its more sophisticated class consciousness, in the leadership role. In power, Lenin favored collectivization of agriculture via two organizational forms, the state farm and the peasant-run production cooperative. (He apparently did not take the position, which was widespread in his party, that state farms were the superior form because they represented a higher level of socialization.) Lenin's emphasis on the worker–peasant alliance and his interest in agrarian cooperatives resonated with the thinking of his Nicaraguan contemporary Sandino, or so it seemed to the Sandinistas some decades later.

The Sandinista Front had its own experts on agrarian matters when it came to power in 1979. Two of the best researched works on the farm export sector were written by Jaime Wheelock and Orlando Núñez, who were to become Minister of Agriculture and head of the ministry's research center.[16] But having long focused on agro-export development, Wheelock and many who worked for him tended to view the farm economy and rural politics in terms of modern export enterprises. The emphasis on large-scale, technologically advanced agriculture in Marxism-Leninism reinforced this tendency. As a result, the peasant half of the worker–peasant alliance received little political attention in the early years of the revolution and rural economic planning often ignored the potential of Nicaragua's numerous small and medium-sized farms.

## The Emergence of the State Farm

The FSLN'S early attitude toward agrarian issues can be gauged by the party's 1969 "Historic Program." In it, the party defines itself as an organization based on a worker–peasant alliance and commits itself to a "massive" and "immediate" agrarian reform, affecting all large "capitalist and feudal" estates. The reference to capitalist holdings indicates that even modern agro-export enterprises would not be excluded. The land would be redistributed to peasants without charge. The program makes no mention of state farms, but would encourage peasants to form cooperatives.

At the time the 1969 document was issued, the FSLN was struggling to build a guerrilla movement in the countryside. But the insurrection that finally brought the FSLN to power was largely urban-based and the Sandinistas' bourgeois allies in the struggle against Somoza included many wealthy farmers. By 1979, the FSLN's positions on agrarian questions were neither as radical nor as decisive as they had been in 1969. The party was committed to the program of the national unity government, issued shortly before Somoza fled Managua, which called for the seizure of estates belonging to the dictator and those closely associated with him, but implied that other efficiently exploited rural properties would be respected.[17]

The Sandinistas were well aware of the costs that agro-export development had imposed on Nicaraguan society. But there is no evidence that the new government or the National Directorate – which reserved for itself final authority over agrarian reform decisions – ever considered dismantling the agro-export system. The Nicaraguan economy had grown dependent on the dollar income that farm exports provided. Not just luxuries, but basics from petroleum to medical equipment had to be purchased with dollars on the international market. The FSLN hoped to undo the human damage while retaining the benefits of agro-exports. This early decision (or non-decision) shaped the agrarian reform program and the revolutionary regime's relations with private farmers by favoring the preservation of large, modern, export estates.

Two of the initial decrees of the revolutionary government provided for expropriation of Somocista farms, some of which had already been occupied by peasants. With these properties – comprising, it was believed, 50–60 percent of arable land – the new regime had obtained a rich bonanza at minimal political cost. In the eyes of most Nicaraguans, rich or poor, the expropriated property was simply being recovered from thieves. Since no significant foreign holding was involved, the new government did not risk the external tensions that had accompanied the Cuban revolution's early seizure of American-owned sugar mills.

The key agrarian policy decision facing the revolutionary government in late 1979 concerned the disposition of the expropriated farms.[18] The Sandinistas' apparent commitment to the preservation of the agro-export sector and the practical need to restart an economy devastated by war favored their retention intact as state farms. The Somocista properties included many of the country's major export estates — modern, integrated, well-capitalized enterprises that employed thousands of workers and accounted for a sizable proportion of the country's foreign exchange earnings. There could be no question of carving them into family-sized parcels, despite peasant demands for land.

The farms might have been titled to their workers as cooperatives, but there was doubt among Sandinista agricultural officials that the workers would be able to manage them and concern that cooperative members might revert to growing subsistence crops on individual plots. In addition, turning a large estate over to a relatively small resident labor force seemed inequitable. Public ownership would allow profits to be used to finance schools, health clinics, and other social projects.

Finally, there was a well-founded fear that passing out the Somocista properties to individuals or cooperatives would encourage invasions of non-Somocista estates by land-hungry peasants. (As it was, the FSLN had to invest its own prestige in persuading peasants who had occupied Somocista lands to give them up to the state.) A new wave of land invasions would affect production, cut into export income, and undermine the FSLN's political strategy of alliance with the bourgeoisie.

The Sandinista leadership's ideological inclinations also favored the state farm solution. Early comments by Jaime Wheelock – who quickly emerged as the Directorate's voice on agrarian matters – revealed a commitment to socialized forms of agrarian organization. In September 1979, Wheelock told *Barricada* that the agrarian reform policy would favor state farms. Peasant smallholders would be urged to unite in cooperatives. "[T]he land is the patrimony of the Nicaraguan people. We are going to build an agrarian reform that tends to establish state ownership of the means of production. We are going to promote a cooperative movement to socially organize individual peasant production."[19]

Official statements began to reflect an implicit hierarchy in the value of rural property forms, based on the degree of socialization. State farms were superior to cooperatives, production cooperatives superior to service cooperatives, and – ironically – capitalist estates superior to peasant farms. The more advanced forms were identified with greater productivity and higher social consciousness. They could exploit the advantages of scale and sophisticated technology. On the other hand, the peasant smallholder was regarded as the victim of his life experience, technologically and ideologically underdeveloped.

In language that often recalls Marx's comments about the French peasantry, Sandinistas stressed the need to rescue the Nicaraguan peasant from his "isolation and backwardness."[20] Wheelock spoke of varied cooperative projects designed to "[lead] the peasants in a process of increasing socialization . . . progressively develop the social awareness of the peasants and change their traditional and explicably individualistic mentality."[21] Just as capitalism, from a Marxist point of view, was a progressive advance over pre-capitalist forms of organization, so the rural proletariat was an advance over the peasant smallholder. The FSLN's 1977 *Platform* was explicit about this: "Because of its direct involvement in capitalist production, the [urban and rural] working class has acquired collective habits, working discipline, mental and manual ability . . . and other traits which put them (*sic*) in the vanguard . . . of the masses . . ."[22] Wheelock and many other Sandinistas rejected the idea of distributing the expropriated land to peasants precisely because "this type of land reform destroys the process of proletarianization and constitutes a historic regression."[23]

The Sandinista view of the Nicaraguan peasantry – like Marx's conception of the French peasants – was a stereotype with some basis in fact. Their years in the mountains had exposed many Sandinistas to the isolation and backwardness they lamented. In some rural areas illiteracy reached 85 percent. Primitive methods of cultivation limited production on peasant farms. Corn is the quintessential peasant crop throughout Central America. International statistics show that per-acre corn yields in Nicaragua were the lowest in the region, though bean yields compared more favorably.[24]

Given the reigning Sandinista conception of agrarian development, the decision to convert the Somocista properties into state farms was almost inevitable. Party leaders were disappointed to learn, in November, that the confiscated farms did not cover half of the cultivatable land, as had been imagined, but something closer to 20 percent. This meant that large and medium farmers remained in control of the agro-export economy.[25] November's revelation was a setback for those among the Sandinista leaders who viewed the expropriated land as the basis for a rapid transition to a socialist society. Nonetheless, the new state sector included 43 percent of the estates over 850 acres and a 15 to 20 percent share in the production of the principal farm exports.[26] This stake, Sandinistas hoped, contained the germ of a new society.

## From State Farms to Cooperatives

In its initial incarnation, the Sandinista agrarian reform favored the state farm and protected the (non-Somocista) agrarian capitalist. But it offered little to the peasant. The landless and land-poor, many of them victims of the expansion of export agriculture, had been led by wartime Sandinista propaganda to expect massive land redistribution. The FSLN's program for the medium and large peasant seemed limited to official exhortations (largely ignored) to join together in cooperatives. The attention of agriculture officials was focused on assimilating Somocista properties.

If the Sandinista vanguard expected the peasant masses to passively accept its policies, it was soon freed of this illusion. Early 1980 saw a new wave of land occupations by peasants, some spontaneous, others promoted by ATC, the Sandinista-affiliated rural union. At the same time, the more prosperous peasants in certain areas, attracted by promised access to cheap inputs and credit were joining producer associations organized by large landowners. Wheelock charged that the big growers were "trying to take advantage of the cultural and ideological weaknesses of the peasants and small producers to isolate them from the revolution."[27]

In February, an ATC-organized demonstration brought some 30,000 peasants and rural workers to Managua to press an array of demands on behalf of the rural poor.[28] The FSLN cooperated with the demonstration, which was addressed by Wheelock. But the comandante's speech may have disappointed some in the audience.

On behalf of the Sandinista Front, Wheelock acceded to a key demand of the demonstration and pledged that "not one inch" of the land that had already been seized (including non-Somocista properties) would be returned. He promised technical advice and material assistance to peasant smallholders who formed cooperatives and held out hope that land would be found for peasants who needed it. But Wheelock appeared to limit future expropriations to "idle lands." He insisted on the need to end "anarchistic and spontaneous" land seizures, asserted the economic impossibility of raising rural wages, and lectured agricultural workers on the need to reverse the precipitous decline in rural labor productivity that had begun with the triumph of the revolution.[29]

A few months later, at ceremonies commemorating the first anniversary of the victory over Somoza, Daniel Ortega revealed that the government was preparing a new agrarian reform law. Ortega – whose rhetoric on this occasion was alternately passionate and pragmatic – tried to reassure the agricultural bourgeoisie that the law was not aimed at those who were effectively exploiting their land but warned,

> It is not acceptable that while there are peasants who have to scratch among the rocks to sow their crop, there should be landlords with fertile land unused except for contemplation by its owners . . . there is great pressure for land. Thousands of dispossessed peasants are taking over cultivated land because they feel like farmers, while there are hundreds of thousands of acres totally unused. Therefore, by expropriating idle land, we are protecting the good producer, the efficient producer, protecting him in this way from the natural pressure of the landless peasants.

A follow-up press conference by Wheelock and an editorial in *Barricada* reemphasized Ortega's basic theme: the government was acting under pressure from land-hungry peasants and was attempting to protect the efficient capitalist producer.[30]

The new law was drafted in the Agriculture Ministry, but it was not forwarded to the Council of State for enactment. The Sandinista media fell silent on the topic. For the moment, agrarian reform was hostage to the FSLN's relations with the bourgeoisie, which were in almost continual crisis through 1980. Major agricultural interests were resisting even the mildest of reforms. The Sandinista leadership was reluctant to risk undoing the national unity alliance, especially after peasant land occupations dropped off in the latter part of the year. [31]

The FSLN's own division over agrarian policy probably contributed to inaction on the reform law. An internal debate was developing, which – setting aside the nuances of individual positions – can be described in terms of two basic positions. At one pole were the Sandinistas who supported state farms and heavy investment in large-scale, capital-intensive projects, such as sugar mills and regional irrigation works. They favored a relatively rapid transition to a centralized socialist economy, which, they believed, could be achieved through modern agriculture. These people resisted encouraging peasant agriculture and especially opposed the distribution of small parcels to individuals (a process they labeled "repeasantization") because it ran counter to their program of rural modernization, reinforced an individualistic mentality, and broadened the social base of support for capitalist agriculture. They also feared that land distribution could reduce harvest labor supply.

On the other side of the debate were those who placed strong emphasis on the peasant farmer and peasant-run cooperative, believed in simpler, locally controlled technologies, and were willing to accept a slower process of rural socialization. The Sandinistas who took this position had greater faith in the peasant's capacity for social and technological change but they also believed that the direction and pace of change should be determined by the peasants themselves, even if that meant individual land grants or cooperatives whose members farmed individual plots – measures which apparently ran counter to the ultimate goal of socialized agriculture.

The first position was strongly represented in the upper reaches of the Agriculture Ministry, especially in the early years of the revolution.[32] The second found its most important institutional bases in UNAG, the Sandinista farmers' organization, and CIERA, the research arm of the agriculture ministry. Many officials held views which were variants on these two. A few, especially non-Sandinistas in the government banks and marketing institutions, were resistant to all socializing schemes.

Ultimately, agrarian questions had to be fought out in the National Directorate, where the same basic positions were represented. The collegial character of the Directorate may have contributed to the indecisiveness of Sandinista agrarian policy, which tended to drift with changing tides of political circumstances. Even when decisions were made, basic issues were often left unresolved and policy remained ambiguous.

Although the revolutionary government did not produce an agrarian reform law in 1980, it did take two measures designed to help the peasant farmer. One was the imposition of a legal requirement that unused land be made available at very low rental prices to those willing to cultivate it. The other was a generous program of crop financing for small farmers. Neither was especially successful. Landowners frequently ignored the rental requirement. Even the administrators of state farms – who were also covered by the decree – resisted renting out idle land to needy peasants.[33] Credit was passed out mindlessly under the crop financing program. In some remote areas, ministry officials arrived by helicopter to offer cash to startled peasants. Little thought had been given to how these isolated borrowers were to market their crops.

Most peasants had little experience with credit. A rural priest working on the agricultural frontier reported that when peasants received money, they "'would go to the nearest cantina and then go buy radios.'"[34] In the end, grain prices were held so low that even responsible borrowers were unable to cover their debt. Wheelock later attributed the program to revolutionary "romanticism."[35]

In 1981, the land issue returned to the top of the Sandinista agenda. The months leading up to the second anniversary celebration brought a new round of land occupations by peasants. Again Daniel Ortega used the July 19 celebration to announce an agrarian reform law. The reform would eliminate the cause of farm seizures, which, Ortega warned, would no longer be tolerated.[36] This time the law was enacted.

Political circumstances had changed. The recently installed Reagan administration represented a new external threat, requiring the FSLN to consolidate its lower-class support. Moderate domestic policies had failed to improve political relations with the bourgeoisie. And the FSLN was growing impatient with the entrepreneurial performance of the private sector, which it now accused of consciously running down its investments to the detriment of the national economy. As in July 1980, the revolutionary government may have doubted its ability to protect bourgeois property without somehow responding to pressure from below.

Sandinistas remained divided over agrarian issues, but the balance in the debate was shifting against partisans of the state farms. The state sector was not proving especially profitable. Fears that distributing land would cut into harvest labor supply were countered by a study conducted for the Agriculture Ministry. Above all, the Sandinistas were concerned with preserving peasant support.[37]

The 1981 legislation was directed against inefficient and pre-capitalist uses of the land.[38] In contrast to many previous reforms (including the Cuban reform), it placed no upper limit on the size of well-run estates – in effect immunizing most modern export enterprises. The first article of the law "guarantees" the property of owners who farm their land "productively and efficiently." The law targeted farms that were underutilized or not cultivated by their owners. With the exception of land which has been abandoned or was being farmed under sharecropping arrangements, only very large holdings, exceeding 850 acres, were subject to the provisions of the law.[39] In most cases, landowners would be compensated for their property with bonds.

Peasants and rural workers – men and women – were to receive land under the reform free of charge. The law was the first in Latin America to specifically provide for the inclusion of women. Title would be given in perpetuity to the beneficiaries and their descendants. But agrarian reform property cannot be divided, sold, or rented. When these provisions were debated in the Council of State, the Sandinista majority argued that while the peasant farmer would not willingly give up his land, it was important to remember "history and the idiosyncrasies of the Nicaraguan peasantry."[40] In other words, the lesson of Nicaraguan history is that peasants, unprotected by the law, lose their land to fraud, violence, and their own folly.

The 1981 law, reflecting continuing division over agrarian policy, did not dictate how affected property was to be organized. It could be turned into family farms, cooperatives, or state farms. But the law tended to favor cooperatives and, by the end of 1983, 80 percent of the land distributed under its provisions had gone to groups of rural families organized into production cooperatives. Most of the remainder had gone to individuals.[41]

This pattern of land distribution was a defeat for the partisans of state farms within the Agriculture Ministry. But the state sector continued to dominate the ministry's budget, consuming resources which might have gone into organizing and supporting the cooperatives. The ministry was launching a series of enormously expensive, large-scale, high-tech rural projects, concentrated in the state farm sector. Among the most costly were an advanced sugar complex near Managua and an intensive grain production program, also based in the Pacific region. The latter required heavy investment in irrigation infrastructure.

These elaborate ventures, says an American agriculture advisor generally sympathetic to the revolution, are rooted in "technofascination": a naive faith in the redemptive power of sophisticated technologies. Such technologies may be inappropriate to Nicaraguan conditions and are certain to increase dependency on foreign financing and imported components.[42] The very scale and complexity of these projects placed them beyond the control of peasant farmers or cooperatives, leading to an undemocratic centralization of power over economic resources.

Sandinista agrarian policy was now moving on two tracks: while land was redistributed to peasant cooperatives, other resources were largely reserved for the state sector.

## The Crisis of Sandinista Agrarian Policy

By the mid-1980s, it was apparent that Sandinista agrarian policy was failing on many fronts. The flaws inherent in the programs worked out in 1980 and 1981 were intensified by the dual strain of economic decline and external attack. With the very survival of the revolution at stake, the Sandinista leadership was compelled to address the following problems.

### Continuing demand for land

At the beginning of 1984, the agrarian reform had barely touched the needs of the rural poor. About 5 percent of the arable land had been distributed under the 1981 law to fewer than 20,000 families – a fraction of the landless and land-poor peasantry.[43] The war was creating new demands. Some 40,000 rural families, Wheelock reported in early 1986, had been displaced by the fighting and needed to be resettled.[44] But the moderate character of the existing legislation, the leadership's fear of further alienating the

**Table 4.2**  Mean estimates of grain production
(millions of quintales)

|          | Corn | Beans | Rice |
|----------|------|-------|------|
| 1978–79  | 5.72 | 1.45  | 1.26 |
| 1979–80  | 3.46 | 0.80  | 0.88 |
| 1980–81  | 4.15 | 0.79  | 1.32 |
| 1981–82  | 4.30 | 1.11  | 1.69 |
| 1982–83  | 3.57 | 0.94  | 1.68 |
| 1983–84  | 3.99 | 0.96  | 1.83 |
| 1984–85  | 3.57 | 0.90  | 1.91 |

*Source:* See n. 46.

bourgeoisie, and bureaucratic concentration on the state farms all slowed
the pace of the reform. Production cooperatives – the form in which most
land was distributed – were difficult to organize. Peasants, who were not
accustomed to working collectively, wanted individual land grants, especially after the cooperatives became favored targets of the contra forces.

In 1984 and 1985, the government was compelled to use force to
dislodge peasants who were invading private farms in various parts
of the country. During the same period, Sandinista rural organizations
and local FSLN members, sensitive to peasant demands, were pressing
a reluctant national leadership to intensify the agrarian reform.[45]

*Inadequate grain production*

By 1984, food shortages had turned into the single most troublesome
domestic political issue facing the FSLN. For a growing number of
Nicaraguans who were becoming disaffected from the revolution, the
food deficit was proof of the Saninistas' inability to manage the economy.
Deflecting popular anger over shortages had become a daily struggle for
the party's grassroots organizers.

The problem centered on basic grains, especially corn, the major
staple in the popular diet. With the 1981–2 harvest, grain production
appeared to be returning to pre-revolutionary levels (see table 4.2).[46]
But after that year, corn and bean production sank. Only the rice crop
continued to expand. While the domestic grain supply was shrinking,
the national population was growing – it probably increased more than
20 percent from 1979 to 1985.[47] And export earnings, which the country
needed to pay for food imports, were also falling.

Weather conditions and contra aggression have contributed to Nica-

**Table 4.3** Indices of export production (1977 = 100)

| Commodity | Year | Nicaragua | Costa Rica | El Salvador | Guatemala |
|---|---|---|---|---|---|
| Coffee | | | | | |
| | 1977 | 100 | 100 | 100 | 100 |
| | 1978 | 110 | 121 | 90 | 100 |
| | 1979 | 112 | 128 | 155 | 105 |
| | 1980 | 93 | 101 | 109 | 97 |
| | 1981 | 107 | 135 | 98 | 78 |
| | 1982 | 114 | 133 | 105 | 62 |
| | 1983 | 114 | 152 | 119 | 108 |
| | 1984 | 84 | 159 | 120 | 96 |
| | 1985 | 83 | 172 | 110 | 120 |
| Cotton | | | | | |
| | 1977 | 100 | n/a | 100 | 100 |
| | 1978 | 111 | n/a | 114 | 105 |
| | 1979 | 98 | n/a | 108 | 124 |
| | 1980 | 17 | n/a | 105 | 110 |
| | 1981 | 63 | n/a | 60 | 77 |
| | 1982 | 51 | n/a | 63 | 53 |
| | 1983 | 67 | n/a | 73 | 31 |
| | 1984 | 71 | n/a | 11 | 42 |
| | 1985 | 57 | n/a | 47 | 46 |
| Beef | | | | | |
| | 1977 | 100 | 100 | 100 | 100 |
| | 1978 | 130 | 108 | 187 | 79 |
| | 1979 | 136 | 98 | 276 | 82 |
| | 1980 | 39 | 82 | 69 | 55 |
| | 1981 | 35 | 104 | 19 | 79 |
| | 1982 | 58 | 76 | 56 | 71 |
| | 1983 | 55 | 42 | 68 | 66 |
| | 1984 | 41 | 64 | 44 | 38 |
| | 1985 | 25 | 78 | 41 | 74 |

*Source:* Food and Agriculture Organization, *Trade Yearbook* (Rome, 1977–85), v. 31–9.

ragua's grain supply difficulties. Floods washed away part of the 1982–3 crop and droughts reduced the 1983–4 harvest. The contras attacked grain-producing cooperatives and government grain shipments, while recruitment of peasants into the armed forces cut into the rural labor force. However, the government's own policies – designed to hold down the cost of basic foods for the urban popular classes – have been the most consistent source of the supply problem.

Until 1985, the government spent a sizable chunk of its budget subsidizing retail food sales. In addition, the government's marketing agency displaced the intermediaries who had long cheated the peasant and contributed to inflated food prices in the city. But the intermediaries, who were typically truck owners, had also sold peasants urban goods they needed (machetes, clothing, boots, radio batteries, etc.) and transported the grain to the cities – services the government could not immediately replace. Grain producers were required to sell at official prices and strongly pressured to sell directly to the government. But the official prices were low, relative to other prices in the economy, and slow to rise, in spite of an accelerating rate of inflation. (Government bureaucrats, complained the head of the Sandinista farm organization UNAG, were guilty of "turtle'ism" in setting producer prices.[48]) Only the rice growers escaped this pricing pattern. Rice, unlike corn and beans, is not a peasant crop. Virtually the entire rice crop is produced on a few large, modern farms, and the growers were able to force the government to pay attractive prices.

The peasant response to this situation was – or should have been – predictable. Peasants reduced their sales of corn and beans. They ate more of what they produced or shifted to other, more profitable crops. In some cases, they actually bought corn, at the government's attractively subsidized retail prices, instead of growing it.[49]

### Declining export production

The volume of Nicaragua's three major exports, the source of most of its foreign currency earnings, declined well below prerevolutionary levels (table 4.3). Export production was afflicted by most of the same problems as domestic food production: unfavorable weather, contra attacks, and unattractive prices. Production throughout the region was affected by sinking international prices, but Nicaragua's neighbors with similar export profiles – Guatemala, El Salvador, and Costa Rica – were generally more successful in maintaining production levels. In Nicaragua, the government reduced incentives for export producers by reserving a part of export income for its own purposes.[50] By paying low prices for export commodities and additionally taxing growers, the government was, in effect, transferring income from generally affluent exporters to school children, hospital patients, soldiers, and bureaucrats. The FSLN's strained political relationship with the bourgeoisie also contributed to declining export production. Increasingly hostile to the revolution and unsure of the future of the private sector, wealthy farmers cut back their investments by lowering herd size or acreage planted, reducing long-term maintenance, and selling off farm machinery.[51]

### State Farm Inefficiency

The state farms proved to be a financial drain on government resources. While production rose after 1980, costs were well in excess of those on comparable private farms. According to one knowledgeable student,

"[S]tate farm accounts became one of the most closely guarded secrets in Nicaragua," apparently because of heavy losses.[52]

*Weakened rural support*

By 1983–4, there were clear indications that the FSLN's rural support was slipping. The rapidly expanding contra army across the border in Honduras – though led by former National Guardsmen – consisted largely of peasants from northern Nicaragua.[53] The resettlement of rural families noted above was undertaken in part for their own protection – some peasants fled conflict zones spontaneously – but also because authorities suspected that peasants in certain zones were sympathetic to the contras. Sandinista leaders privately conceded, and sometimes publicly suggested, the presence of an "internal front" of medium-sized farmers who were willing to provide logistical support and "safe houses" for contra fighters.[54]

Contra propaganda effectively played on ill-founded peasants' fears that the revolution threatened their farms and their God. "The Sandinistas are going to take away your land," warned contra broadcasts from Honduras.[55] "They're communists and they want to make the state the owner of everything." The peasantry, noted Luis Carrión in 1983, "is the social class to whom the counterrevolutionaries direct their propaganda . . . they [take] advantage of many things, such as the almost fanatic religious mentality of the peasants."[56] (Ironically, Carrión himself had been drawn into the revolution out of Christian conviction.)

But the Sandinistas had contributed to their own problems in the countryside. The government certainly had little interest in seizing small land-holdings, but the independent peasants of the north resented pressures to join cooperatives. Low grain prices did not win friends for the revolution among the peasantry nor did efforts to compel peasants to sell their grain directly to the government collection network, nor the declining purchasing power of rural wages, on which many peasants depended for at least part of their income.[57]

To be sure, the revolution had delivered benefits to rural people – some land had been distributed, access to credit improved, schools built, and health services extended. Many farm workers found their first year-round jobs on state farms. The 1980 literacy campaign had substantially reduced illiteracy in the countryside and expanding educational opportunities filled many rural people with new hope. "The revolution woke me up," a state farm worker told the author in 1982, "Before the revolution I never set foot in a school." Said one of his co-workers, "The important thing is the chance for my children to study. Our children won't be like us. We didn't have opportunities." But the most isolated areas had probably received the smallest benefits and the war was forcing contraction of social programs, both through budgetary pressure and contra attacks on schools, clinics, cooperatives, and other social symbols of the revolution.

The FSLN had not effectively carried its political message into rural areas. In some regions there was very little party presence.[58] One revealing indicator was the relative distribution of membership in the mass organizations. Although the urban and rural populations were of similar magnitude, the urban-based CDSs had over half a million members, while rural ATC and UNAG combined had fewer than 150,000.[59] Given the superiority of urban organization, it is not surprising that food policy was more responsive to the needs of the urban popular classes than those of the peasant farmer.

Party leaders and cadres were generally of urban origin and many had little understanding of rural life. Daniel Núñez, one of the few ranking Sandinistas with a rural background, became president of UNAG in 1984. Nuñez was critical of the "narrow" thinking that had developed in the organization. UNAG did not understand the "peasant mentality." Its officials had begun "to prostitute the word bourgeois, calling [anyone] with 10 cows or 200 cargas of coffee a 'bourgeois,' without knowing the sacrifices that he had made to get them." These small farmers, Núñez warned, were becoming disconnected from the revolution and were easy prey for the counterrevolution.[60]

## The Transformation of Sandinista Agrarian Policy

It did not take the National Directorate long to recognize that its rural policies were in trouble, especially in the north, where the contra challenge was growing. In mid-1983, the Directorate decided to shift the direction and accelerate the pace of the agrarian reform. The Directorate recognized that the policy of organizing peasant-beneficiaries into production cooperatives was slowing the reform. The problem, Wheelock later wrote, was especially serious in the "scattered and very backward peasant communities" of the northeast. "Although the cooperative form of social property that we had been favoring . . . represented a significant advance over the old patterns of the individualist and traditional peasant economy, we decided to undertake a massive campaign of distributing individual property to the peasants especially in the north and east."[61] The decision was unambiguously political and taken, as Wheelock's comment suggests, with some ideological regret, to bolster Sandinista support in the areas of greatest contra challenge.

During 1983 and 1984, the pace of land distribution was more than double what it had been in 1982. But, despite Wheelock's dramatic language about massive distribution of "individual property," most land was given in cooperative form. Few farms were handed over to individuals. The "campaign" to which he refers was, in fact, an accelerated titling program to legalize the claims of squatters in the north. The beneficiaries of titling were typically peasant cultivators who had lost their land in the Pacific region to agro-export expansion and fled to the agricultural frontier. There was reluctance in the ministry to issue such titles because they would have the effect of reinforcing primitive and ecologically damaging agricultural practices. But strong peasant desire for legalization and the contra political threat forced the issue. In 1984, government titlers handed out deeds to over 2 million acres, 17 percent of the arable land in the republic.[62]

Another sign of change in Sandinista agrarian policy was the transformation of UNAG into a broader, more independent and aggressive organization. Looking back in a 1986 report, UNAG recognized that it had devoted "almost exclusive attention to the cooperatives, while the small, medium, and large patriotic producers were not included in our policies." In October 1983 – not long after the National Directorate's reexamination of rural policy – UNAG decided to "broaden its base by attracting the largest possible number of producers, especially those still to be drawn to the People's Popular Revolution."[63]

The selection of Daniel Núñez as UNAG president a few months later reflected the organization's new orientation. Núñez, a passionate man and charismatic leader, had built himself into a substantial cattleman before he joined the armed struggle against Somoza. After the war, he became a member of the Sandinista Assembly and – having donated his own land to the agrarian reform – an Agriculture Ministry official.

By virtue of his prewar background, Núñez represented a social sector that the FSLN was especially anxious to win: the rural *burguesia chapiolla*. This Nicaraguanism, which means something like "rustic bourgeoisie," refers to farmers who are more successful than the prosperous peasant, but lack the cosmopolitan polish, connections, and outlook of the urban-based, agro-export entrepreneur. The *chapiollo* may drive a new pick-up truck, but he does not routinely accompany his wife on shopping trips to Miami.

Núñez and other Sandinista spokesmen began to draw a sharp distinction between the *chapiollos* (or simply "small and medium producers") and the rich landowners who oppose the revolution and support COSEP, the conservative national business organization. In one interview, Núñez described the latter group of farmers as the "pedigreed elite of growers, who are unpatriotic, pro-imperialist, who discriminate against the peasants."[64] The FSLN was beginning to realize that its early conception of a polarized rural society – the agro-export bourgeoisie vs. the semi-proletariat – was missing a middle sector of farmers who were, collectively, substantial landowners and producers, Many Sandinistas who dealt with agrarian policy concluded that the *chapiollo* was continuing to invest in his farm and expand production at a time when the COSEP landowners were disinvesting. The *chapiollo*, the reasoning went, did not have the option of running off to Miami or Caracas.[65]

There was doubtlessly an element of wishful thinking in the neat distinction these Sandinistas were drawing between the two groups. Núñez knew that much of the *burguesia chapiolla* was sympathetic to COSEP. He saw his organization as locked in a struggle with UPANIC, COSEP's rural affiliate, for *chapiollo* loyalty.[66]

UNAG's positions on agrarian issues reflected its determination to recruit members and gain support for the revolution wherever it could. UNAG backed the land-titling program and urged stepped-up distribution of land to the rural poor. It viewed cooperativization as desirable but insisted that it be voluntary and not a prerequisite to receiving land. UNAG sought better prices for peasant grain producers and better provision of agriculture inputs and basic consumer goods in the countryside. The organization was even ready to defend a large, efficient producer whose land had been invaded or unjustly seized by the agrarian reform. There were obvious tensions in this program, reflecting conflicts among UNAG's diverse constituencies, but tension was built into UNAG's inclusive political strategy.[67]

UNAG played an important role in the events of 1985, a critical year for the agrarian reform, when the focus of attention shifted from the isolated north to the densely populated region around Masaya, in the center of the country.[68] There, land pressures and disaffection from the FSLN had been building together. Masaya was a crucible of agro-export development. Land-holding was polarized between a few modern export plantations that monopolized most of the land and thousands of subsistence plots, too small to support their owners. Most peasants depended on seasonal work on the plantations to maintain their families. Inflation was depressing the value of their wages and government efforts to regulate the commercialization of food was cutting into the income they had earned by carrying their own crops to urban markets.

The restrained 1981 land reform, protective of large, efficiently managed export farms, had disappointed the Masaya peasants. "[T]he law passes through the clouds," they said, "it doesn't touch anybody."[69] A peasant movement in 1982 calling for the expropriation of several large estates stirred no response in the Agriculture Ministry. By 1984, the peasants were demonstrating their attitudes through what observers described as a "political strike" – boycotting Sandinista rallies and refusing to participate in UNAG. In the November elections, Masaya's vote for the FSLN was noticeably behind the national average.

A few months later, Masaya peasants were joining a protest movement, led by UNAG's regional president, to demand distribution of land to individual families. After demonstrations in June 1985, several plantations, among them state farms, were occupied by armed peasants. The events in Masaya set off protests by land-hungry peasants in other parts of the country – encouraged in some cases by local FSLN and

UNAG officials, trying to bolster flagging peasant support and pressure national officials into deepening the agrarian reform.

The spreading protest movement, coming on top of the land pressures created by the war, forced the party's leadership to reexamine, yet again, what Sandinistas began calling "the peasant problem." In Masaya, exercising a little-used provision of the law allowing for the creation of "agrarian development zones," the government distributed land taken from state farms and land expropriated or, more typically, purchased from private owners. Nationally, the agrarian reform distributed 30 percent more land in 1985 than in 1984 and sharply increased the proportion of agrarian reform land grants to individuals. Excluding special land concessions to indigenous communities on the east coast, grants to individual farmers rose from 6 percent to 44 percent of the land distributed.[70] The reform program was becoming much more responsive to peasant opinion. In Masaya, Wheelock told a group of peasants that they would have to be the ones to determine how expropriated lands were to be organized. "Obviously, we don't know how to do these things," he is reported to have said, "so it's up to you."[71]

In January 1986, the government announced a new agrarian reform law.[72] Like the 1981 law, the new legislation placed no upper limit on the size of private land-holdings and reaffirmed the rights of all farmers who use their land efficiently. But the new law eliminated one of the most conservative features of the 1981 law: the lower limit on affectability. Now the government could take land-holdings of *any* size. Even well-exploited land could be bought or expropriated under special circumstances, such as resettlement of war refugees or providing for the needs of the rural poor in areas of extraordinarily high land concentration.

These changes clearly reflected the experience of 1985. Hobbled by the provisions of the 1981 law – which generally protected even poorly exploited farms if they were under 850 acres – the government had distributed state lands and spent heavily to buy private land so it could meet pressing needs. The possibilities of the 1981 law had been exhausted, or, as Jaime Wheelock later put it, "we ran out of ammunition."[73]

The new agrarian reform law, like its predecessor, allows the government to redistribute land in any organizational form it chooses. But Sandinista leaders publicly confirmed that they would continue to respond to peasant desires for individual land grants. Speaking for the National Directorate, Luis Carrión told UNAG's First National Congress:

[A]t the same time that we warmly support the process of cooperativization, it should be clear that the FSLN categorically rejects the use of coercion or force to organize cooperatives. The distribution of land to peasants who demand it should not be used to force cooperativization. . . .Cooperatives should only develop as a product of the free will of the peasants.[74]

The leadership continued to believe that collective forms of agriculture were socially and, in the long run, economically superior to peasant smallholding. Unless peasants were willing to join together in some way, it would be difficult to offer them credit and technical advice, much less tractors and irrigation works. But the party would yield to what its leaders saw as the backwardness and obstinacy of the peasant – and to the reality of the war. "It may be that social property is better in some sense, we don't doubt that," Wheelock told the UNAG Congress. "But in the final analysis, the crucial thing is the international correlation of forces."[75]

The party hoped that the peasantry would evolve toward a "higher" social consciousness. Until then, policy would be flexible. Peasants who were not open to cooperatives could receive individual titles. Without giving up their titles they could join credit and service cooperatives. The members of production cooperatives would be allowed to organize their affairs as they wished. Many were choosing to operate as so-called "dead furrow cooperatives," dividing their land into individually worked plots (separated by uncultivated furrows) but sharing equipment and activities such as plowing.

During the first year under the new law, the accelerated rate of land distribution achieved during 1985 was maintained. Some 41 percent of land titled went to individual households. Another 14 percent was organized into "dead furrow" cooperatives or credit-service cooperatives – both suggesting family-farm operations. Individual land grants were especially common in areas of high contra activity.[76]

While the Sandinista leadership was reshaping its approach to agrarian reform, it was struggling with another aspect of the peasant problem: the production of basic grains. In 1985 and 1986 government policy moved closer to a strict market rationality, in the hope of providing better incentives for peasant grain producers. Retail food subsidies were dropped. Producers were allowed increasing freedom to set their own prices and sell outside official channels, at least within their own regions. In general, government policy aimed to reverse the declining terms of trade that had placed rural producers at national disadvantage. UNAG played an expanding role in grain marketing and supplying peasants with the urban goods that would restore their economic links to the city.[77]

In his speech to the UNAG congress in April 1986, Wheelock announced a national free market in corn and beans. But this striking piece of news was downplayed in *Barricada's* coverage of his remarks. At the same time, the Agriculture Ministry was moving ahead with the large-scale grain project mentioned earlier. By 1986, the state farms involved were producing 14 percent of the grain supply, according to a ministry economist. But the project was the subject of considerable criticism, inside and outside the government, because of its dependence on high-cost imported equipment. By mid-1987, free trade in basic grains was, according to Daniel Ortega, official policy, though there was apparently still some bureaucratic resistance to its implimentation.[78]


## The Future of Sandinista Agrarian Policy


"This is a law to state-ize the lands of Nicaragua," declared an UPANIC official when the 1986 agrarian reform law was published. "It is a law to transform the peasant into a peon of the state, a slave of the state who will do what the state says, how it says."[79] In fact, the 1986 law reveals very little about the intentions of the FSLN beyond a determination to extend the agrarian reform. But judging from the direction of Sandinista agrarian policy since 1983, the law is likely to have the opposite effect from the one anticipated by UPANIC.

**Table 4.4** Changes in land tenure

| | *Percent of farmland* | | | | |
|---|---|---|---|---|---|
| *Type of Size of Landholdings* | *1978* | *1982* | *1983* | *1985* | *1986* |
| Individual, Total | 100.0 | 74.1 | 74.8 | 71.7 | 70.1 |
| Over 875 acres | 36.2 | 15.9 | 14.0 | 10.9 | 9.8 |
| 350 to 875 acres | 16.2 | 12.6 | 12.6 | 12.6 | 12.6 |
| 18 to 350 acres | 45.5 | 42.6 | 44.0 | 44.0 | 44.0 |
| Less than 18 acres | 2.1 | 3.0 | 4.2 | 4.2 | 4.5 |
| Production cooperatives | 0.0 | 1.9 | 4.7 | 9.1 | 11.6 |
| State farms | 0.0 | 24.0 | 20.5 | 19.2 | 17.5 |

*Source:* Andrew Reding, "Nicaragua's New Consitution," *World Policy Journal 2 (Spring) 1987.*

The common thread that runs through the Sandinista response to the agrarian crisis of the mid-1980s is its emphasis on the individual farmer. The titling program, the renaissance of UNAG, the burst of individual land grants, and the evolution toward market incentives all follow a consistent pattern. And while the Sandinistas were developing new policies to favor the private farmer, the state sector was shrinking, from 24 percent of arable land in 1982 to 17.5 percent in 1986 (see table 4.4). An Agriculture Ministry spokesman predicted in 1986 that the state sector would decline to 10 percent, "in the next few years."[80]

These recent developments should not be surprising. Since 1979, Sandinista agrarian policy has moved, more or less steadily, away from its initial emphasis on the state farm — driven by the recurrent protests of land-hungry peasants. The 1981 land reform, in practice a charter for production cooperatives, was the first great step. Peasant dissatisfaction with the cooperative model and the political pressures created by the war set the stage for further movement away from state agriculture.

But the wealthy planters whom UPANIC represents can take little consolation from these facts. Running through Sandinista thinking on agrarian matters is the commitment, as old as the party itself, to a worker–peasant alliance. In the midst of a war, the FSLN is certainly not seeking a new confrontation with the bourgeoisie; but satisfying the peasantry means taking land away from those who have it in abundance. As table 4.4 indicates, the proportion of land in large estates, like the proportion in the state sector, is shrinking. Two comments by Wheelock in the wake of the 1986 legislation encapsulate the politics of Sandinista land policy: "We know that in order to defend the alliance with the peasants we must accelerate the land distribution process" and "Between a . . . property owner who can live with other resources and 500 peasant families, we prefer to respond to the latter."[81]

Ironically, the policies of the mid-1980s, from the titling program to the Sandinistas' new-found enthusiasm for the *burguesia chapiolla*, all point toward the ultimate triumph of rural capitalism – even if it comes at the expense of the biggest agrarian capitalists. Individual titling and land grants are especially important in this regard, since they are creating a powerful *fait accompli* – an expanded class of smallholders – which cannot easily be undone by the FSLN.

But the tension between Sandinista ideology and practice and the tensions within the FSLN over agrarian policy remain unresolved. Every pledge to respect the desires of the peasant is coupled to the expectation that the peasantry will evolve to a more socialized consciousness. The Agriculture Ministry, as its high-tech grain program suggests, has not abandoned the two-track policy under which much of its budget is devoted to large-scale state farm projects. At this juncture, an astrologer may have as good a chance as anyone else of divining the long-term direction of Sandinista agrarian policy.

# 5
# The Bourgeoisie and the Revolution

The earthquake that leveled Managua in December 1972 jolted the Nicaraguan bourgeoisie out of its civic lethargy and propelled it on an improbable – and still unfinished – political odyssey. For nearly four decades, the bourgeoisie had lived, and generally prospered, under the Somozas. The years after World War II brought a real bonanza. The export economy diversified and thrived. Export earnings and the opportunities offered by the new Central American Common Market encouraged industrial growth. New fortunes were made and old ones refurbished.

But the political power of Nicaragua's planters, bankers, industrialists, and merchants had not grown to match their expanding wealth. Sandinista leader Bayardo Arce later described the Nicaraguan bourgeoisie as a class that had dominated the rest of society without exercising political dominion:

> [The] bourgeoisie, as a class, never had political hegemony. What it had was a dictatorial military power that represented its class interests and that made it hegemonic in the context of other classes. Because, at the hour of a strike, the manager or owner called the National Guard. The Guard came and beat up the workers and that was that. There was no way to make a mistake.[1]

## The Structure of the Modern Bourgeoisie

On the eve of the Sandinista revolution, the private economy was composed of four entrepreneurial strata:(1) the Somoza group, (2) the Banco de Nicaragua and Banco de America groups, (3) the middle bourgeoisie, and (4) small producers and merchants. A large part of the national economy was controlled by the major economic groups in the first two strata.[2] The Somoza family and its close associates ran an extensive economic empire of agricultural, commercial, industrial, and financial enterprises, built with the help of state power and resources during four decades of family rule. In the 1970s the family's private fortune was independently estimated at $400 million to $900 million.[3]

The Banco de Nicaragua (BANIC) and Banco de America (BANAMERICA) groups emerged in the 1950s and 1960s, in part as defensive responses to the Somozas' relentless aggrandizement. Each was a coalition of businessmen and families that controlled diverse enterprises crystallized around a bank. Together the BANAMERICA and BANIC groups controlled an estimated 20 percent of the GNP.

The "middle bourgeoisie" included all modern producers and major retailers not tied to the big economic groups. This category, which had grown in numbers and affluence in the postwar years, contained many enterprises that were relatively small – for example, a 100-acre farm growing coffee for export or a factory with a few dozen workers producing cosmetics. But the businesses controlled by the middle bourgeoisie could be distinguished from the multitude of peasant farms, artisan shops, neighborhood stores, and street peddlers in the bottom stratum by their application of modern technology and administrative methods. This chapter will be largely concerned with the middle bourgeoisie, the most dynamic of the four strata through the 1970s and 1980s, but the term "bourgeoisie" will be used more broadly to refer to the two middle strata.

## The Bourgeoisie and the Somoza Regime

The attitude of the bourgeoisie toward the dictatorship during the postwar decades was inevitably ambivalent.[4] Businessmen resented the expanding economic power of the Somozas, their arbitrary seizures of property, and their use of government resources and regulatory mechanisms to gain private advantage. The Somozas kept the rich at arm's length from power, but they also favored them with labor, taxation, and development policies tilted toward business. As Somoza reminded his peers, they needed him: "My opponents should remember that we, the better people [*gente decente*] are only 6 percent; if trouble arises, the 94 percent may crush us all."[5]

Responses varied. Many members of the bourgeoisie simply avoided politics. Others looked after their own interests by cutting cynical political deals with the Somozas – for example, providing token opposition in meaningless elections in exchange for a share of the spoils. One result of this tendency was the factionalization and delegitimization of the traditional upper-class dominated Conservative and Liberal parties.

Between 1948 and 1967, some members of the bourgeoisie – typically drawn from prominent families of the opposition Conservative party – participated in a series of armed conspiracies against the Somozas. All failed and none gained broad bourgeois support. The most spectacular of these defeats was led by Pedro Joaquín Chamorro, publisher of *La*

*Prensa.* Inspired by the victory of the Cuban revolution five months earlier, Chamorro trained a guerrilla force of about 100 and hired two C-47 transport planes to deliver men and arms to remote sites in Nicaragua. The invaders were quickly detected and captured by the National Guard.[6]

Many on the left were disdainful of such bourgeois adventurism. Tomás Borge, commenting on Chamorro's attempt was more charitable: "I don't ridicule that effort the way some have ridiculed it, like those who never fought. . . .in the end, someone who takes up a gun deserves more respect, even though he's finally captured, than someone who never did."[7]

By the 1970s, the most significant opposition to the regime was coming from the emergent middle bourgeoisie, whose members were by and large not well represented by the traditional parties, not individually powerful enough to make attractive deals with the regime, and generally more progressive than the established rich.

The organ that best represented the middle bourgeoisie was COSEP, the umbrella organization of private-sector associations. In the 1960s, COSEP periodically clashed with the regime over specific matters of economic policy and regulatory corruption. But gradually COSEP turned its attention toward broader social and political concerns. The organization shared the reformist outlook that motivated the Alliance for Progress – a sense that moderate change was the best prophylactic barrier to radical revolution. COSEP, its statutes declared, hoped to contribute to "development" and "social justice" from a viewpoint that was "democratic and within Western Civilization."[8]

Somoza's relations with the private sector degenerated sharply in the aftermath of the 1972 quake. Businessmen were resentful of the Somozas' systematic monopolization of reconstruction opportunites and alarmed by evidence of spreading popular discontent. In the 1970s, the middle bourgeoisie became increasingly determined in its opposition to the regime. Its members backed and led UDEL and FAO, the two broad opposition coalitions that sought Somoza's removal. (COSEP was one of the member organizations of FAO.) In contrast, the more conservative BANIC and BANAMERICA groups held themselves aloof from efforts to depose the dictator.

The leadership of the FSLN took careful note of the evolution of the bourgeoisie. One of the party's persistent concerns was that the bourgeois opposition might dislodge the dictator prematurely, thereby foreclosing a Sandinista victory and erecting a regime the FSLN described as "Somocismo without Somoza."[9] The Tercerista alliance with the anti-Somoza bourgeoisie was in part a preemptive tactic. The Tercerista strategy assumed that the FSLN would control the revolutionary movement. "The bourgeoisie," states the Tercerista-written 1977 *Platform,* "will not be a vanguard in the struggle against tyranny or in the revolutionary process. . . .The FSLN will win and maintain hegemony within the [Anti-Somoza] Front."[10]

The assassination of Pedro Joaquín Chamorro in 1978 shocked the bourgeoisie. Chamorro was more than an opposition leader. He was the scion of an old and prominent upper-class family. His murder violated the implicit code of conduct that has traditionally regulated behavior among gentlemen in Latin American politics. "One does not," explained a Nicaraguan banker some years later, "kill people of a certain social condition." A government might, on occasion, shoot peasants or workers. Members of the bourgeoisie are subject to deportation, perhaps prison, but murder was beyond the pale.

The business-led national strike that followed Chamorro's assassination was widely observed but failed to achieve its underlying objective – Somoza's departure. In the months that followed, the organized middle bourgeoisie lost the political initiative to the FSLN. The Terceristas captured popular imagination with dramatic strokes such as the seizure of the National Palace in August. While the efforts of the bourgeois opposition failed to budge the dictator, they contributed to the rapidly expanding popular mobilization that fed the ranks of FSLN supporters. For example, a national strike, called by FAO after the National Palace operation and strongly backed by business organizations, helped set the stage for the massive September insurrection, led by the FSLN.

As the Sandinistas gained the political initiative, bourgeois attitudes toward the FSLN were shifting. Many sons and daughters of bourgeois families joined the Sandinista Front. These links and the relatively moderate political rhetoric of the Terceristas drew an expanding sector of the bourgeoisie to the FSLN. But it was the mindless brutality of the regime's response to the September insurrection that crystallized the change in bourgeois thinking. In the wake of that disaster, even the conservatives of BANIC and BANAMERICA (now fearful of an FSLN victory) supported talks between FAO and the government designed, once again, to induce Somoza's voluntary departure.

Many members of the middle bourgeoisie went even further and began actively supporting the insurgents with money, arms, shelter, and other forms of assistance. Reservations about the FSLN were set aside. All attention was focused on a single goal: toppling Somoza. As one anti-Somoza activist recalls the period, the prevailing attitude in middle-bourgeois circles was, "There is no alternative. Come what may – it can't be worse than this."

## The Bourgeoisie and the Consolidation of Sandinista Power

In planning the government that would assume control on July 19, 1979, the FSLN chose to ease its own transition to power by emphasizing the same broad alliance strategy that had characterized its approach to the last phase of the military struggle. Well before Somoza fled Managua, the middle bourgeoisie was offered significant participation in the new government and important legal guarantees for its political and economic interests. Alfonso Robelo, a COSEP activist who headed his own political party (the reformist Nicaraguan Democratic Movement, MDN),and Violeta de Chamorro, widow of the assassinated publisher, were named to a five-member junta on which the FSLN had only one official representative, Daniel Ortega. The key economic-policy posts in this national unity government – the Planning and Finance Ministries and the Central Bank – all went to men whose solid business and banking backgrounds were reassuring to both the local private sector and international financial interests. Many sub-cabinet posts also went to anti-Somoza moderates.

The general program announced by the new junta in June foresaw a "mixed economy" of private, state, and joint enterprises. The state would "recover" the properties "usurped" by the Somozas and their allies. There would be an agrarian reform and substantial reorganization of the financial sector and of foreign and domestic commerce. However, the junta promised that the state sector would be of "precise extent and clearly delimited characteristics" and that the "properties and activities of the private sector" would be "fully guaranteed and respected."[11]

What was being proposed sounded like a social-democratic experiment, potentially acceptable to the middle bourgeoisie – especially the reform-minded business leadership that had risen to prominence during the 1970s. The middle bourgeoisie would hardly object to the expropriation of the Somocistas. Reorganization of the financial sector and foreign commerce were most likely to affect the major economic groups and might actually benefit lesser capitalists. The middle bourgeoisie seemed prepared to adapt to the mixed economy delineated by the junta. Moreover, the program contained reassuring guarantees of formal democratic rights – an important opening for the press, parties, and political money controlled by the bourgeoisie. COSEP and the bourgeois parties would receive a substantial block of seats in the Council of State, the national assembly sharing legislative powers with the junta.

Some bourgeois politicians may have even believed that they would be the politically dominant force in the revolutionary government. Edgar Chamorro, a relative of Pedro Joaquín and, for a time, part of the contra leadership, recalls a conversation with Alfonso Robelo in Managua not long after the junta came to power. Robelo's conception of the new regime was simple: the guerrillas would be the soldiers and people like himself would take control of the government.[12]

The Sandinista view of the new order was quite different. The leaders of the FSLN valued their alliance with the bourgeoisie and worked to maintain it. They believed that their allies possessed administrative and technical skills that would be useful to the young government and essential to the reconstruction of the war-damaged economy. They also understood that the bourgeoisie was the key that would open the door to friendly financial and diplomatic dealings with the West. But the Sandinistas also feared that the bourgeoisie might use its economic weight and international connections to defeat the larger goals of their revolution. They therefore felt the need to capture the "hegemonic" power, referred to above, within the new government.[13]

The Sandinista Front viewed the national unity government within the context of the two-phase revolutionary schema described in chapter 1. The reunification agreement that brought the Sandinista factions together in March 1979 anticipated a regime whose goals would be "the neutralization of potential internal and external enemies, while we accumulate the military and mass forces that guarantee the continuity of our [revolutionary] process."[14] The 1979 "72 hours document" similarly describes the post-victory order as "transitional" and leading toward a "transformation in the relations of production corresponding to the state sector [of the economy] . . . the fundamental modif[ication] of the relations between class forces in favor of the oppressed."[15]

The Sandinistas also regarded the political role of the bourgeoisie as transitional. The 1977 *Platform* described the alliance with the anti-Somoza bourgeoisie as "tactical and temporary."[16] In an interview in early 1979, Daniel Ortega used precisely the same language for this alliance.[17] A terminology had grown up within the Front, reflecting the two-phase conception that distinguishes short-term, *tactical* arrangements from long-term, *strategic* goals. These terms convey a deceptive sense of precision. There was always disagreement in the party over how "temporary" tactical might be and exactly what strategic goals were. But the minimal intentions of the party, from the beginning, were to contain the political influence and circumscribe the economic power of the bourgeoisie.

By the time Nicaraguans celebrated the first anniversary of the victory over Somoza, the FSLN had moved decisively to consolidate its own power, undermining the optimism that the government's original program had inspired in the bourgeoisie.[18] The balance of forces on the five-member junta was less fluid than had been assumed. Three of the members were Sandinista militants acting under party discipline. Robelo and Chamorro, feeling themselves powerless, resigned in April 1980. Several months earlier the cabinet had also been reshaped, eliminating conservatives and asserting Sandinista control. In laying the groundwork for the Council of State, the Sandinistas diluted the representation of the bourgeois parties and private sector organizations that had been agreed to in the June program by increasing the representation of the mass organizations tied to the FSLN.

It soon became apparent that all significant lines of power were converging on the members of the National Directorate. They dominated the junta and the Council of State, controlled the military, and personally held the most important cabinet portfolios, including Defense, Interior (police), Planning, and Agriculture.

Political control enabled the FSLN to strengthen the state's capacity to direct the economy. Two critical steps taken in the first year were the nationalization of the entire financial sector and of the commercialization of major exports. These measures assured the Sandinistas control over the disposition of investment credits and use of precious foreign exchange. By monopolizing the major sources of hard-currency income, the state limited the ability of the bourgeoisie to pressure the government and protect its own interests by moving capital abroad.

The bank takeovers, together with the nationalization of Somocista properties, shattered the major economic groups. A few large firms that had been associated with the BANAMERICA and BANIC groups remained. But the private sector had been radically restructured. The medium-sized enterprises of the middle bourgeoisie now predominated.

## 1980: The Bourgeois Political Challenge

In the wake of the FSLN's political consolidation, the first in a series of bourgeois–Sandinista political crises began to develop. By early 1980 a confluence of economic and political developments was feeding bourgeois fears about the direction of the revolution.

Freed from the restraints imposed by the Somoza regime, labor unions were organizing workers who had never had representation in the past and making aggressive demands on employers. In the absence of a more reasonable system of control to replace the bone-crunching tactics of the National Guard, labor discipline declined to a level that undermined efforts to rebuild the national economy. Workers, exhilarated by their sudden release from the *patron's* daily humiliations, were enjoying what was described as "a historic holiday." Work days declined to four hours or less in many enterprises. Employee seizures of factories and farms were common. Some were subsequently expropriated by the government.

The Sandinista Front, whose immediate concerns were economic reconstruction and maintenance of the alliance with the bourgeoisie, tried to restrain labor excesses. But the party's own revolutionary rhetoric sometimes undercut these efforts. Even worse, in the early months of the revolution, the FSLN did not have full control over its own cadres in the labor movement. The party was also facing a challenge from ultra-left groups that were attempting to force the radicalization of the revolution through strikes and seizures.[19]

Bourgeois concern about the security of private property was exacerbated by the promulgation of a "decapitalization" law at the beginning of

March. Decapitalization refers to disinvestment through such devices as allowing plant and machinery to run down while profits are pocketed or paying high salaries to family members who have no active participation in the firm. The law presupposed worker participation in detecting disinvestment and economic sabotage – an implicit attack on traditional management prerogatives. In light of these developments, COSEP and other private sector voices began to demand that the government clarify its attitude toward private enterprise.

Businessmen were also unsettled by political developments, which did not appear to be leading toward the Western democratic institutions which the bourgeoisie had anticipated. According to a diplomatic observer with extensive private sector contacts, the bourgeoisie believed "that the only way to protect themselves economically was to have political rights."

The strain developing between the Sandinista Front and the bourgeoisie was reflected in a struggle for editorial control of *La Prensa*. In April the paper was shut down by a strike that pitted publisher Xavier Chamorro, who had taken over the paper after his brother's murder, against family members who were growing skeptical of the FSLN. When the family majority faction attempted to remove Xavier, most of the staff walked out in support of the publisher.

The larger political confrontation was brought to a head by Robelo's resignation from the junta over bourgeois representation on the Council of State, on April 23 – days before the Council was to be inaugurated. Robelo had not, in fact, functioned as a private sector representative on the junta, either by actively championing bourgeois interests or by serving as an intermediary between the government and the bourgeoisie, which had come to regard him as a renegade. But coupled with the quieter departure a few days earlier of his colleague Violeta de Chamorro and the unannounced resignation of Central Bank president Arturo Cruz, Robelo's resignation in protest challenged the legitimacy of the Sandinista political system. The bourgeoisie seized the moment to press its demands on the government. COSEP entered into direct negotiations with the National Directorate, mediated by US Ambassador Lawrence Pezzullo.

The settlement they reached provided government reassurance of respect for the private sector, most concretely embodied in a new *ley de amparo*, a law providing court protection in the event of arbitrary administrative action against persons or property. The National Directorate also agreed to announce dates for elections and to protect democratic rights generally. A parallel family settlement at *La Prensa* returned the paper to the stockholding majority and provided Xavier and his supporters with the resources to start *El Nuevo Diario*, a new pro-Sandinista daily.[20] With these concessions, COSEP representatives took their seats in the Council of State when it was inaugurated on May 4, in an atmosphere of reconciliation and harmony. Later that month Robelo and Chamorro were replaced on the junta by two men of suitably bourgeois backgrounds: banker Arturo Cruz and Rafael Cordova Rivas, an affluent lawyer.

The settlement of the April crisis appeared to promise a renewal of the bourgeois–Sandinista partnership. Instead, it proved to be a momentary truce in a developing political war. The conflict broke into the open again in November. The month began with the election of a new, reactionary American president (a development, the Sandinistas later argued, that encouraged bourgeois intransigence). In Nicaragua there were sharp exchanges between the authorities and Robelo's MDN, over the government's denial of permission to hold an outdoor rally in the town of Nandaime and the sacking of MDN headquarters in Managua by a Sandinista mob. Government and party spokesmen suggested that the planned rally amounted to electoral campaigning, which was legally proscribed until at least 1984.[21] (The FSLN had already announced that elections would be delayed until 1985.) On the tail of these events, COSEP issued an elaborate analysis of government policies, bitterly critical of the FSLN, and withdrew its representatives from the Council of State.

The COSEP analysis censures the treatment of MDN, the FSLN's continuing vagueness about elections,[22] and the expanding power of the state sector. But the document's most striking passages deal with its authors' perception of the national political atmosphere being created by the FSLN and the media and mass organizations tied to it. They find "a state of political uncertainty in which the specter of Marxist-Leninist socialism looms in the panorama of national life" and conclude with the charge that "the most radical sectors of the FSLN Party, with open Marxist-Leninist tendencies," are working to implant a "communist" system in Nicaragua.[23]

These accusations seemed to move the conflict to a new plane, but whatever attention they might have attracted was immediately undercut by news that Jorge Salazar, vice-president of COSEP and head of its farmers' affiliate UPANIC, had been killed in a shoot-out with state security agents. The authorities reported that Salazar and several less-known private sector figures had been involved in a conspiracy to overthrow the government, that Salazar had been transporting arms when he was stopped, and that he had died resisting arrest. The government conceded that Salazar himself was unarmed at the time of the incident.

Salazar's death further hardened attitudes on both sides. Sandinista suspicions about the loyalty of the bourgeoisie were confirmed (although only Salazar among the top leaders of the private sector was involved). In bourgeois circles it was generally believed that Salazar had been the victim of entrapment, drawn into the plot by government agents and ultimately executed in the encounter with security agents.[24] Whatever the case, his death reinforced the message that had been delivered publicly to the bourgeoisie a few days earlier by a member of the National Directorate. Avoid "adventures," warned Comandante Carlos Núñez. "[The FSLN] took power by arms and created the instruments to defend power. We will do everything within our reach to defend this revolution."[25]

Thus, by the end of 1980, the FSLN had demonstrated its determination to meet any political or military resistance from the bourgeoisie. By then also, a loose coalition of conservative groups opposed to Sandinista rule – here labeled the bourgeois coalition – had emerged. At the center of the coalition was the middle bourgeoisie, represented by COSEP. Other key members were the editors of *La Prensa*, most of the hierarchy of the Catholic church, and several bourgeois political parties. These elements were united by a sense that the Sandinistas were opposed to political democracy and capitalism and, more vaguely, represented a threat to their way of life. The coalition was committed to the West and was supported, in varying ways, by several Western governments.

The bourgeois coalition unquestionably constituted the most significant internal opposition to the FSLN, though its members were not the revolution's only domestic opponents. Others included two small, non-Sandinista labor confederations that frequently associated themselves with initiatives of the bourgeois political parties, and several ultra-left political and labor groups.

## 1981: The July Decrees and their Aftermath

On July 19, 1981, the second anniversary of the victory over Somoza, the government unveiled a stunning package of economic measures, including a stringent new decapitalization law, a broad agrarian reform law, a decree expropriating 13 major private firms, and a law providing for the expropriation of properties belonging to individuals absent from the country for more than six months. All of these measures reflected the FSLN's growing frustrations with the economic performance of the private sector. In announcing them, Daniel Ortega denounced "unpatriotic investors and producers who have decapitalized factories and farms." Ortega went on to accuse the bourgeoisie of limiting investment in order to force its will on the country. "This is a private sector that is consciously playing with fire, that wants to destroy popular power in order to impose the power to rob and oppress the workers."[26]

In months preceding the anniversary celebration, decapitalization had become a critical issue for leaders and supporters of the revolution. "Against decapitalization – confiscation!" had become a popular revolutionary slogan. A government economist described the problem as endemic. "It's not as if there are just four or five of the big guys," he told an American agricultural advisor. "If there were, you could round up one or two and make an example of them." The bourgeoisie was subjecting the country to "death by a million cuts."[27]

Estimating the level of decapitalization was difficult. A government economist placed the total loss at $140 million in 1980, a large annual figure for a small economy, but a Western embassy economic attaché guessed $30 million the following year.[28] There was ample evidence of decapitalization in the critical agro-export sector. Ranchers were depleting their herds and evading government taxes and exchange controls by driving cattle across international borders to be sold. Big cotton growers were pocketing part of their crop loans, while running up heavy debts. Coffee growers stopped replanting and cut back on routine maintenance, a strategy that increased short-term profits but resulted in declining production after several years.[29]

On one level, the July measures could be read as a benign restatement of the official attitude toward private enterprise: operate efficiently, maintain your investment, obey the laws concerning labor, health, and so on, and you can keep your business forever. The agrarian reform law, for example, placed no limit on the size of private holdings as long as they were farmed fully and efficiently. In announcing the new legislation, Ortega responded to bourgeois concerns by pledging the government to fight "lockouts, strikes, seizures, all of the ways which the rank and file can deplete capital."[30]

The bourgeoisie, however, interpreted the decrees as new evidence of government hostility. Businessmen viewed the expropriation decrees as arbitrary and regarded the decapitalization and agrarian reform law as a threat to the future of private enterprise. While willing to concede that some of the nationalized firms were decapitalizing, they argued that others had not and that even the guilty firms were taken without regard to proper legal procedures – for example, enterprises expropriated after being occupied by their workers. When bourgeois leaders saw the land-reform legislation, they were more impressed with the prohibition of court appeals than with the liberal attitude toward large land-holdings. Business leaders concurred with government assertions that private investment had fallen to anemic levels, but they blamed the situation on the investment climate created by the policies of the Sandinista government.

More generally, the bourgeoisie and the FSLN had conflicting attitudes toward private property. What the bourgeoisie regarded as a right, the Sandinistas saw as a privilege, subject to social control. No one, the Sandinistas believed, had a "right" to decapitalize or leave land fallow while the country was underdeveloped and malnourished.

The bourgeois counterpoint to charges of decapitalization was the demand for clarification of the "rules of the game." Private enterprise, observed COSEP's November 1980 analysis, operated "under a permanent threat of expropriation or illegal seizure." Bourgeois spokesmen asserted that business confidence could not be restored unless the government established stable rules that clearly defined the limits of the state sector within the mixed economy and put an end to arbitrary confiscations.

In the initial years of the revolution, bourgeois economic behavior and Sandinista response set up a dynamic of their own. The industrialist who ran down his plant while paying generous dividends, the farmer who left land idle in the sight of land-hungry peasants, and the cattleman who took out a government herd-expansion loan that he quickly converted to dollars to be banked abroad – all were contributing to the country's economic problems and stimulating popular political pressures on the government for corrective action. But anti-decapitalization legislation and anti-bourgeois rhetoric intensified the behavior they sought to control by undermining private-sector confidence in the future of the mixed economy.

In this atmosphere, what Sandinista leaders said was at least as important to the bourgeoisie as what the Sandinista government did. Thus the bourgeois reaction to the new measures was shaped by the accompanying rhetoric, which suggested a shift in the attitudes of the National Directorate. Jaime Wheelock had gone on record in June questioning the mixed economy: "If we are going to have an economy here that robs and decapitalizes, we prefer to close that type of economy down completely."[31] At the July 19 celebration and in the months that followed, the top leaders of the revolution placed renewed emphasis on class and class conflict.

On July 19 the class theme was present in the passage from Ortega's speech quoted above and in subsequent remarks by Tomás Borge. Borge picked up Ortega's discussion of the "unpatriotic" bourgeoisie. After making it clear that he regarded them as constituting a vast majority of their class, Borge asked the Sandinista crowd: "Who decapitalized the country? Who assassinated Sandino and celebrated in an orgy of champagne and blood? Who made contributions under the table to Somoza's election campaign? Who grabbed up the peasants' land and has kept the workers under the yoke of oppression?" To each question the audience responded, "The Bourgeoisie!"[32] A month later, Humberto Ortega returned to class themes in a speech before a Sandinista military audience, which soon leaked into the public domain. Ortega defined Sandinismo as Marxist-Leninist and stated flatly, "we are against the bourgeoisie."[33] While some speeches by members of the National Directorate were more conciliatory than those quoted, they did not alter the effect of the blunter statements.[34]

The bourgeoisie presented its response to the FSLN in a sharply worded letter to Daniel Ortega, as chairman of the junta, from the officers of COSEP. Written October 19, the letter appeared in *La Prensa* the next day and was picked up by the international press. Its character is revealed in an early passage: "Upon reflecting on the conduct of domestic policy and foreign policy ... we identify an unmistakable ideological line, Marxist-Leninist in pattern, which is confirmed in the discourses of the members of the National Directorate." The letter seldom addresses specific policies. It focuses almost entirely on the rhetoric of the Sandinista leaders and the undisclosed political agenda regarded as implicit in their language. The Sandinistas are accused of advancing "a Marxist-Leninist project behind the backs of the people," of preparing a "new genocide" (this in response to another extravagantly phrased speech by Humberto Ortega), and of leading the nation to "the doors of destruction."

The COSEP letter was published at a time when the Sandinista revolution was under attack in the Western news media and by spokesmen of the Reagan administration. It was interpreted by the FSLN leadership as part of a coordinated international effort to destroy the revolution – in the words of an official statement, "a frank and open destabilizing effort complementing plans which international reaction and the defeated Somocistas are attempting to unleash from abroad."[35] Almost immediately, the government ordered the arrest of the authors, simultaneous with that of the leaders of CAUS (Center for Trade Union Action and Unity), an ultra-left labor organization, which had been harassing the government with aggressive labor actions and radical criticisms of Sandinista policies. The two groups were tried together under public-security legislation on charges couched in terms of a destabilization campaign. Within ten days of the publication of the COSEP letter, sentences were handed down: 7 months for the COSEP leaders, 29 for the CAUS officials.

Under intense international pressure, the Nicaraguan authorities released the COSEP prisoners in February, halfway through their sentences. (The CAUS prisoners were left to languish in jail.) The Sandinistas had reacted sharply to the letter because of COSEP's international weight. Now, facing a severe balance-of-payments problem and increasingly explicit threats from the Reagan administration, the government felt compelled to release the prisoners for the same reason. The COSEP leaders had received strong support from Mexican President José López Portillo, a key international backer of the Sandinista revolution, who reportedly acted in the COSEP matter under considerable pressure from his own organized private sector.

## 1982–1984: Producers Without Power

After the release of the COSEP prisoners, Sandinista policies attempted to restore a working relationship with the bourgeoisie in economic matters without conceding bourgeois political rights. The objective, as described by Comandante Jaime Wheelock, was "[a] *bourgeoisie that just produces without power*, that limits itself to exploiting its means of production and that utilizes these means of production to live, not as instruments of power, of imposition."[36]

In early 1982 the Sandinista Assembly called for the establishment of "guarantees" for "principled entrepreneurs" who contribute to the national economy and for the negotiation of "patriotic production agreements between the state, the private sector, and the working classes."[37] A few days later, the government announced a new program of incentives for export producers.

If by "guarantees" the Assembly meant new legal guarantees for private property, none was forthcoming. But the government did begin to negotiate production agreements with the private sector, covering such matters as price, production levels, credit, and access to foreign exchange. The government generally avoided dealing with established business organizations, such as COSEP and its affiliates, which the Sandinistas regarded as political in character. In manufacturing there were accords with individual firms and some industrial sectors, but the most significant agreements were the crop-by-crop understandings that covered most of the agricultural bourgeoisie.

The agreements in agriculture varied substantially, reflecting the relative economic and organizational strength of the producers. At one extreme were the rice growers, technically sophisticated, few in number, represented by a strong national organization, and facing robust demand for an annual crop, vital to the national diet. Each of these factors contributed to the growers' bargaining power and enabled them to obtain a generous price and other economic concessions. The coffee planters presented a sharp contrast to the rice producers on virtually every count. In particular, they were saddled with a perennial crop, which reduced their capacity to withhold production in the face of low prices. Unlike rice farmers, coffee growers claimed to be losing money during most of this period.

In late 1983, government and private economists informally estimated private participation in the economy at 55 to 60 percent of the GNP. But both businessmen and Sandinista officials recognized that such figures overestimated the position of private enterprise in the mixed economy since government regulation had curbed managerial freedom to set prices, lower or raise wages, fire workers, buy raw materials, redeploy capital, obtain credit, or buy foreign exchange. Some Sandinistas spoke of the entrepreneurial class an an "administrative bourgeoisie." Moreover, private participation in the economy was slowly declining through expropriation and the shrinking private contribution to new investment (most new investment was being made by the government).

The Sandinistas had managed to rein in the radicals who had been responsible for factory and farm seizures in the initial years of the revolution. Nonetheless, new expropriations did not consistently conform to the rule of immunity, implicit in the 1981 legislation, for producers who operate efficiently and maintain their capital. Sometimes the government used eminent domain as a rationale for expropriation, a legal wild card that did not require the authorities to demonstrate that a firm was violating the law.

On occasion, authorities expropriated property for political reasons. Officials of COSEP and its constituent organizations were favored targets. When UPANIC president Ramiro Gurdian, an unbridled critic of the revolution, publicly recognized "the right" of the United States to cut off Nicaragua's sugar quota, Sergio Ramírez, one of the Sandinistas on the junta, announced that Gurdian's banana plantation was being nationalized. Gurdian, explained Ramírez, could not "be a member of the revolutionary state because we need owners who are clear regarding the danger represented by this measure taken by the United States."[38] Eminent domain and political expropriations were relatively rare, but their unpredictable nature reinforced the notion that there were no secure rules for business under the Sandinistas.

The capacity of the bourgeois leaders to respond publicly to Sandinista policies they disliked was severely limited after the government imposed a "state of emergency" in March 1982. The decree, issued in the wake of a series of CIA-inspired contra attacks on civilian targets in Nicaragua, suspended most constitutional guarantees, including the freedom of the press, the right of assembly, and the right to strike. The state of emergency assured firm control of labor unions but also brought prior censorship of *La Prensa* and tight restrictions on the public activities of bourgeois political parties.

In private, Nicaraguan businessmen continued to express their political opinions freely. Interviews with executives and private-sector leaders conducted periodically from 1982 to 1984 revealed deep, often passionate, bourgeois disaffection. The views expressed suggested that no significant sector of the bourgeoisie supported the revolution. Even businessmen whose firms had positive relations with the government harbored negative attitudes toward the Sandinistas. An industrialist who was receiving attractive investment loans and cheap foreign exchange to import machinery contended that the government was wrecking the economy, had created a perilous political situation, and wanted to convert Nicaragua into "another Cuba." ("They think it's beautiful," he added sarcastically.) Another industrialist, operating profitably in a sector he described as strongly supported by the government, said of the Sandinista leadership: "They have no capacity to govern. They want to do away with us. All their speeches contain an open or implicit threat. It's them or us." A major entrepreneur, who ran a profitable mixed enterprise and reported that he was treated well by his Sandinista partners, said he supported COSEP, which "represents the feelings of the majority of the private sector."

A rare member of the bourgeoisie who maintained friendly relations with the FSLN (in part, because of family ties) and had worked to bridge the gap between the private sector and the government was almost apologetic about his position: some aspects of the revolution frightened him, the mass organizations were too powerful, they were "dangerous"; certain of the comandantes were "extremists" and had done enormous damage with their rhetoric. He admitted that he had been criticized by others of his class for his contacts with the government but he argued that the only way to influence events was to participate in them. He would, he said, rather be in the ring contending with the bull than up in the stands watching.

As some of these remarks suggest, the bourgeoisie suspected that the Sandinistas' ultimate intention was the total elimination of private enterprise. A rice grower with an American agronomy degree commented: "We believe that when all the technocrats they are training in Cuba and the USSR return, they will confiscate us." Asked what the government wanted from the private sector, a major cotton planter responded, "'Obey! Produce as long as I want you to. I'll cut your throat when I want. Be my servant. Do as I say until I'm ready to dispose of you . . . If they don't fall, the private sector is condemned."

Bourgeois attitudes toward the FSLN were reflected in their assessments of American foreign policy. Publicly, bourgeois representatives were noncommittal about the American-supported contras. But by 1984 they were supportive in private. Asked about US policy, a top business leader responded flatly, "I love it." A leading industrialist contrasted the Carter and Reagan approaches. He prefered the latter: "A demonstration of force . . . it's the only thing the Sandinistas understand." Such appraisals represent a shift from earlier attitudes. Interviews with private-sector leaders conducted in January 1982, when the contra operation was only getting under way, had revealed patriotic resentment of the rhetorical threats then emanating from Washington.

In 1984 there was a division of bourgeois opinion on one key matter: the prospect of US invasion. While some clearly favored such a move, others (including the two men quoted above) were leery of its consequences for an already war-battered nation and hopeful that the existing military and economic "pressures" could force some sort of compromise between the Sandinistas and their domestic opponents.

## Sandinista Visions

"As long as they continue to produce, they can continue," a ranking party official said of the bourgeoisie in mid-1984. "We need to take advantage of the experience of the private sector . . . [but] politically in this country they have no future. They will have to fit into the economic plans of the state." About the same time, a vice-minister concerned with economic policy predicted: "As long as they don't question the authority of the revolution, they will continue. There is no political project to do away with the private sector. It depends entirely on their willingness to participate." These comments, like Wheelock's earlier remark, center on the notion of capitalist "producers without power" in a mixed economy, managed by the state.

A very different conception of the future of the mixed economy is implied in remarks made by Bayardo Arce to leaders of the Moscow-line Nicaraguan Socialist Party in May 1984. Discussing the FSLN's strategy "to advance the construction of socialism" in the midst of a war with the United States, Arce comments:

> [F]or us it is useful, for example, to be able to present an entrepreneurial class and private production within the regime of mixed economy that we proclaim, at the same time that we advance in *strategic aspects* [of the revolution]. The important thing is that the entrepreneurial class no longer controls all the economic means for its own reproduction. It no longer controls the banks, it no longer controls foreign commerce, it no longer controls the source of foreign exchange. And, therefore, the entire investment project of our country is state. The bourgeoisie no longer invests, it subsists.[39]

Arce, of course, is regarded as one of the most dogmatic members of the National Directorate, and his remarks must be assessed in context. His speech, delivered a few months before the 1984 elections, seeks communist support for the policies of the FSLN.

Wheelock is identified with the pragmatists who control the National Directorate. But if his "producers without power" represents their "strategic" intention, it leaves unanswered questions. In particular, are the owners of the means of production ever "powerless"? The example of the rice growers suggests that they have the potential to be quite powerful. Could a powerless bourgeoisie be productive, or does the investor confidence that appears to be a prerequisite to capitalist dynamism depend on bourgeois power over the state? The performance of the Nicaraguan bourgeoisie under Sandinista rule suggests a negative answer.

## 1984: The FSLN, the Bourgeoisie, and the Elections

In early 1984, the government announced that national elections would be held in November. The Sandinista Front and the political representatives of the bourgeoisie approached the campaign with two common assumptions. One was that the FSLN was likely to win. The other was that foreign sympathy – especially from the Western democracies – was the real object of the electoral contest.

When the FSLN postponed elections in 1980, the party left some doubt as to what sort of political competition it envisioned. Speaking for the National Directorate, Humberto Ortega had described the revolution as "irreversible," and asserted that the purpose of elections was "to improve revolutionary power, not to raffle who has power."[40] Three years later, Daniel Ortega, addressing the fourth anniversary celebration, flatly stated, "[N]either bullets nor ballots will defeat this revolutionary power, this Sandinista power, this popular power!"[41] The party never repudiated these statements. But in early 1984, facing a growing military threat on its borders, the party hoped to gain international political legitimacy by holding Western-style elections. The revolution was increasingly criticized from abroad for its curtailment of political pluralism under the 1982 emergency law. Especially in the wake of the October 1983 American invasion of Grenada (with its implicit threat that US forces might also be used in Central America), the Sandinista leadership was anxious to shore up its sagging support in Western Europe and Latin America.[42]

The bourgeois opposition developed its approach to the elections through the Democratic Coordinator, a political front composed of COSEP, four conservative-to-moderate political parties and two labor federations (one with Christian Democratic connections and the other linked to the US-based American Institute for Free Labor Development). The parties were weak, some existing only on paper, others compromised by their performance under the old regime. Sandinista restrictions had limited their development under the revolution. A Western ambassador gave this assessment of them in 1983: "They have no leaders, no program, and so few members that they would have a hard time coming up with poll watchers in a election."

Sharing the Sandinista assumption that the FSLN was unbeatable, the members of the Coordinator asked themselves, "Why participate?" A minority argued that the campaign offered the opposition a chance to take part in open political debate and contribute to the development of democratic institutions which might be used in the future to challenge the FSLN. They suggested that the Coordinator could always halt its participation, generating bad publicity for the Sandinistas, if the campaign appeared unfair.

The abstentionist argument was made most forcefully by the COSEP representatives, who proved to be the dominant force within the Coordinator. The abstentionists questioned the FSLN's long-term commitment to liberal democracy and contended that joining the campaign under any circumstances would only help legitimize Sandinista rule, both at home and abroad. Even before the government had set the date for the balloting, the bourgeois opposition had decided not to compete.[43]

The Coordinator's political strategy in 1984 was to discredit the Nicaraguan elections, especially among foreign audiences. "We have to play on two fields," explained a ranking Coordinator official interviewed in mid-1984. "We cannot forget the internal, but much of the game is on the international field." The leaders of the bourgeois opposition had concluded that their best hope of influencing events in Nicaragua lay with the United States and the contras. American pressure might force a broad restructuring of the regime or escalate into the removal of the Sandinistas by US forces. Internationally recognized elections in Nicaragua would undermine these possibilities.

Months before the campaign began, the Coordinator had announced that it could not participate because the Sandinistas were not creating the minimum conditions for fair elections. Its minimum conditions ranged from the lifting of press censorship to the opening of negotiations between the government and the contras.[44] In late July, the Coordinator named a standard-bearer, former junta member (and future contra official) Arturo Cruz, but refused to register him as a candidate. Cruz flew from his home in Washington to Managua, where he made a few campaign appearances and then left the country for a political tour of Europe, where he was accompanied by contra leader Eden Pastora. About the same time, the US-backed contra group FDN (Nicaraguan Democratic Force) endorsed the activities of the Coordinator, which in effect had become its internal political representative.[45]

While the Coordinator held itself aloof from the electoral process, the left-center to ultra-left parties that ultimately did participate won significant concessions on campaign conditions from the Sandinistas. They were able to mount lively campaigns highly critical of the revolution and win about one-third of the seats in the National Assembly.

In the last month of the campaign, Cruz and Bayardo Arce held talks with the encouragement of the Socialist International at the organization's meeting in Rio de Janeiro. The two apparently reached an agreement under which the elections would have been delayed for several months in exchange for the Coordinator's agreement to participate. But the understanding collapsed when Cruz was unable, or unwilling, to publicly commit the Coordinator to its terms. There is no indication that Cruz had ever controlled the group, whose strategy precluded taking part in the campaign.[46]

The preelection maneuvering completed the political transformation of the middle bourgeoisie. Wartime ally of the Sandinistas and partner in the national unity government, the middle bourgeoisie had become the core of the domestic political opposition and finally the political wing of the contra movement.

## Three Who Stayed

Backstage from the clash of national politics, bourgeois families carry on still-comfortable lives, haunted by insecurity about the future. Three families illustrate their experience.[47]

Antonio Gutiérrez is an industrialist. He inherited a factory and a small coffee plantation from his father. Antonio's grandfather was a physician, coffee grower, and sometime cabinet minister. After getting a degree in industrial engineering from the University of California, Antonio returned to Nicaragua in the 1960s, married the daughter of an upper-class Matagalpa family, and went to work for his father's company. The factory is small – employing 20 to 30 people – but even in the mid-1980s it provided enough income to maintain what would qualify as an upper-middle-class home by US standards, keep two cars in the driveway, and pay for travel abroad.

Although Antonio has few complaints about the way the government has treated the Gutiérrez firm, he despises the FSLN, which he believes wants to "do away with the private sector." He has little hope of leaving the factory to his children. "Education," he says, "is the only thing I can give them now." After the government decreed conscription, he sent his three teenage sons to study in the States, a response typical of bourgeois families that rapidly depleted the student bodies of many private schools. (None of his friends' kids or his kids' friends has served in the army, he says.) Señora Gutiérrez complains that she misses her sons and Antonio worries about how to pay for their education. By 1986, $80,000 he had in US accounts had shrunk to $40,000, even though he regularly exchanged money on the black market to send abroad. Antonio has talked to people he knows in the State Department in Washington about changing his sons' immigration status, a move he hopes will lead to cheaper tuitions. He has no intention of leaving Nicaragua himself. He breaks into rusty English to explain, "I refuse to let them drive me out."

The Sandinista revolution, which Jacinto Arias sometimes describes as part of a worldwide communist conspiracy, has not forced him to lower his standard of living. His home is large, modern, tastefully furnished, and well maintained. He drives a new pick-up truck – a rarity in Nicaragua – and regularly travels abroad. His trips are generally to the United States to see his children, but recently he accompanied a group of friends to a Black Sea resort in the Soviet Union, on a packaged tour that he describes as absurdly cheap and quite enjoyable.

Jacinto is a major rice grower. He holds an agronomy degree from Louisiana State University and was able to educate his children in the United States. A daughter earned an MBA, married an American, and settled in the States. One son became a doctor; after two unhappy years working for the Sandinistas' state medical system, he returned to Texas. A second son, with an agronomy degree, is working with Jacinto, who has already given this son some land and would like to see him inherit the family's entire holdings. But he sees little chance of that happening. Jacinto ascribes little significance to the fact that the government has treated the rice sector well. Like Antonio Gutiérrez, he is convinced that the Sandinistas intend to eliminate the private sector. "There aren't many of us left," he says of the large planters. But Jacinto's attitude might be described as qualified pessimism. The Sandinistas have been in power for a while without achieving their aims, he observes. Perhaps they've missed their chance. Perhaps there's been more resistance than they expected. Jacinto intends to stay and see what happens.

Cipriano Martínez does not live as well as Gutiérrez or Arias, and his children are unlikely to mix with theirs, but he shares their attitudes toward the Sandinista revolution. Cipriano is a rancher who characterizes himself as "100 percent peasant" ("I live by nature: I know why a dog barks and what a cow is feeling and never to cut wood by the full moon"). Some Sandinista analysts would describe Cipriano as part of the *burguesia chapiolla*, whose support the revolution would like to win. He owns about 230 acres of land and 300 head of cattle – modest holdings by local standards. Having lost most of his herd in the anarchy of 1979, he rebuilt with the help of a low-interest government loan. Cipriano never required business credit before and seems to resent rather than appreciate the help. His consuming business concern is to save enough money to replace his aging jeep with a newer vehicle. He is trying to get some help from UNAG with this, although he has nothing but contempt for the Sandinista farmers' organization.

Cipriano and his family share a rustic but comfortable middle-class home in a provincial capital, where his wife runs a small business. To protect his 18-year-old son from the draft, he sent him to live with relatives in Los Angeles and enroll in a public high school. Cipriano has been to Los Angeles several times himself and has great admiration for the United States. The Sandinistas, he thinks, have been foolish to get on such bad terms with the United States, which he regards as the ultimate source of all prosperity. He points to the refrigerator and several other expensive appliances in his kitchen. "You see these things. They come from the US. That's where dollars come from." Cipriano says that "in a future life" he would like to be "reborn a Texan – a cowboy with a ranch." He concedes that a dark-faced Cipriano Martínez might encounter discrimination in Texas, but he has a solution: "I will be reborn an American." Cipriano also has a solution for Nicaragua's problems: direct American intervention. But he devotes more time to worrying about how to get a new jeep.

A large portion of the pre-revolutionary bourgeoisie has left Nicaragua. Those who remain, like the Gutiérrez and Arias families, typically have substantial assets to protect and a standard of living that they could not easily transfer elsewhere. But they are sending their children abroad, generally to the United States, which is obviously their economic and cultural reference point. Thus, the Nicaraguan bourgeoisie is not reproducing itself socially. Marginal families like the Martínez will find it harder to reestablish themselves outside the country, however much some may want to be "reborn American." They are likely to take advantage of the opportunities that the Sandinistas offer them, as Cipriano has, and might even gain advantages by filling holes in the mixed economy left by despairing members of the bourgeoisie.

## Comandantes and Capitalists Face the Future

In the late 1980s, the bourgeoisie and the FSLN have one thing in common: a sense that existing arrangements are transitory. A well-known industrialist describes the country as a giant roulette game: "Other places they bet on horses. Here everything is on the line." He and the rest of his class would like to be rid of the Sandinistas when the wheel stops spinning. At least some Sandinistas would like to be rid of the bourgeoisie. Neither group is likely to have its wish fulfilled soon.

The bourgeoisie, having been stripped of the weapons characteristic of this class in Latin America, is in no position to challenge the FSLN. It no longer controls the financial system, and most foreign-exchange earnings are beyond its reach. Thus, it cannot strangle the national economy, however much its undynamic performance might contribute to economic stagnation. Its press has generally been censored or padlocked since the beginning of the war. It cannot appeal to the military, since the military is unambiguously Sandinista.

However, as the negotiating strength of the rice growers and the 1982 release of the COSEP prisoners suggest, the bourgeoisie is not defenseless. It has powerful supporters, including the hierarchy of the Catholic church, Western governments and other political forces in the West, and, of course, the contra movement itself. Unless the Soviet Union is ready to commit its own power to Nicaragua's defense and assume the full burden of Nicaragua's faltering economy – it does not appear anxious to do either – the Sandinistas will have to remain sensitive to the reactions of West European and Latin American governments, and to political groups from the Socialist International to the liberal wing of the Democratic Party. A decisive move against the bourgeoisie, such as the declaration of a fully socialized, command economy, would alienate the sympathy that remains in these quarters and leave the Sandinistas vulnerable to direct attack from the United States. At the same time, the revolution, as its leaders have repeatedly acknowledged, is in no position to dispense with the services of the bourgeoisie, on whose managerial and technical talents the national economy still depends. The departure of people like Antonio Gutiérrez or Jacinto Arias would certainly be reflected in reduced output in their economic sectors.

The Sandinistas' initial conception of their revolution assumed limits on bourgeois political power in a first stage and a radical restructuring of class relationships in the second stage of revolutionary development.

From the beginning there was some disagreement within the party over the meaning of the second socialist stage.

The pragmatic vision of the future of the bourgeoisie is expressed in Wheelock's phrase "producers without power," which pictures a mixed economy, guided by a strong government, in the interests of the poor majority. Bayardo Arce's remarks to the Socialist Party (also quoted earlier in this chapter) suggest that more dogmatic conceptions of socialism are still represented at the top of the party. In this vision, the powerless bourgeoisie is a transitory phenomenon on the way to a society without capitalists. The sobering experience of managing the country appears to have strengthened the pragmatists. The preeminence of Daniel Ortega, especially after 1984, and the evolution of Sandinista agrarian policy point in this direction.[48]

After nearly a decade of Sandinista rule, comandantes and capitalists find themselves locked in an embrace which neither desires and neither can escape. About half the economy remains in private hands. This, in itself, is remarkable. (The Cuban economy was almost entirely socialized after two years of revolution.) But the mixed economy has not been a happy union and is not sustainable in its present form. Perhaps the end of the war will compel the reluctant partners to reach a new understanding.

# 6
# Christians: The Church and the Revolution

In the mid-1970s, Padre Uriel Molina would celebrate outdoor masses in the working-class barrios of his Managua parish. One day, just as he finished the service, a little boy handed him a note. "I am nearby, in a house," it said. "I'll wait for you tonight. Don't fail me. Tomás Borge." The note startled and frightened Molina, but he followed a guide to the house, where he found Borge, sitting in a small, low room "with one machine gun on either side of him. There was a candle on the table lighting up a book by Marx, *Capital*."

Borge and Molina had been boyhood friends in Matagalpa, but had lost contact when Molina went abroad to study for the priesthood. Borge knew that Molina was teaching the new "liberation theology" and working with progressive Christian groups in his parish. Now Borge wanted Molina and these lay groups to work for the FSLN. "At that time," the priest would later recall, "I was not ready to listen to that. And I said, 'No, I'm not going to allow those who have no faith to use those who do. I know that we can go part of the way together, but then we split up. Your way and mine are different.'"[1] But Molina was already more identified with the coming revolution than he cared to admit. Nicaraguan Christians, from the nation's bishops to the members of lay groups in urban slums, were being drawn inexorably into the anti-Somoza movement. By the time of the 1979 insurrection Molina and many of his parishioners would be deeply involved in the armed struggle.

The collaboration that Borge was urging would have been unthinkable a decade earlier, when the conservatism of the church and the Marxist orthodoxy of the party made even dialogue impossible.

## The Marxist Background

Marx, both his friends and enemies remember, called religion "the opium of the people." But the meaning of that phrase, cut out of context, has been distorted – in fact, inverted. Marx wrote:

> *Religious suffering* is at the same time an *expression* of real suffering and a protest against real suffering. Religion is the sigh of the oppressed creature, the sentiment of a heartless world, and the soul of soulless conditions. It is the *opium* of the people.[2]

Marx's point here is not that religion is oppressive but that it is a symptom of oppression, even a protest in the face of oppression.

As a materialist, Marx rejected the idea of a transcendental realm outside of human history. Like most European progressives of his time, Marx viewed religion as an ideological prop to the established order. But he rejected the notion that anything could be achieved by attacking religion directly. Religious ideas are rooted in oppressive social conditions, he reasoned. Therefore, only by liberating themselves from oppression could people free themselves from religion.[3]

Lenin adopted Marx's basic position on religion. But he gave greater emphasis to the tenacity and the counterrevolutionary power of religious ideas. Choosing cruder imagery than Marx's, he described religion as "spiritual booze" in which the "slaves of capital" drown their hopes for emancipation.[4]

Lenin's main concern when he wrote about religion was with developing effective political tactics for his fledgling party. Although he characterized the party's outlook as "absolutely atheistic and positively hostile to all religion,"[5] he warned that aggressive anti-religious propaganda could easily backfire, playing into the hands of conservatives. Lenin urged the party to support state policies of religious tolerance and even suggested accepting believers into the party as a way of "educat[ing] them in the spirit of our programme."[6]

Borge and Fonseca were exposed to Marxist ideas about religion as high-school students in Matagalpa when they read Engels's *Anti-Dühring* (1878) and Bukharin's popular Bolshevik primer, *The ABC of Communism* (1919).[7] Engels dismissed "all religion" as "nothing but the fantastic reflection in men's minds of those external forces which control their daily life," but he ridiculed Dühring's proposal to constitutionally "abolish" religion in a future state and predicted that religion will die "*a natural death*" under socialism.[8]

Bukharin — who was also read by some younger Sandinistas in the late 1960s — is similar to Engels in theory but less tolerant in spirit. Like Engels, he opposes the illusion of religion to the truth of "science." He rejects as "radically false" the notion that one can be both a believer and a revolutionary. Bukharin supports the right of religious freedom but calls for an active struggle "against religious prejudices" — in the schools, for example, where children should be rendered "immune to all those religious fairy tales they hear at home."[9]

Against this background — and the antediluvian conservatism of the

Nicaraguan church – it is hardly surprising that there were no identifiable Christians among the early leaders of the FSLN. For some time, even left-leaning Christians were regarded with skepticism by Sandinistas. Christianity, they thought, was at best idealistic and given to a conciliatory view of society – tendencies that undermine a revolution based on class struggle.[10]

The Sandinista Front was less concerned with dogma than with practical revolutionary politics. In the 1960s, when the FSLN was competing with the reformist Social Christian Party (PSC) for the support of university students, Fonseca accused the PSC of "demagoguery" and "capitalist hypocrisy" for propagating a doctrine based on "reconciliation of social classes."[11] But in the late 1960s party leaders began to seek out sympathetic priests. In the 1970s, the party was quick to recognize the revolutionary potential of a new breed of radicalized Christians, such as Padre Molina and the people in his study groups. It was not worth getting bogged down in philosophical debates about Marxism and Christianity, suggested one of the party's top leaders, when people share "strategic objectives."[12]

## A Changing Church

For 450 years the Nicaraguan Catholic church has defended the status quo – except on occasions when the rich and the powerful were divided among themselves.[13] The church was an integral part of the Spanish colonial regime. In the decades after independence from Spain, when the bourgeoisie split into Conservatives and Liberals, the church often found itself at odds with anti-clerical Liberal governments. But as anti-church attitudes of the Liberals faded and the ideological differences within the bourgeoisie blurred, the church in Nicaragua, as elsewhere in Latin America, returned to unhesitating support of the established order.[14]

Multiple links bound the bishops and the bourgeoisie to each other. They shared living standards, education, and a cosmopolitan experience which separated them from most Nicaraguans. The bourgeoisie provided financial support for church institutions. The church educated the children of the rich and the bishops presided at their weddings. Above all, the leaders of Nicaraguan Catholicism and capitalism shared conservative social values, including, in the twentieth century, deep anti-Marxist convictions.

In the late 1920s the Nicaraguan bishops opposed Sandino, backed the incumbent Liberals, and welcomed the US Marines. For more than a generation they held the Somozas in a fawning embrace. In 1942, the bishops officiated at an elaborate ceremony in the National Stadium, where they honored Somoza's teenage daughter with a gold crown symbolizing the Virgin of Candelaria and proclaimed her "Queen of the Army." When Somoza García died in 1956, he was buried with the high honors, although he had not been a practicing Catholic. The Archbishop of Managua offered 200 days' indulgence to Catholics who joined prayers for the departed dictator's soul.[15] These gestures must have endeared the bishops to Somoza's two sons who were then struggling to preserve the family's political power.

For the most part, the Nicaraguan bishops took scant interest in political matters during the Somoza era. They joined the Cold War chorus, denouncing "atheistic communism," which they characterized as "a species of religion" directly opposed to Catholicism – in effect, a substitute faith.[16] They criticized the 1950 national constitution for proclaiming such principles as freedom of religion and secular public education. But that same year, they came close to declaring their God to be the Somozas' silent partner: "[A]ll authority comes from God. God is the Author of all that exists, and from the Author comes Authority; [faithful Catholics] should remember that when they obey the Political Authority, they do not dishonor themselves, but rather they act in a way that basically constitutes obeisance to God."[17]

The authors of these words would not have recognized the church of the 1970s that helped bring an end to the Somoza dynasty. The hierarchy's defection from the status quo came at a time when a large part of the bourgeoisie was pulling away from the regime. But the church was also changing from within. Few of the bishops who had led the church in the late 1960s remained in the early 1970s.[18] A younger hierarchy was more open to the spirit of renovation that had been sweeping through the church worldwide and especially in Latin America since the 1960s.

The transformation of the universal church received its major impetus from the Second Vatican Council (also known as Vatican II), which was convened in Rome in the early 1960s to conduct a broad reassessment of Catholic practice. The council called for a church that was more worldly in its concerns, more sensitive to questions of social justice, and more pluralistic as an institution. It rejected the narrowly individualist, otherworldly piety of the traditional faith. It urged that theology be rooted in the concrete realities of human experience. It redefined the church as the whole "people of God," rather than simply the Pope and his fellow bishops, and challenged the laity to assume greater responsibility in the church and to carry the church's social message into the world.

Nowhere were the revolutionary implications of the council's work more quickly appreciated than in Latin America. There, Vatican II inspired the development of a new theology and new forms of clerical and lay activism.

In the 1960s, Latin American theologians began fashioning what became known as liberation theology.[19] Their starting-point was not scripture or church doctrine, but the social reality around them, examined from the bottom, the vantage point of the poor. To comprehend the underdevelopment, mass poverty, and political oppression which they found, they drew on the Marxist-inspired class analysis and dependency theory of contemporary Latin American social science.

The liberation theologians reexamined the scriptures, just as they had their own societies, from the bottom up. Drawing on such material as the Biblical accounts of the Exodus and the life of Jesus, they concluded that what God requires of people is this: love of others, especially of the poor, expressed in action on their behalf. Gustavo Gutiérrez, one of the best known of the liberation theologians, writes, "[We] met God on our encounter with men; what is done for others is done for the Lord. In a word, the existence of poverty represents a sundering both of solidarity among men and also of communion with God. Poverty is an expression of sin."[20] Conversely, struggling on behalf of the poor is, by the light of liberation theology, the path to salvation.

Ultimately, liberation theology draws Christianity out of the seminaries and the cathedrals into the streets. The old piety of rosaries, candles, and plaster saints is overshadowed by the new commitment to social justice. Liberation theology has persuaded many to work among the poor and some to take up arms on their behalf.

In tandem with the new theology, a new form of grassroots organization was growing up within the Latin American church, known as the Christian base community.[21] Base communities are lay groups of 10 to 25 people, generally residents of a peasant village or urban slum. Many have been organized by priests, nuns, and lay activists inspired by liberation theology and strongly committed to the poor. Christian base communities emphasize *concientización* – the development of social consciousness and moral commitment through reading and reflection. Typical meetings center on discussions of Biblical texts, which participants are encouraged to interpret in the light of their own lives. Pharaoh of Exodus invites comparisons with the current dictator. Parables of Jesus among the poor suggest the human dignity of the dispossessed.

From such discussions, peasants and slum dwellers gain a new awareness of their own circumstances and growing confidence in their own judgements. Some groups move beyond reflection to community improvement projects and, finally explicitly political activities. Especially under regimes, such as Somoza's, that severely restrict routine political activity among the poor, the base communities can become a crucial source of revolutionary leadership and organization.

The changes that had been quietly brewing in the Latin American church received forceful public expression when the Conference of Latin American Bishops met at Medellín, Colombia, in 1968. At Medellín the bishops endorsed the formation of Christian base communities and issued a series of path-breaking documents that reflected the influence of the liberation theologians who helped prepare the conference. The prelates blamed the continent's endemic poverty and violence – which they described as "sinful" – on the self-serving behavior of national elites and international capital. They assumed a burden of guilt for the church's own complicity in upholding the status quo. The church, the bishops concluded, must place itself unequivocally on the side of the poor, on the side of change.

In later years, a single phrase came to symbolize the message of liberation theology and Medellin: *"A preferential option for the poor."*

## The Church and the End of the Old Regime

In the late 1960s and early 1970s, the spirit of renovation in the church worldwide began to make itself felt within Nicaragua.[22] A new generation of Nicaraguan priests – men such as Molina and Ernesto Cardenal – was returning from study abroad. Foreign missionaries, including the Jesuits, the Maryknoll sisters, and the Capuchins were expanding their activities in Nicaragua. These religious workers were carriers of the new theology and new conceptions of the church. In January 1969, over 200 priests and nuns and three bishops met to consider the meaning of Vatican II and Medellin for the Nicaraguan church. Under pressure from this conference, the Nicaraguan bishops officially adopted the Medellin principles, though many of the prelates resisted their practical implementation.[23]

This period was marked by a florescence of innovative Christian activity much of it directed at the poor. Some examples:

A young Spanish priest, José de la Jara, started organizing Christian base communities in his lower-class Managua parish in 1966, setting off a movement that extended to other parts of the city.[24]

In 1969, the Jesuits started the Evangelical Committee for Agrarian Advancement (CEPA), a rural movement designed to provide technical agricultural instruction, biblical reflection, and leadership training for peasants in the Pacific zone.

About the same time, in the sparsely settled eastern half of the country, the Capuchins were organizing Christian base communities and training hundreds of "delegates of the word." The delegates were lay preachers, drawn from the communities, who provided literacy and health instruction, in addition to promoting religious reflection.

In the city of Estelí, a Catholic renewal movement known as *Cursillos de Cristiandad* ("Christian Seminars") took an unexpected turn. In Estelí, the Cursillos – a normally conservative, middle- or upper-class movement, promoted from Spain – became a vehicle for increasingly radical Christian reflection. Soon, Curcillistas were organizing progressive Christian groups in the city's working-class barrios and traveling to other provincial cities to promote similar grassroots efforts.[25]

One afternoon in November 1971, a group of college students – most of them from upper-class Managua families – arrived at the door of Padre Molina's parish house. They had come to form a Christian community, they said, and to be close to the poor. Molina, who was also a university teacher, responded, "Sure, come here." The students left and returned shortly "with mattresses, sheets and everything."[26]

All of these group undertakings stressed *concientización* through religious reflection. In the course of the 1970s, they grew increasingly political in their intentions and gradually developed links with the FSLN. In Managua, the process was accelerated by the Somoza regime's unbridled looting of relief supplies destined for victims of the 1972 earthquake, which was especially resented in the poorer barrios. Soon after the quake, recalls Sandinista leader Monica Baltodano, "[T]he whole Christian movement was being oriented in one way or another by the Front."[27] Organized Christians supported the 1978-9 insurrections as fighters and as members of the FSLN's clandestine support network.

The Nicaraguan bishops, like the Christians in the grassroots movement, were turning against the dictatorship, but more hesitantly and from a more moderate political perspective.[28] The bishops, in contrast to the grassroots movement, devoted most of their criticism to the political abuses rather than the socio-economic failings of the existing order. Although they were, by the late 1970s, calling for improvements in such areas as health care, education, and land distribution, the bishops thought in terms of reform rather than the sweeping transformation of Nicaraguan society favored by radicalized Christians.

While the grassroots movement was drawn to the FSLN, the episcopate was oriented toward the bourgeois opposition and suspicious of the Sandinistas. In a 1977 pastoral letter that unleashed one of their most uncompromising denunciations of the dictatorship, the bishops warned of "movements that call themselves liberators ... but end up putting new bosses in charge, without benefit to the growth of human liberties."[29] The bishops shared the opposition bourgeoisie's preference for a negotiated solution to the political crisis, achieved with American help that would ease Somoza from office, replace him with a moderate government, and exclude the FSLN from power. The archbishop of Managua, Miguel Obando y Bravo – who had distinguished himself as a plain-spoken opponent of the regime – persisted in the search for such a solution into the final days of the insurrection. The bishops long resisted the idea of armed rebellion. Not until June 2, when the insurgents were beginning their final offensive against Somoza's forces, did the bishops offer support for taking arms against "evident and prolonged tyranny."[30]

## After the Fall

As the triumphant Sandinista forces poured into Managua on July 19, 1979, Archbishop Obando celebrated a victory mass attended by thousands.[31] The event was symbolic of broad Christian support for a popular insurrection – a development without precedent in Latin American history. Two priests held positions in the newly appointed cabinet: Foreign Minister Miguel D'Escoto and Minister of Culture Ernesto Cardenal. Several other priests and dozens of lay Christians were also appointed to important government posts. An alumnus of Molina's Christian commune, Luis Carrión, sat on the FSLN's National Directorate. The leadership of ATC, the party's rural affiliate, was largely Christian. The revolution enjoyed the support of a national network of Christian organizations.

But it would soon be apparent that the fall of the old regime had left a latent division between two tendencies in the church that paralleled the tension between the FSLN and the anti-Somoza bourgeoisie. On one side were the Christians in the FSLN and the revolutionary government; radicalized church workers, including priests and nuns from several missionary orders; lay participants in the popular Christian movement; and theologians associated with several Managua-based, Christian "think tanks" dedicated to promoting liberation theology. On the other side were the episcopate plus the conservative clergy and the (heavily middle- and upper-class) laity that sided with the bishops. In this chapter, the former (sometimes referred to as the "popular church" or "church of the poor") are labeled *the revolutionary church*, and the latter are called *the conservative church*.[32]

In the midst of the euphoria of national unity that followed Somoza's departure, the revolutionary Christians and the Sandinista leadership, mindful of the episcopate's reluctant attitude toward the insurrection, anxiously waited for the bishops to define their attitude toward the revolution.[33] A pastoral letter issued by the episcopate on July 31 shows that the bishops were no less uneasy. They alluded to "the hopes and joys" of the new era, but their message was criss-crossed by dark shadows: "[we must not] enslave men all over again"; "without God there can be no liberation"' "to conscientize is not to impose something alien." These warnings seemed to be directed at both the FSLN and the revolutionary church.[34]

A few months later, in November 1979, the episcopate distributed a remarkable pastoral that exactly reversed the mood of the July letter. "It would be grave infidelity to the Gospel," wrote the bishops, "to [allow ourselves to be ruled by] fears and suspicions or the insecurity that all radical processes of change create or by the defense of individual interests, large or small, and miss the critical opportunity to concretize [the Church's] *preferential option for the poor* . . ." The bishops warned of the dangers of a new tyranny, but they also declared themselves open to "socialism." Liberation theology is unambiguously the interpretive basis of this message, which encourages the Christian base communities and calls on the church to learn to see the world from the perspective of the poor.[35]

But in an open letter to the National Directorate written in October 1980, the bishops reversed themselves again, abandoning all the positions they took the previous November. The successive twists of episcopal opinon during this period suggest an ideological struggle among the bishops, through which the conservatives regained the initiative. Whatever happened among them, the prelates were clearly responding to changing national political circumstances.

The immediate context of the October letter to the Directorate was an exchange over the FSLN's attitude toward religion, set off by the revelation of an internal party memorandum written the previous December. Signed by Julio López, then the party's national propaganda chief, and directed at regional propaganda officers, the memorandum dealt with the Christmas celebrations about to begin. López viewed the holiday as a folk tradition, which can be given a new, "fundamentally political" content. But he warned that a direct confrontation with "a tradition 1,979 years old would bring us political conflicts and we would lose influence among our people." The Soviets, he noted, have not fully eliminated religion after 62 years of revolution. "[P]ropaganda campaigns are not what erases a tradition with profound ideological roots from the [popular] consciousness. It is the transformation of material life that will create the objective conditions . . . for a labor of education and ideological formation among our people."[36]

Although the sentiments of the López memorandum were anti-religious, the document reflected Marx and Engels's *laissez-faire* attitude (religion will "die a natural death") rather than Bukharin's militant atheism. The status of the memorandum within the party was harder to decipher. It certainly expressed the views of some Sandinistas, but others thought differently, and without the imprimatur of the National Directorate, the López memorandum was not a weighty document.

The memorandum had been in the hands of *La Prensa's* editors almost from the moment it was written.[37] But they had chosen to publish it at a time that would maximize its political impact. In late 1980, the alliance that had linked the FSLN and the anti-Somoza bourgeoisie was unraveling and conservative forces were agitating religious questions as part of the surrounding debate. With the publication of the López memorandum, the party was compelled to publicly define its attitude toward religion.

The 1980 "Official Communiqué on Religion," released by the Directorate in early October, conceded that "some authors" have regarded religion as a source of false consciousness, a mechanism to justify class exploitation. This view has some "historic validity," the comandantes observed, but it does not agree with "our experience." In Nicaragua, "basing themselves on their faith," Christians played a heroic role in the insurrection and remain "an integral part of the Sandinista popular revolution." The Nicaraguan experience demonstrates that "one can be a believer and a committed revolutionary at the same time." This discovery may well have significance for future revolutions in other places.

The October communiqué committed the party to support religious freedom – a position the FSLN had taken at least as early as the 1969 *Program*. It declared that party membership was open to believers and non-believers without discrimination, that the party would not take positions on religious matters, or allow its members to do so in any official capacity, and that the FSLN opposed the political manipulation of religion. Here the comandantes offered a critical warning: if others attempt to turn popular religious activities into "political acts *against the revolution* (as has happened sometimes in the past), the FSLN declares it also has a right to defend the people and the revolution . . ."[38]

With the 1980 religion communiqué, the FSLN took an extraordinary step – demonstrating its indifference to Marxist-Leninist orthodoxy, its willingness to be guided by experience. The Directorate went beyond the perfunctory acknowledgement of the right to religious freedom common to even the most dogmatic Marxist authors. They accepted believers as full members of the party. (By comparison, most Marxist-Leninist parties, including the Cuban and Soviet parties, have barred all believers from membership.[39]) Revolutionary Christians had won this right *by their actions*, that is, by bearing arms, by spilling blood – no small matter for a party that reveres its martyrs.

The comandantes had not, however, disposed of the religious question, as their final cautionary note reveals. The religion communiqué anticipated that religion would continue to be used against the revolution by its enemies and implied that Sandinista religious tolerance had political limits.

The bishops' October 1980 open reply to the FSLN religion communiqué repudiated the optimism of their November 1979 pastoral.[40] The bishops had given in to the fears they warned themselves against. Their earlier hopes for change, "preferential option for the poor," and openness to socialism had all vanished. These concerns never reappeared in the episcopate's statements.

Two related themes ran through the long text of the bishops' letter, both concerning imminent threats from an unnamed source – which could only be the FSLN. The first was the threat to democracy represented by those who set themselves up as the "'Representative'" (vanguard?) of the

people, who would create a new "Pharoah" and open the country to a
new "interventionism" (the Soviet Union?). The second was the threat
to the faith from those who would use religion to destroy democracy,
who ultimately intend to "eliminate religion" and replace it with a
system that is "materialist" (a codeword for Marxist) and "atheist." This
"instrumentalization" of faith was evident to the bishops in the political
mobilization of believers by the revolutionary church, the use of priests in
high government positions, and Sandinista participation in popular religious
festivals, such as "La Purisima," the traditional celebration of the immacu-
late conception. The intention was to divide the church: Christ, recalled the
bishops, denounced those who "wound the Pastor to disperse the sheep."

The October letter suggests that the bishops had come to regard any
Sandinista association with religion as a direct challenge to the *magisterium*:
the sacred teaching authority of the church (conferred, according to
Catholic tradition, on Peter and the apostles by Jesus and passed to
successive popes and the bishops they appoint).[41] More broadly, they
were convinced that the Sandinistas intended to appropriate the power of
religion for their own purposes. Obviously, the bishops regarded the López
memorandum rather than the National Directorate's religion communiqué
as the best guide to the intentions of the FSLN. Interpreted in that light,
the party's very openness to Christians became a threat to the church.

The October letter represented the episcopate's response to the consolidation of Sandinista power and the political eclipse of the bourgeoisie
in the course of the preceding year. The bishops had placed themselves on
the side of the bourgeois coalition in the emerging political conflict.

## Symbolic Struggles

The period following the October 1980 exchange will be remembered
for the often extravagant, symbolic struggle over religion waged between
the revolution and its enemies. The brief, well-publicized career of the
"sweating Virgin" is emblematic of these years. The sweating Virgin was
a plaster of paris statue of the Virgin Mary that inexplicably exuded
moisture through her "pores" – a sign, said anti-Sandinista interpreters,
that the Virgin was crying over Nicaragua's Marxist revolution. The statue
turned up in the home of a Managua couple in early December 1981 – just
before "La Purisima," high-point of the Nicaraguan religious calendar –
and received extensive, front-page coverage in *La Prensa*. Hundreds lined
up to receive the Virgin's blessing, among them, the paper reported, a
13-year-old boy who was apparently cured of epilepsy. A cotton swab
used to absorb the holy moisture miraculously burst into flame in
the hands of a *La Prensa* reporter without burning him. Archbishop

Obando came to pray with the crowd and examine the statue, which he found worthy of further observation. His auxiliary bishop found the phenomenon "extraordinary" and inexplicable. But after the archdiocese took possession of the Virgin, she apparently stopped sweating, and was quietly forgotten. The Sandinista press later reported that the head of the household where she was found had a long criminal record.[42]

Another Marian miracle, similarly interpreted and promoted by *La Prensa*, proved more enduring. The Virgin reportedly appeared to a peasant near the town of Cuapa, told him to recite the rosary, and promised her protection. An elaborate cult developed around the "Virgin of Cuapa," and in 1982 a shrine was consecrated in her honor by the head of the diocese, Bishop Pablo Vega, like Obando, a determined anti-Sandinista. Sandinistas could not help wondering how the Virgin, who had ignored Nicaragua through long centuries of sin and suffering, found time for two visits in 18 months.[43]

These events reflect an effort by conservative Catholics to turn the country back to a traditional, pre-Vatican II religiosity, built on personal spirituality and obedience to the bishops.[44] The Virgins, rosaries, and miracles of this Catholicism are intended as a challenge to the prophetic Jesus, political commitment, and social objectives of the revolutionary church. (In November 1982, the bishops reminded Nicaraguans of their traditional faith with a series of open-air masses consecrating the nation to Mary.)

The new, conservative religiosity was enthusiastically taken up by *La Prensa* and the rest of the bourgeois opposition. Businessmen commonly displayed religious posters bearing obliquely anti-Sandinista slogans in their salesrooms and offices. An upper-class critic of the Sandinistas noted a religious revival among his friends.[45] Affluent Managuans crowded the Sunday masses presided over by Archbishop Obando; and when the archbishop was decorated by the Venezuelan government, Nicaraguan business firms paid for full-page advertisements in a special edition of *La Prensa* honoring him.[46]

The apotheosis of the archbishop became part of the bourgeois political strategy. Enrique Bolaños, president of COSEP, later commented, "Monsignor Obando is our most respected figure, not only because he wears a cassock but also because of his personality. He has a historic role and is well prepared for it. Marxism-Leninism being a sort of religion, it can only be confronted by another religion."[47] Obando was in fact well suited for his new role. His modest origins, stamped on his Indian features and dark skin, and his history of resistance to the Somozas contributed to his popular appeal. He did not hesitate to turn religious occasions into symbolic substitutes for the opposition political activity restricted by the Sandinistas.

Obando's political potential was also appreciated by conservative forces outside the country. Programs administered by his diocese were supported by USAID and, it appears, at least one American corporation. The

Washington-based Institute on Religion and Democracy (a right-wing think tank), the Latin American Bishops' Conference (controlled by traditionalists since the 1970s), and Vatican conservatives have all helped promote Obando's career, which culminated in his elevation to cardinal in 1985.[48]

One arena of conflict between the conservative church led by Obando and the Sandinista leadership was education policy. Tension over educational issues had been growing since the 1980 literacy campaign. The bishops and their conservative supporters objected to school texts that celebrate the FSLN, its leaders, and political principles. They viewed Marxist-influenced textbooks in areas such as history or science as an inherent challenge to faith, even though the texts avoid religious questions. Opponents of the revolution feared that the government might abolish the largely Catholic private schools that educate middle- and upper-class Nicaraguans. Instead, the government instituted a unified curriculum which it required all schools to follow. The national curriculum is secular. Public schools do not tell their students what to think about religion, but church schools – many of which are subsidized by the government – are free to teach religion classes, whose content they determine. This solution did not satisfy the bishops and their conservative backers, since it restricted the church's control of education to an explicitly defined religious sphere.[49]

During the early eighties, the hierarchy's anti-Sandinista policies were more typically aimed at revolutionary Christians than at the government or party. The bishops began undercutting the revolutionary church by transferring priests associated with it, often over the protests of their lower-class parishioners. The targeted priests were moved to unsympathetic middle-class neighborhoods or even forced out of the country.[50]

Since 1980, the episcopate has also pressured the priests who hold high government positions to resign. Under most circumstances, such service violates rules established by the Vatican. But for both the episcopate and the FSLN the crux of the issue is the Christian legitimization of the revolution implied by a clerical presence in the government. A 1981 compromise allowed the priests to continue temporarily, but the bishops subsequently renewed their demands, and only the tenacity of the cleric-revolutionaries and the intricacies of canon law have kept them in place.[51]

While the episcopate was struggling to contain the influence of the revolutionary priests, the official church was training a new generation of priests, presumably indoctrinated with a conservative theology and traditional notions of ecclesiastical authority.[52]

## Confrontations

The strain that had been accumulating in church–state relations since 1980 exploded in a week of sometimes violent confrontations in mid-August

1982.[53] That week was preceded by several months of growing political tension generated by the emerging contra war. In March the government had declared a state of emergency in response to attacks by the US-backed Nicaraguan Democratic Force (FDN). Political conflict soon spilled into the religious sphere. In late July, the removal of a popular revolutionary priest from his working-class parish precipitated a bitter controversy – the subject of highly charged stories in the Managua papers – between neighborhood Sandinista activists and church authorities. About the same time, FDN forces killed 14 peasants in the village of San Francisco del Norte and left written on the walls of their houses the words, "in the name of God."[54]

On Monday August 9, Sandinista mobs began a series of occupations of small fundamentalist churches. The Sandinista press had been charging that these sects, which were typically American-based and had expanded rapidly since 1980, were part of a CIA-orchestrated campaign of ideological subversion of the revolution. On Wednesday, the Managua papers published a letter from Pope John Paul II to the Nicaraguan bishops concerning the "fragile and threatened" unity of the Nicaraguan church – a strongly worded denunciation of the "popular church" and reaffirmation of the authority of the bishops.[55] This very political document was written shortly after a visit to Rome by Archbishop Obando. The government added to the letter's political weight by initially prohibiting its publication. (Responding to the Pope some days later, revolutionary Christians rejected the label "popular church" along with its implication of schism. They insisted on their loyalty to the Roman church and respect for the doctrinal authority of the hierarchy, while recalling the Vatican II conception of the church as the whole "People of God.")

The day the Pope's letter was published, Archbishop Obando's spokesman, Father Bismarck Carballo, was dragged naked into the street of an affluent Managua neighborhood, detained by Sandinista police and photographed by pro-government newsmen. On Friday, images of the nude priest appeared in *Barricada*, the semi-official *Nuevo Diario*, and on Sandinista Television. According to the Sandinista press, the incident grew out of the priest's involvement in "a classic triangle of passion" – to quote *Barricada*'s uncharacteristically florid language.[56] Surprised in the arms of his lover by an enraged husband, Carballo had the good luck to be rescued by the Sandinista police. Carballo's rendition of the incident asserted that he had been in the midst of a pastoral visit to the woman concerned, when armed men abruptly appeared and forced him to disrobe. Many Nicaraguans were, at the same time, skeptical of Carballo's explanation and outraged at what appeared to be the calculated humiliation of a priest. Clerics in official positions protested the government's actions.

Over the weekend, Sandinista activists fought with seminarians accompanying Archbishop Obando on a visit to Masaya, a provincial capital close to Managua. Events climaxed on Monday, when students at Catholic schools in several cities went on strike to protest the Carballo incident. The strike incited new clashes between Sandinistas and conservative Catholics – the worst of them at a Catholic school in Masaya occupied by protesters, where shooting broke out and at least two Sandinistas were killed. The government subsequently seized the school and arrested nearly 100 people.

Borge blamed these events on the CIA and suggested that they were somehow associated with the military plans of the contras. But Borge's own Interior Ministry, which supervises both the police and the office of press censorship, was widely regarded as responsible for the Carballo incident.[57] In the wake of Monday's violence the National Directorate issued a cautiously worded communiqué, reaffirming its positions of tolerance on religion and warning the party's press and supporters to exercise restraint.[58] The Masaya school and most of the evangelical churches that had been seized were returned to their owners, all but a few of those arrested were released without charge, and Borge was sent on an extended tour of Eastern Europe.[59]

The surface calm of earlier months returned to church–state relations and endured into 1983, only to be shattered on March 4, the day the Pope came to Nicaragua.[60] The Sandinistas had courted the papal visit, part of a Central American tour, which they naively saw as an opportunity to focus world attention on American aggression against Nicaragua and demonstrate the compatibility between Christianity and their revolution. They may have even believed that they could recast the Pope's own views. But John Paul had his own, unambiguous agenda: to strengthen what he regarded as a beleaguered church and reinforce the position of his bishops.

A collision course was set on the tarmac at Sandino Airport, where John Paul proclaimed the guiding theme of his visit – obey your bishops – and Daniel Ortega denounced American imperialism. On the receiving line Culture Minister Ernesto Cardenal, one of the priest-officials whose resignation the episcopate had been demanding, kneeled before the Pope to kiss his ring. John Paul pulled back his hand, and shook a finger at Cardenal, warning him to "straighten out" his situation with the bishops. Ortega's welcoming remarks recalled the long history of US military intervention in Nicaragua, whose most recent victims, he noted, were 17 teenage militiamen, killed by the contras and buried by their families the previous day. Ortega also reminded the pontiff of the FSLN's policies of religious tolerance. The Pope looked pained.

John Paul's 11-hour visit to Nicaragua reached its denouement at an open-air mass in Managua's July 19 Plaza. Over half a million people attended (a substantial proportion of the national population) with the help of free transportation provided by the government. The Pope opened his homily with an expression of "affection and esteem" for Archbishop Obando and then turned to the politically charged topic of church unity. Elaborating on the contents of his 1982 letter, John Paul warned of the threats posed to the church by "unacceptable ideological commitments," "materialism," misguided priests, the "popular church," and a "parallel *magisterium*." The Pope made no concessions to Vatican II reforms. "[O]bedience to the bishops and the Pope" is the rock on which the church rests. The *magisterium* was conferred by Christ and deviation from it is "absurd and dangerous."[61]

Anxious to avoid incidents that would embarrass the revolution, the FSLN had carefully prepared its supporters for the papal visit, emphasizing the great respect due the "Holy Father," as *Barricada* piously referred to him. But the party had also allowed people to hope that the pontiff would back Nicaragua's calls for peace and pray for the country's war-dead. Halfway through the homily it was apparent – if only from John Paul's angry tone – that neither was going to happen, and Sandinista self-restraint began to break down.

The party's current slogans rang out in the plaza: "We want peace!" "People's Power!" "*Silencio!*" replied the Pope. A group of mothers whose sons had perished in the insurrection or in the contra war (including mothers of the 17 boys just buried) began to press forward. Dressed in mourning, many bearing aloft large photographs of their sons, they wanted, "A prayer for our martyrs!" At this point the Pope might have halted the gathering storm with a neutral prayer for *all* the victims of Nicaragua's wars, but he refused. "*Silencio!*" "We want peace!" "*Silencio!*" "People's Power!" "We want church on the side of the poor!" The habits of many, many political rallies – often in this very plaza – were taking over.

Initially, some of the Sandinista dignitaries in attendance tried to calm the tumult, but they were soon drawn into it. By the time the Pope finished his homily, the entire National Directorate was on its feet, and Borge and Humberto Ortega were chanting and clapping in time with Sandinista partisans in the audience. The ceremony broke up in chaos.

The National Directorate issued another conciliatory communiqué, reaffirming its 1980 position on religion and vainly appealing to John Paul's "wisdom" to understand Nicaragua's situation. But there was no getting around the fact that the Sandinistas had handed their domestic and international enemies an enormous victory. "The Pope is with us," claimed an FDN poster captured in May.[62]

## Faith and Revolution

The irony of the Pope's attack on the Sandinistas and their Christian allies is that religion was thriving in Nicaragua, while the strength of the revolutionary church had dwindled. In the 1980s, by all accounts, there were more churches with more people in them, more processions, more denominations, more clergy, and more seminarians than ever before. Under Sandinista rule, Nicaragua was undergoing a religious revival. [63] The following observations from the author's fieldnotes reflect the atmosphere of the period:

> Matagalpa, March (Lent) to August, 1984. Yesterday I ran into another religious procession. About 500 people moved down a narrow street in the middle of town and turned onto the main street, bearing aloft a Christ shouldering his cross and accompanied by two kids dressed as Roman soldiers. A small band played a dirge. In the vanguard, small boys, slightly ahead of their schoolmates in choirboy garb, darted about, occasionally throwing rocks at one another. In the rear, an old man, a campesino with a weather-beaten hat in his hands, his steps halting but determined. These processions are held daily in the late afternoon and in the very early morning (4.30 a.m.). The first time I heard the band, the dirge, and the priest intoning through a loudspeaker at that hour, I thought I was dreaming – it was surreal, out of Fellini. No one else would be allowed to make so much noise so early. One day I saw a procession of about 300 people march around the Cathedral square, past the police station, where some young police came out to watch the spectacle.
>
> The level of religious activity here stuns me. A couple of days ago, compelling revival music drew me to an open door in Fanor Jaens Barrio, which opened into an assembly hall of unexpected proportions. The structure seemed to be still under construction. Several hundred people clapped their hands ecstatically to the music, men on one side of the room, women on the other. Some of the women wore mantillas [a traditional Hispanic Catholic practice]. Some people carried Bibles. A man near the door told me that they were evangelicals. Every day I seem to run into some church I didn't know existed. I notice that the 7th Day Adventists have their own school in town.
>
> I ran into three young guys carrying Bibles on the path up to Walter Mendoza [a shantytown of about 5,000]. They tell me that they are members of Assemblies of God [the domination that includes American TV-evangelists Jimmy Swaggert and Jim Bakker] and have churches in central Matagalpa and Walter Mendoza.
>
> Near the 7th Day Adventist School, a shriveled old woman sits before a lively display of baskets and other straw items. I stop to look. Seeing nothing to buy, I thank her and start off, but she stops me. A beatific expression on her face, she insists on giving me two tiny prayer leaflets (Catholic-inspired). When I have time, she says, I'll read them. And, she tells me, don't worry. It's not the fault of the "Junta de Gobierno," but of subversives ("Infiltrados") in the bureaucracy. But everything will be all right. All this with no coaxing from me.

The revolutionary church has remained strong in some parts of the country, such as parishes with progressive priests, certain rural zones served by resilient lay movements, and the diocese of Estelí, where base communities were encouraged by a rare sympathetic bishop. But in most of Managua, the grassroots communities did not retain the dynamism of the late 1970s. In

Matagalpa, the strong Christian revolutionary movement of the insurrection period had vanished by the early 1980s. In much of the country the revolutionary church was small or invisible by the time of the Pope's visit.

Why had the revolutionary church failed to thrive in revolutionary Nicaragua? The bishops contributed by removing or intimidating priests supportive of the revolution. At the same time, much of the lay leadership developed by the Christian movement during the insurrection was being drained off by the government, party, and mass organizations. The multiple demands that the revolution make on activists left them little time to work with Christian base communities. Finally, the role of the revolutionary church had changed. Once a political vehicle for mobilizing protest against an unpopular regime, it came to be viewed, perhaps unfairly, as an apologist for a revolutionary government, whose support was declining in hard times.

As early as May 1982, revolutionary Christians meeting for a week of theological reflection recognized the situation and began to organize a campaign to regain lost ground. The Pope's visit seemed to give new impetus to their efforts. But in the mid-1980s most Nicaraguans – excepting the conservative privileged classes – identified with neither the official nor the revolutionary tendency in the church. And while the vast majority of Nicaraguans continued to consider themselves Catholics, no religious movement could match the dynamism of the rapidly expanding fundamentalist churches.

## After the Pope

In the aftermath of the Pope's visit, relations between the official church and the revolutionary state grew even more conflictive. When the government – in reply to rising contra attacks – promulgated a military conscription law in late 1983, the bishops responded with a statement that questioned the very legitimacy of the Sandinista state, asserting that no one who disagreed with the FSLN should be obligated to serve. One Sunday a few weeks later, Sandinista demonstrators disrupted religious services in churches, largely in Managua, where they charged anti-conscription activities were being organized. The government expelled two priests whom it accused of encouraging draft resistance.

In 1984, the episcopate issued an Easter message calling for national "reconciliation," but their less than conciliatory text is full of hostile allusions to the FSLN and the revolutionary church.[64] Treating the expanding conflict as a civil war, the message fails to acknowledge the National Guard roots or American control of contra forces. The bishops called for dialogue among all Nicaraguan parties, including negotiations with "those who have risen in arms," a course demanded earlier by bourgeois opposition parties and flatly rejected by the FSLN. Coming on top of the pastoral letter on conscription, the Easter message was inevitably read by Sandinistas as support for foreign aggression. Daniel Ortega angrily called the bishops "false prophets," directed by the CIA and the US embassy. *Barricada* published a lurid cartoon of a bishop transforming a cross into a swastika.[65]

For supporters of the revolution, the failure of the episcopate to react to contra human rights abuses underscored the partisan position the bishops were assuming. In the face of accumulating evidence from international human rights organizations and from the church's own clergy in conflict zones, Archbishop Obando asserted that no dependable information was available on the contra abuses. When six children were killed by contra mortar fire, Bishop Vega's reaction was, "to kill the soul is worse than to kill the body." The episcopate never responded collectively to rebel abuses, but three bishops from the frontier dioceses of Estelí, Matagalpa, and Bluefields broke with their colleagues to condemn the murder of 30 telephone company workers by contra forces in December 1984.[66]

During the three years following the Pope's visit, Obando and Vega, the prelates most hostile to the revolution, were at the zenith of their influence. A supportive Pope elevated Obando to cardinal in 1985. Back from his investiture in Rome, Obando threw himself into a series of appearances around the country that assumed the atmosphere of an anti-Sandinista campaign tour. "[T]he Lord speaks through his mouth," announced *La Prensa*.[67] In fact, Obando had become the chief spokesman of the bourgeois opposition. Vega verged on identifying himself with the contras in his public statements, especially those directed at international audiences. He defended "a people's right to insurrection" before a Managua press conference, and addressed a Washington audience supportive of administration policy (with several contra leaders in attendance) on the eve of a critical contra-aid vote in the House of Representatives.[68]

The FSLN never knew how to respond to a hostile church. It was easier, Tomás Borge thought, to confront 10,000 contras than a few bishops.[69] In late June 1986, the government stopped the cardinal's spokesman, Father Bismarck Carballo, from returning to the country after a trip to the United States and Europe. A few days later, state security agents picked up Bishop Vega and delivered him to exile at a Honduran border crossing. This move precipitated the expected international torrent of protests from governments and church authorities, but it also notified the bishops and the Vatican that the Nicaraguan church could not openly side with the contras without endangering its own apostolic mission.

The revolutionary church had its own answer to Obando and Vega, organized by Father Miguel D'Escoto, Nicaragua's foreign minister. While Obando was touring the country in July 1985, D'Escoto began a month-long fast to protest US aggression and the official church's own complicity. In February 1986, he led a "*Viacrucis* for Peace," turning the traditional

Nicaraguan "way of the cross" from a modest local procession into a national protest march from the Honduran border, through the major provincial capitals, and into the center of Managua. D'Escoto seized on the rich symbolism of the *viacrucis* to equate the American empire with its Roman antecedent and the war-suffering of Nicaragua with the agony of Jesus on the cross. The implied role of Nicaraguan bishops in this portable passion play could easily be imagined.

In Estelí, the sympathetic but usually reticent Bishop Rubén López blessed the marchers and opened his cathedral to them – a moral victory for D'Escoto, which must have rankled some of López's episcopal brothers. Close observers of the bishops know that they are divided over the war and Obando's confrontational approach to the Sandinistas but are under considerable pressure to avoid public discord.[70]

The *viacrucis* ended a week later, in Managua, where 72 priests (about 30 percent of the priests in the country) led the pilgrims and a large crowd in the mass before the ruins of Obando's earthquake-shattered cathedral. In an impassioned sermon, D'Escoto addressed himself directly to the cardinal:

> Miguel Obando, brother in the priesthood that you have betrayed. . . .Listen: if you had the television or radio on, don't turn it off! Don't turn it off, Miguel Obando! God, through his humble people . . . who have suffered the aggression of which you have been the principal accomplice, that God, the God of Life, God of Love . . . has mercy on you. . . .God and his entire people want your repentance. [Until you repent], IN THE NAME OF GOD . . . WE SAY THAT YOU MUST CEASE CELEBRATING THE HOLY MASS, BECAUSE THAT CELEBRATION BY ONE WHO IS AN ACCOMPLICE IN THE ASSASSINATION OF HIS PEOPLE IS A SACRILEGE AND AN OFFENSE TO THE FAITH OF OUR PEOPLE.[71]

## Religion and the Sandinista Front

The conflict between the official church and the FSLN is typically presented as a collision between two monolithic forces. But there is a range of attitudes on both sides. At one end of the spectrum within the FSLN are cadres whose opinions reflect the more dogmatic strains in FSLN's Marxist heritage.[72] They are militant atheists, who regard religion as inherently reactionary, and would like the party to take more aggressive anti-church action. Among younger militants, who typically lack the practical experience of the leaders of the insurrection, such attitudes are encouraged by training in Soviet bloc countries, by reading the Soviet and Cuban political manuals that circulate in Nicaragua, and by some of the instruction now given in Nicaraguan universities.

The 1979 López memorandum, whose revelation in 1980 compelled the FSLN to define its attitude toward religion, was a warning to this dogmatic sector of the party. Such damaging actions as the humiliation of Father Carballo in 1982 and the disruptions of Sunday services in October 1983 reflect the influence of militant atheists. In Sandinista circles, according to a publication of the pro-FSLN, Jesuit-run Central American Historical Institute, their presence has tended to "intimidate Christians involved in the revolution, to make them ashamed of their faith, unsure of it, or inclined to disguise their Christian sentiments."[73] But in 1985, according to a clergyman with close party ties, militant atheists unsuccessfully resisted the appointment of a priest, Fernando Cardenal, to the crucial post of Education Minister (Cardenal replaced another Sandinista Christian, Carlos Tunnerman).

At the other end of the ideological-religious spectrum within the party are those party members who are identified as practicing Christians and regard their faith as integral to their revolutionary commitment. A few (5 of 104) members of the Sandinista Assembly fit this description, including the three priest-cabinet ministers (D'Escoto and the Cardenal brothers), one vice-minister, and the head of ATC, Edgardo Garcia. (From its inception, the Sandinista rural union was permeated with Christian cadres.) Other prominent Christian revolutionaries in the party include Carlos Tunnerman, now ambassador to the United States; Miguel Vigil Icaza, Minister of Housing; Reinaldo Tefel, Director of the Social Security Institute; and Emilio Baltodano, Controller General of the Republic. [74]

Most Sandinista militants probably fall between these polar categories. Their positions range from the *laissez-faire* atheism of Marx and Engels ("religion will die a natural death") to non-practicing Christian faith. Some are conflicted about their beliefs or have simply set the question of faith "in parentheses" for the moment. This broad category includes militants who were Christian activists during the insurrection but drifted away from their faith as their revolutionary commitment grew. For them, liberation theology provided an ideological way-station on the road to a Marxist materialist position. At least six members of the Sandinista Assembly fit this description. The most important of the ex-Christians is National Directorate member Luís Carrión, originally part of Padre Molina's Christian student commune, who told a meeting of Christian revolutionaries in late 1979:

> I became involved in the revolution through a religious experience. My first motivations were of this type. My growing concern with the concept of justice, my first search for identification with the people took this road. . . . As I began to advance and grow as a revolutionary, I found other reasons and other motivations. I developed an objective consciousness of the roots of exploitation, of the suffering of the people, and I began to see things from another perspective.[75]

The attitudes of other members of the National Directorate are harder to gauge. None is publicly identified as a practicing Christian, though Daniel Ortega has had his children baptized and Tomás Borge frequently attends the mass at his friend Molina's church. Borge, enigmatic as ever, has taken a special interest in religion – covering a wall in his Interior Ministry office with an array of crosses, sprinkling his speeches with references to the Bible, and frequently addressing church audiences. He seems drawn to the ideals of liberation theology and maintains close relations with several Sandinista priests. He is capable of tantalizing a liberal Christian audience by suggesting that if being a Christian means loving the poor and practicing such Christian virtues as humility, he is or at least aspires to be a Christian. He is also the comandante who has spoken most menacingly about counterrevolutionary religious activity.[76]

The personal views of Wheelock and Humberto Ortega might be deduced from two rare public statements on religion. Wheelock, addressing a working-class audience, declares, "We openly state that there are some in the Sandinista Liberation Front who, on the basis of their ideas, their ideology, their studies, their questions, have begun to believe that God does not exist. We state this openly. There is no need to discuss it." But in the same speech he recalled the role of Christians in revolution and repeated the Sandinista slogan. "Between revolution and Christianity there is no contradiction."[77] Humberto's remarks to a Sandinista army audience reveal grudging tolerance but betray no enthusiasm for Christian participation in the revolution: "If [people] want to believe in God, let them believe . . . .[W]e are [not] going to attack some little old lady who goes around saying the rosary. . . ."[78]

All members of the party are politically bound to the positions of tolerance prescribed by the 1980 religion communiqué. But that declaration – quite daring from a Marxist-Leninist perspective – has never persuaded conservative Christian critics of the revolution, who believe that the party's long-term objective is the eradication of religion in Nicaragua. Their fears are fed by the continuing friction between the party and the church and promoted by those whose interests run, more generally, counter to revolutionary change.

There are good reasons, however, to take the Sandinistas at their word. For one, the broad, programmatic, internal party documents that anticipate a long-term attack on capitalism contain no provisions for a "two-stage" atheist revolution.[79] Under Sandinista rule, religion is flourishing in Nicaragua – especially the U.S. based, fundamentalist faiths that are, at very least, suspicious of Sandinismo. While religious activities have occasionally been disrupted by Sandinistas, their motivation has always been explicitly political, rather than anti-religious.

Sandinista leaders frequently preface discussions of religion with the observation that the Nicaraguans are a very Christian people. They know that any attacks on religious belief could easily split their movement and undermine their popular support. Although there are few practicing

Christians in the upper reaches of the FSLN, the revolutionary Christians appear to have many sympathizers in the party, including some members of the National Directorate. In Managua, more than a few middle-ranking government officials wear crosses around their necks. In the lower-class barrios of Matagalpa, most CDS leaders have a sacred heart of Jesus poster, a cross, a corner shrine, or a picture of the Pope hanging in their homes. Typical supporters of the revolution in these neighborhoods are Catholics who know as little of the "good news" of liberation theology and as of the bad news of church–state antagonisms. A Sandinista assault on religious faith would certainly shake them out of their religious lethargy and open them to anti-revolutionary political appeals. The FSLN has little reason and no apparent inclination to take such a risk.

## The Roots of Conflict

Running through all the theatrics of religious affairs in Nicaragua – from the sweating Virgin and the naked priest to the Pope heckled in the plaza and the cardinal called to repentance on the radio – is a pattern of steadily worsening relations between the Sandinista revolution and the official church. Why? It would be a mistake to ignore the obvious. The Nicaraguan church is an institution that has upheld the established order for centuries, and has long viewed the world from an anti-communist perspective. The FSLN is a revolutionary party rooted in Marxism, a system of thought that is, at best, tolerant but contemptuous of religion. Neither the powerful message of Medellin nor the experience of Christian participation in the insurrection was enough to overcome the burden of the past. Although the bishops were open to change and the comandantes welcomed Christians as partners in the creation of a new society, the leaders of the church and the party regarded each other with deep suspicion from the beginning of the revolution.

In the political context of a revolutionary upheaval, it was unlikely that the episcopate and the Directorate would find a *modus vivendi*. The bishops shared the values of the bourgeoisie – including a commitment to Western democratic institutions. They rapidly forgot their own admonition to see the world from the perspective of the poor. When the FSLN moved to consolidate its own power, the hierarchy sided with the bourgeoisie, as it had done for many decades. Conservatives in Washington, at the Vatican, and within the Conference of Latin American Bishops – mindful that collaboration between a Marxist revolution and Christian radicals posed a powerful example for the rest of the Third World – worked to strengthen the Obando–Vega tendency within the episcopate. Finally, the war – in which the bishops assumed attitudes toward the Sandinista state ranging from neutral to treasonous – raised the church–revolution conflict to a level from which it will not easily recover.

The FSLN and the Catholic church are remarkably similar institutions and their similarities have contributed to their confrontation. Both are hierarchical organizations that concentrate doctrinal authority and administrative power at the top. The National Directorate and the Episcopal Conference are collegial bodies, neither of which is accountable, in a democratic sense, to the lower ranks. Both the church and the party draw a sharp distinction between members (priests or militants) and non-members. Absolute discipline and values favoring subordination to the institution (modesty, self-sacrifice) are expected of members. Indiscipline or doctrinal deviation are regarded as threats to the very existence of the organization. (The church, John Paul reminds Nicaraguans, is preserved by "one Lord, one faith, one baptism, one God and Father." The party, warns the National Directorate, is threatened by "the maintenance of divisionist, sectarian, or factional positions . . . which sabotage the internal cohesion of the organization."[80])

The vanguard and the *magisterium* are parallel concepts, representing claims of privileged access to truth. Both the church and the party claim a transcendental mission – building the Kingdom of God or a New Nicaragua. Accordingly, both demand the ultimate loyalty of all Nicaraguans.

The church and the party, like two great, sovereign powers attempting to occupy the same continent, are drawn inexorably into frontier clashes and finally into war. The problem rests on expansive ambitions and obscure boundaries. When the government names priests to the cabinet, cultivates the revolutionary church, or expands its control of education, the vanguard is threatening the church. When the bishops instruct the country on the draft or lend their authority to anti-Sandinista Virgins, they are extending the *magisterium* into the realm of politics.

The official church asserts that it suffers religious persecution. It could, more reasonably, claim to be the victim of political persecution, since Sandinista harassment of the church has always grown out of political conflict. According to Borge, Christ had the answer: "What Christ said is still valid. Render to Caesar the things that are Caesar's and to God the things that are God's."[81] But, Borge, who has preached many sermons, must know that God and Caesar would have a hard time figuring out who gets the revolutionary church or the Virgin of Cuapa.

In retrospect, the period from the 1982 Carballo incident to the 1986 expulsions of Father Carballo and Bishop Vega may be seen as the high tide of church–state confrontation in Nicaragua. In 1987, Vega and Carballo were informed that they could return to Nicaragua. (Vega chose to remain in exile). By then both sides had recoiled from the level of conflict reached earlier. The bishops may still pray for the demise of the FSLN, but within the episcopate and the Vatican there is growing recognition that the revolution is likely to survive and the church, for its own good, will have to adapt to that reality. The comandantes were never so deluded, dogmatic, or despotic as to think that they could root out the church, but they would have liked to relegate the authority of the bishops to a narrowly sacramental realm. The end of the war will allow the leaders of the church and the revolution to work out their separate peace.

# 7
# *Yankees and Sandinistas*

To Sandinistas and other Nicaraguan nationalists Anastasio Somoza Debayle was "the last Marine."[1] The title was doubly appropriate. Somoza had been educated at an American military academy. He was also the last in a long line of Nicaraguan rulers who built their careers on American power.

## Sandinista History: Betrayal and Redemption

The first of these men was, oddly enough, an American who became president of Nicaragua. In 1855, Nicaraguan Liberals, on the losing side of a civil war with the ruling Conservatives, invited help from abroad. A group of American investors battling Cornelius Vanderbilt for control of the lucrative inter-oceanic transportation concession across Nicaragua were also interested in a change of government. They recruited an American adventurer named William Walker to help the Liberals. With the aid of private American financing, superior firepower, and no small amount of luck, Walker and his band of Yankee mercenaries overcame the Conservatives. But instead of handing the country over to his Liberal sponsors, Walker set up a puppet regime, which was recognized by the United States.

Walker subsequently had himself "elected" president of Nicaragua. After his inauguration (to the tune of "Yankee Doodle"), he legalized slavery, established English as a national language, and began to seize land from those who opposed him. Courting the support of Southern slaveholders, he publicized his intention to place "a large portion of the land in the hands of the white race," a category that presumably excluded most Nicaraguans. Walker told his men that they were "the advance guard of American civilization."[2]

In the age of "Manifest Destiny," Walker, who had a flair for self-promotion, became a popular American hero. In Nicaragua he is hated to this day. One of his final gestures, before he was driven out of the country in 1857 by a united Central American army, was to order the destruction of the 300-year-old city of Granada – a task which the advance guard of American civilization completed with drunken abandon.

In the early decades of the twentieth century, the United States backed the Nicaraguan Conservatives. In 1909, the US Navy helped the Conservatives despose the Liberal government of José Santos Zelaya, a strong leader whose policies had frequently clashed with American diplomatic and business interests. American corporations in Nicaragua gave the conspirators financial support, and some of their employees participated in the rebellion. Among them was Adolfo Díaz, an officer of an American mining corporation that was unhappy with Zelaya. With American help, Díaz soon became president of Nicaragua.

In exchange for American support, the new Conservative regime negotiated a series of unneeded loans from American banks and gave control of the country's customs receipts, national bank, railroads, and steamship lines to US bankers as collateral. The new government had sacrificed authority over its own financial affairs and left the country deeply indebted to win the affection of State Department officials and New York financiers. Much of the cash that flowed into the government's coffers by these arrangements soon escaped into the pockets of Díaz and other regime insiders. According to American diplomatic records, one Conservative family, the Chamorros, received $500,000. [3]

In 1912, Emiliano Chamorro, Díaz's ambassador in Washington, signed a treaty under which Nicaragua, in effect, renounced its rights to build an inter-oceanic canal in exchange for a one-time payment of $3 million. Engineers had long regarded Nicaragua as an attractive alternative to Panama, where the Americans were already at work. When the Chamorro–Bryan Treaty – infamous to subsequent generations of Nicaraguan nationalists – was ratified in 1916, most of the $3 million went directly from the US Treasury to the American bankers who held Nicaragua's debt.

These policies did not win the Conservative regime a large popular following. American troops were required to put down a Liberal rebellion in 1912 and supervise the one-candidate election that confirmed Díaz in office. Thereafter, the United States maintained a permanent Marine detachment in Managua as a reminder of American support for the governing party. With American guidance, Emiliano Chamorro and his uncle Diego Manuel Chamorro succeeded Díaz in the presidency. Since the State Department, backed by the Marines, guided Nicaragua's political affairs and US banks controlled its finances, it required some imagination to think of Nicaragua as an independent republic.

But even from Washington's perspective, the American-managed regime in Nicaragua was not a success. Its financial health was undermined by the rapaciousness of the Yankee bankers and corrupt Nicaraguan officials. Its political stability was continually threatened by intra-party Conservative intrigues and the armed conspiracies of the majority Liberals. The occupying Marines involved themselves in ugly incidents with Nicaraguan civilians and drew criticism at home.

US policy makers dreamed of finding a new political formula that would simultaneously incorporate the Liberals, replace the Marines with a "non-political, native constabulary," achieve political stability, and insure continuing Nicaraguan submission to Washington's desires.

When the elder Chamorro died in office in 1923, the existing system collapsed. Three presidents passed through Managua in rapid succession, before the United States managed to maneuver its perennial favorite, Adolfo Díaz, back into place. But the Yankees also had to recall the Marines, who had just been sent home, to protect Díaz from a Liberal uprising. By early 1927, there were eleven American warships in Nicaraguan ports and 5,400 Marines occupying its principal cities.[4] In Washington, the Coolidge administration was explaining to a skeptical Congress that the American troops were needed to protect Nicaragua, and ultimately the Panama Canal, from the advance of Mexican "Bolshevism" – the State Department's misconception of the contemporary Mexican revolution.

Faced by a choice between defending Díaz against the superior forces of the Liberals or absorbing the humiliation of his defeat, the administration sent a special envoy, Henry L. Stimson, to Nicaragua to find a political solution that would preserve American influence. Stimson, a Wall Street lawyer and sometime cabinet officer, found two Nicaraguans that he could deal with: President Díaz, ready as ever to follow American instructions, and José María Moncada, the military leader of the Liberal forces, a man who had repeatedly followed his political ambitions from party to party and accepted the US presence in Nicaraguan affairs as a fact of life.[5]

Stimson was also impressed with a young man on Moncada's staff, Anastasio ("Tacho") Somoza García, who spoke good English and got on well with Americans from Marines to diplomats – so well, in fact, that he became known as "El Yanqui." Somoza became Stimson's interpreter.[6]

The key provision of the agreement that Stimson worked out with Moncada at Tipitapa on May 4, 1927, was that Díaz would remain in office until the end of his term in 1928, when open elections would be held under American supervision. It was assumed that such elections would produce a Liberal victory. (Stimson had already satisfied himself that the Liberals were not planning a revolutionary regime modeled on Mexico.)

With help from Stimson and Díaz, Moncada was able to offer the Liberal generals political rewards and financial incentives to hand over their arms and accept an amnesty decreed by the government. But one leader resisted these inducements. "*I am not for sale,*" Augusto Sandino wrote his erstwhile ally Moncada, "*I do not surrender*: you will have to defeat me. I believe that I am doing my duty, and I want to leave my protest for posterity, written in blood."[7] As far as Sandino was concerned, Moncada had betrayed both the Liberal cause and his country. He was also convinced that Stimson had promised Moncada the presidency during their Tipitapa talks. Whether or not that was true, Moncada was the successful Liberal candidate in the Marine-supervised election of 1928. Sandino, meanwhile, had retreated north to fight his own war against the Yankees and their domestic allies.

The May 4 Tipitapa Pact and the events surrounding it are the subject of the pivotal myth in the FSLN's reading of Nicaraguan history.[8] Díaz and Moncada were links in a chain of national betrayal that Sandinistas trace back to the Liberals who invited Walker to Nicaragua and forward to the Somoza regime. By his refusal to accept the Liberal surrender to Stimson, Sandino had broken the chain and redeemed national honor.[9] Sandino himself suggested this interpretation. When Moncada proposed that May 4 be observed as a national holiday in honor of the peace accord he had negotiated, Sandino responded that it ought to be celebrated "because that was the day that Nicaragua proved before the world that her national honor is not humbled; that she still has sons who would offer their blood to wash away the stains that traitors may cast on her."[10] (In revolutionary Nicaragua, May 4 is celebrated as the "Day of National Dignity.")

The FSLN's *General Platform*, issued on May 4, 1977, the fiftieth anniversary of Tipitapa, explains that the bourgeoisie will not lead the coming revolution because it "liquidated . . . itself as a progressive political force when it totally surrendered to the interests of Yankee imperialism and allied itself with the most reactionary forces on May 4, 1927."[11] This argument heaps yet another layer of meaning on Moncada's encounter with Stimson. The bourgeoisie referred to here is the Liberal bourgeoisie, which had been in the forefront of economic modernization through the development of coffee exports but was, because of its subservience to the Yankee, judged politically unequal to its historic role.

Sandino's five-year struggle against the Marines and the Marine-led National Guard has often been described as a dress rehearsal for the Vietnam War a generation later. Sandino pioneered the guerrilla tactics of small, mobile units, operating with the help of a sympathetic population.[12] The Americans and their allies had superior numbers and more sophisticated arms, including aircraft, which they employed for reconaissance and, for the first time ever, in strafing attacks. Frustrated by an elusive enemy, the Marine–Guard forces resorted to terror tactics against suspected collaborators and relocations of civilian populations. These methods and economic hard times arising from the world depression increased Sandino's support.

By standing up to the Yankee Goliath and defending the poor against the rich, Sandino became an instant hero throughout Latin America.

The US government always described him as a "bandit," but there was a growing body of liberal opinion in the United States skeptical of this characterization and opposed to the war. If the Marines were so effective against bandits, one US senator suggested, why not send them to Chicago? Some of his congressional colleagues described the Marines in Nicaragua as "ambassadors of death." But the FBI's young director, J. Edgar Hoover, warned that the Communists were planning a propaganda campaign in the United States on Sandino's behalf.[13]

By 1931, President Hoover and his Secretary of State Henry Stimson had decided to withdraw the Marines and leave the fighting to the National Guard. (In Richard Nixon's era, this move would have been called the "Nicaraguanization" of the war.) Stimson instructed Moncada to hold open elections in 1932 and Juan B. Sacasa, a Liberal, won the balloting, supervised by the last of the departing Marines. Sandino, who had made US withdrawal his principal condition for peace, quickly came to terms with Sacasa and abandoned the war.

The National Guard was to be the "non-political constabulary" that the US policy makers had hoped to create since the early 1920s. What they apparently imagined was a stabilizing force, sympathetic to American interests, but riding above the political fray in Nicaragua. The notion of a politically indifferent military looked like another Yankee delusion to most Nicaraguan politicians. But if the idea ever had a chance of success, the Americans guaranteed its failure with their selection of a Nicaraguan replacement for the Marine commander of the Guard: Anastasio Somoza García.

As an official in the Moncada administration, Somoza had continued to build a career on charming the Americans.[14] Ever attentive to American needs, Somoza had ingratiated himself to US Ambassador Matthew Hanna and, by some accounts, even more so to the ambassador's wife. It was at Hanna's suggestion that he was appointed head of the Guard when the last of the Marines departed in early 1933.

Sandino's assassination in early 1934 on Somoza's orders added new substance to the developing Sandinista myth of betrayal and redemption. Somoza later asserted that he had acted in concert with Hanna's successor, Arthur B. Lane, a claim that was gladly accepted by Sandinista historians.[15] But US diplomatic correspondence from the period indicates that Lane attempted to restrain Somoza from taking any action against Sandino and had no advance knowledge of the assassination plot.[16] Somoza seems to have moved under pressure from his own officers, still nursing resentments from the war and uneasy over Sandino's continuing political influence.

The elimination of Sandino helped Somoza consolidate his authority over the Guard, which had been shaky during his first year as its commander. Once he controlled the Guard, it was only a matter of time before he would control the government. Sacasa, a weak and indecisive president, was urged by his advisors to dismiss Somoza. They also appealed to Ambassador Lane for help. But neither man was willing to act. Lane was convinced that an attempt to remove Somoza would precipitate a civil war and he was restrained by Roosevelt's "Good Neighbor" policy toward Latin America, which promised an end to American intervention in the affairs of other nations in the hemisphere. A two-year war of nerves ended in 1936, when Somoza took over the government by brute force. That same year he was elected president of Nicaragua by a remarkable margin: 107,201 to 108.[17]

While Somoza was using the American-created Guard to impose himself on his countrymen, precisely the same script was being played out in the Dominican Republic. Well before the drama reached its inevitable climax in Nicaragua, Lane had morosely concluded that his government had devised, "an instrument to blast constitutional procedure off the map. . . . In my opinion [the National Guard] is one of the sorriest examples . . . of our inability to understand that we should not meddle in other people's affairs."[18]

The US role was even sorrier than Lane suggests. Having built the Guard and selected its chief, the United States stood back and denied responsibility for its own creation. But the United States had achieved most of what it had sought since the early 1920s: a more or less stable regime in Nicaragua that would defer to US interests without the help of US forces.

The process that brought Somoza to power left many clues to the way he and his sons would rule Nicaragua. Their power always rested on two pillars: the National Guard and the United States. Although the Somozas occasionally installed puppet presidents whom they allowed varying degrees of latitude, they always kept a family member at the head of the Guard, in close contact with the most mundane details of its daily affairs.[19]

The United States continued to help train and equip the Guard, maintaining Army and Air Force missions in Nicaragua and offering advanced training to Guardsmen at facilities in the Canal Zone and the States. This intimate involvement with the Somozas' private army – a force that specialized in political repression and was otherwise known for graft, vice, assault, and rape – tied the United States to the worst aspects of an unpopular regime.[20]

The Somozas continued to cultivate close relationships with Americans. Family members were educated from childhood in the United States and the Somoza children spoke English at home. Tacho I and Tacho II (as the first and last of the Somoza presidents were known in Nicaragua) were famous for their colloquial, if sometimes archaic and often obscene English. Dying of gunshot wounds, Tacho I turned to his buddy, US Ambassador Thomas Whelan and said "I'm a goner. They got me this time, Tommy" – lines stolen from some Hollywood gangster.[21]

Washington often sent ambassadors whose subservience to the Somozas was an embarrassment to younger embassy officials and a visible sign to Nicaraguans of American affection for the ruling family. Whelan, who lasted over ten years in his post, helped smooth the critical succession from father to sons after his friend's assassination.[22] Richard Nixon's ambassador, Turner B. Shelton, was so often in Tacho II's company that he seemed to be part of the dictator's entourage. Reporters noted that he had a characteristic way of bowing as he shook Somoza's hand. Shelton helped design the 1971 political pact that enabled Somoza to overcome constitutional barriers to the perpetuation of his power and backed Somoza's efforts to reconsolidate the regime in the chaos that followed the 1972 earthquake. During the same period, the Somozas reportedly donated $1 million to Nixon's reelection campaign. Nixon already held the Somozas in high esteem for the gracious way they received him in 1958 on an otherwise disastrous vice-presidential tour of Latin America.[23]

The Somozas carefully managed popular perceptions of their relationship with the United States, giving ample publicity to any friendly gesture from Washington. The appearance of Yankee support, they understood, was more important than the substance of their relations with the United States. Tacho I's claim – initially to his officers and later in public – that he had US backing for the murder of Sandino was not gratuitous.

US policy makers were not, in fact, always happy with the Somozas. The United States did not sanction the murder of Sandino or Somoza's subsequent seizure of power. After World War II, the United States, in a democratic mood, strongly opposed Somoza's ambition to seek a third presidential term and initially refused to recognize a puppet he placed in the presidential mansion.[24] In the late 1970s, the United States again sought Somoza's departure. But even in these periods of friction there was an ambivalence in US attitudes toward the dynasty, which the Somozas knew how to exploit to local advantage.

The United States found it difficult to reject an ally who maintained stability at home and gave the United States unequivocal support abroad. Tacho I rebounded from the strains of the late 1940s by adopting the rhetoric and policies of the emerging Cold War. He provided bases and some personnel for the CIA's 1954 overthrow of a democratically elected, left-wing government in Guatemala. His sons would give similar support to the Agency's Bay of Pigs invasion of Cuba in 1961 and send troops to back the American intervention in the Dominican Republic in 1965.[25] The dynasty never failed to support the United States on issues before international bodies such as the United Nations and the Organization of American States. Somoza might be bad, conceded a US Embassy cable to Washington in the early 1950s, but he was irresistible:

It seems to have been customary in some quarters to have attacked Somoza's character. The Embassy agrees that he appears to have an insatiable thirst for money and a considerable love of power. Nevertheless . . . he has repeatedly said that he would do exactly as we say, and we know of nothing in his record that shows any inclination to fail us in international matters.[26]

The Somozas were created and supported by the United States. For over four decades they were faithful allies, even though the United States never fully controlled their behavior at home. To the Sandinistas, the Somozas seemed to sum up a long history of Yankee domination. As "sons of Sandino," the Sandinistas assumed the task of redeeming Nicaraguan history – first by liquidating the dynasty of his assassin and then by freeing the nation from the grasp of the power that had always stood behind the dynasty.

## The Crisis of Somocismo

In the late 1970s the United States and the FSLN were engaged in a struggle for control of the crisis that was undermining Somocismo. The FSLN's continuous fear was that the United States and sympathetic forces within Nicaragua would find a political solution which amounted to "*Somocismo sin Somoza*" – the system without the dictator. Humberto Ortega later recalled that the Sandinista Front's October 1977 offensive and its spectacular seizure of the National Palace the following August were specifically designed to undercut such efforts by capturing popular imagination and keeping alive the hope of a true political transformation led by the FSLN. In early 1979, the National Directorate declared, "Today the struggle takes on an anti-interventionist character as the United States forces itself into our affairs and tries to impose its well-known sell-out formulas. The anti-imperialist content of Sandinismo assumes greater relevance and our historical experience warns us of the treachery of US policy."[27]

The United States was slow to grasp the depth of opposition to the Somozas. As a result, American efforts to manage the crisis – first by urging Somoza to restrain his own behavior, then by promoting dialogue between the dictator and his unarmed opponents, and finally by attempting to choreograph his departure and replacement by political moderates – lagged behind events and were often counterproductive.

In the early 1970s, the United States had increased military aid to Somoza to help him fight the FSLN. In 1977, however, the Carter administration (encouraged by human rights advocates in Congress) suspended military and economic aid in belated response to the brutal and indiscriminate campaign of repression unleashed by Somoza's National Guard in 1975 and 1976. Since, as Somoza himself observed, most Nicaraguans believed that "the decision about the survival or disappearance of Somocismo" would be made in Washington, the significance of the cut-off was as much symbolic as material.[28] It encouraged all enemies of the regime, including the bourgeois opposition. Perhaps US support for the dictatorship was not boundless after all.

In mid-1978, however, the United States appeared to shift ground again. Under pressure from Somoza's powerful supporters in Congress and fearful of political instability in Managua, Carter released $12 million in economic aid.[29] In August, the President wrote Somoza, congratulating him on the regime's improved observance of human rights, although there was scant evidence of real change, and urging further progress. These gestures were again laden with symbolic significance for Nicaraguans. By appearing to re-endorse Somoza, Carter inadvertently undermined the moderate opposition and increased support for the FSLN.

Only in the wake of the popular insurrection of September 1978 did the Carter administration recognize that Somoza could not be sustained. From that point on, the United States pursued a series of initiatives designed to ease Somoza out of office through an understanding with the opposition that would preserve as much of the regime as possible (in particular, the National Guard) and keep the FSLN far from power. All failed. Few Nicaraguans were interested in preserving the Guard, and Somoza, encouraged by his allies in Washington and Carter's inconsistent policies, could not be budged.

While the United States toyed with Somoza, the Sandinistas gained strength and support. The moderate opposition in the bourgeois-led Broad Opposition Front (FAO) counted upon the United States to remove Somoza for them through mediation, and when Washington failed, the moderates looked to the FSLN, which had already captured the leadership of the left side of the anti-Somoza movement.

At the end of May 1979, the FSLN launched its Final Offensive and rapidly gained control of every major city outside the capital. As the Sandinista forces advanced, the United States convened a special meeting of the Organization of American States, where Secretary of State Cyrus Vance issued Washington's first public call for Somoza's resignation and outlined a plan involving a cease-fire supervised by an OAS peace-keeping force and transitional rule by a broad-based government that would include elements of the existing regime. Ironically, only the Somoza government supported the American plan, which was widely regarded as a facade for armed intervention to forestall a Sandinista victory and maintain the regime while sacrificing Somoza.[30]

The final American effort to contain the FSLN came in early July when the country was largely under Sandinista control and the National Guard was collapsing before Sandinista forces. The United States offered to obtain Somoza's resignation (which had already been tendered to the US Ambassador) in exchange for the preservation of the National Guard and the dilution of FSLN representation in the recently formed provisional government. Since most Nicaraguans felt that the FSLN had won the moral right to lead the new government and Somoza's defeat was, in any event, imminent, the offer was rejected outright. At that point the United States relented and asked Somoza to leave.

With the initiatives of June and July, US policy toward the Nicaraguan crisis completed its record of failure: having inadvertently undermined Somoza and his moderate opponents, the United States had finally confirmed the Sandinistas' historic suspicion of the United States without blocking their ascension to power.

## From Carter to Reagan

The insurrection that liquidated the Somoza regime – driving the family into exile, dismembering its domestic economic empire, scattering the National Guard, and razing the official party – also destroyed the relationship that had bound the United States and Nicaragua for decades. Both sides came to the task of diplomatic reconstruction seeking amicable relations, but dragging heavy baggage that would inevitably generate hostility in the long run.

The Sandinistas had good reasons to seek friendly ties with the United States. They knew that it would be difficult to obtain the international financing and domestic private sector cooperation that were critical to economic recovery without US support. At the same time, the history of US intervention in Nicaragua (down to July 1979) and the record of US action against left-wing revolutions in Latin America (Guatemala 1954, Cuba 1961, Chile 1973) made the Sandinistas wary of US intentions from the beginning. The immediate fear of the National Directorate, which assumed final authority over foreign-policy matters, was that the United States would use its economic power to deflect the Sandinista revolution from its larger goals.[31]

The Sandinista-led national unity government adopted a formal position of "non-alignment" in international affairs. But, according to the March 1979 reunification accord that created the National Directorate, this stance was designed, "to neutralize . . . the chance of a military intervention by Yankee imperialism. . . . Strategically we will strengthen an alliance with the revolutionary forces of the region and the governments of the socialist camp."[32] In the early months of the revolution, the Sandinista leadership seems to have underestimated the extent to which their anti-imperialist sympathies and "strategic" (that is, long-term) friendships with Soviet bloc countries would evoke aggressive responses from the United States.

The Carter administration approached the new relationship convinced that American hostility had driven the young Cuban revolution into the Soviet camp and determined to avoid a repeat performance in Nicaragua. The administration hoped to build a constructive relationship with the national unity government. It was willing to accept a sweeping transformation of the old order in the hope of strengthening moderate elements in the new regime and holding the government to its self-proclaimed goals of a pluralist polity, a mixed economy, and an independent foreign policy.

This position may not have been shared throughout the Carter administration. It was certainly not universally shared in Congress. In the late 1970s American thinking in foreign policy was moving back toward the Cold War attitudes of the fifties and sixties. Relations with Nicaragua were likely, sooner or later, to be affected by this shift.

Until the final weeks of Carter's presidency, the new relationship between the United States and Nicaragua worked relatively well. The United States committed about $100 million, largely in soft credits, in support of relief and reconstruction efforts through the end of 1980.[33] American influence was used to stabilize and moderate the new order, as when US Ambassador Lawrence Pezzullo mediated between COSEP and the FSLN in the April 1980 political crisis over the restructuring of the Council of State. Pezzullo consistently urged representatives of the bourgeoisie to develop a cooperative relationship with the government. Although the conflict between the FSLN and the bourgeois opposition was growing in intensity, the Sandinistas were usually tolerant of their opponents, allowed a free press to operate, and built economic policy around the private sector. Sandinista support of the Salvadoran guerrilla movement remained limited.

Nonetheless, there were tensions in the new relationship. Washington was unhappy with the dilution of the political power of non-Sandinista sectors in the new government, Nicaragua's warm relations with Cuba, its anti-imperialist rhetoric, and its foreign policy positions, which included support for the Palestine Liberation Organization and abstention on the United Nations resolutions condemning the Soviet invasion of Afghanistan.[34] For Managua, the long, acrimonious congressional debate surrounding aid to Nicaragua and the restrictive provisions imposed on the final legislation were both insulting and threatening. Each side retained deep suspicions about the ultimate intentions of the other.

Two related developments in late 1980 decisively transformed the relationship between the United States and the Sandinista revolution. The first was the election of Ronald Reagan on a platform that, in thinly veiled language, urged efforts to depose the FSLN. While the Carter administration had offered qualified support for progressive change in Nicaragua, the incoming administration regarded any challenge to the *status quo* in Central America as a threat to the United States. Indifferent to the domestic roots of the regional upheaval, the Reaganites viewed Central America as a theatre of East–West conflict.

The second development was the Sandinista decision to ship arms to Salvadoran guerrillas, who were preparing a large-scale "final offensive" for January 1981. As will be shown later in this chapter, Sandinista leaders had resisted supplying the Salvadoran insurgency out of fear that they would compromise their relations with the United States. The open hostility of the Reaganites altered their calculations.

When intelligence of large-scale arms shipments reached Washington, the outgoing Carter administration froze aid to Nicaragua, as required by law. The Reagan administration subsequently informed Managua that aid would be definitively cut off if the movement of arms continued. In reply, Daniel Ortega assured US Ambassador Pezzullo that Nicaragua would respond to American concerns, and intelligence reports soon indicated that the shipments had, fact, ceased.[35] In spite of these positive responses from Nicaragua, the United States announced on April 1 that assistance would not be resumed. By doing so, the administration was sacrificing its remaining leverage with the Sandinistas. "You're throwing away your chips," Pezzullo warned Secretary of State Alexander Haig.[36]

The aid cut-off, Pezzullo's departure, the developing domestic confrontation between the FSLN and the bourgeoisie, and the appearance of military training camps for anti-Sandinista exiles in the United States all contributed to growing tension between Nicaragua and the United States in 1981. In August, a quiet trip to Managua by Assistant Secretary of State Thomas Enders initiated a series of high-level exchanges between US and Nicaraguan officials aimed at reaching a broad settlement of the issues dividing the two countries. But the so-called Enders initiative collapsed in mutual recriminations in October – in part because administration hard-liners had succeeded in phrasing American proposals in a way that inevitably offended the nationalistic sensitivities of the Sandinistas.[37]

## Contras

In Washington, plans for a covert war against Nicaragua were being elaborated even before Enders visited Nicaragua. As early as May 1981, the CIA had channeled seed money to the incipient contra movement.[38] In November, President Reagan signed a formal "presidential finding" authorizing the CIA to create an anti-Sandinista paramilitary force.

Four months later, contra fighters, operating from base camps in Honduras, blew up two bridges in northern Nicaragua. From reports in the American press, the Sandinistas knew the bridge attack was part of a wider US-backed operation.[39] The Nicaraguan government immediately declared a "state of emergency" that suspended most civil liberties for the first time since Somoza's departure. The decree imposed stringent new constraints on the domestic opposition, including prior censorship of the press.

The force created by the CIA was originally small (about 500 men) and obstensibly designed to interdict arms bound for El Salvador – that, at least, is how the operation was explained to congressional intelligence committees. But by 1984, the Nicaraguan Democratic Force (Fuerza Democratica Nicaraguense – FDN), the major beneficiary of the estimated $100 million spent on the war, had grown to 12,000 well-equipped fighters engaged in attacks on both military and civilian targets.[40] While the FDN was not the only contra force active against the Sandinistas, it eclipsed all others in size and level of activity, including the Costa Rica-based forces led by former Sandinista hero Eden Pastora (who also received some CIA funding), and two smaller groups of Miskito Indian fighters on the Atlantic coast.

The FDN was built on an existing band of former National Guardsmen commanded by Colonel Enrique Bermúdez and trained by Argentina's right-wing military regime. It began conducting raids against Nicaragua in 1980. Although the members of the FDN's political front, recruited by the CIA, were generally free of such Somocista ties, the civilians appeared to have little control over their military partners. Both the civilian and military leaders of the FDN received salaries, as high as $7,000 per month, from American intelligence operatives. Thus, the FDN was doubly tainted from the beginning – by its Somocista roots and its political and financial dependence on the United States.[41]

The rank and file of the FDN was composed largely of small farmers and rural workers from the rugged and thinly populated northern reaches of Nicaragua, the FDN's principal zone of operations. While some were former Guardsmen or members of families with National Guard ties (the north was an important recruiting area for the Guard), most claimed objections to Sandinista rural policies as their principal reason for joining the contras. But, according to *Washington Post* reporter Christopher Dickey, who traveled with a contra patrol in 1983, it was the Sandinistas' initial response to the war that crystallized their disaffection. With the first serious attacks in early 1982, Sandinista authorities stepped up their surveillance of the population in the areas of contra infiltration. Those who came under suspicion of collaboration were subject to harassment, jailings, or loss of their land – a process that bred new contra recruits.[42]

The strategy of the FDN emphasized social and economic disruption over military engagement. It launched frequent attacks on civilian targets and employed brutal tactics against noncombatants – a practice reminiscent of Somoza's National Guard, where most FDN commanders, including Bermúdez, began their military careers. Edgar Chamorro, who resigned after four years on the FDN's political directorate, concluded that terror against civilians was the "premeditated policy" of the FDN.[43] A 1985 report on the war by Americas Watch, an independent human rights organization with extensive experience in Nicaragua, found that the FDN made "deliberate use of terrorist tactics," and accused it of murdering unarmed civilians, kidnappings, and indiscriminate attacks on civilian targets.[44] Typical of the incidents investigated by Americas Watch was a July 1985 FDN attack on two agrarian cooperatives in the province of Estelí. In addition to destroying housing, a school and a health center, the contras murdered four people and kidnapped six others. Among the dead was a 76-year-old cooperative member who was tortured and almost decapitated before being tossed in a ditch.[45]

The FDN's CIA handlers were well aware of contra human rights abuses and bore some responsibility for them. In 1983, the official in charge of the contra operation acknowledged in a closed briefing for staff members of the House Intelligence Committee that the contras had murdered "civilians and Sandinista officials in the provinces, as well as heads of cooperatives, nurses, doctors and judges." "After all," said the official, "this is war."[46] About the same time, agency employees produced a manual on psychological warfare for distribution to FDN personnel that advised such tactics as "neutralizing" public officials and hiring "professional criminals" to foment violent confrontations that would create civilian "martyrs" for the contra cause.[47] The manual was apparently part of an effort to persuade the contras to use terror in a less random, more calculated fashion.

The 1985 Americas Watch report also covered abuses by other contra groups and the forces of the Nicaraguan government. It concluded that the FDN had the worst human rights record among the contra groups and that government abuses had declined sharply after the first year of the war. Americas Watch reports from 1985 to 1987 suggest that the Sandinista security forces were not innocent of human rights abuses on the battlefield but their violations were infrequent compared with the massive abuses of their enemies. The Sandinistas did not engage in systematic terror, which has been a theme in virtually every independent report on the FDN contras. The use of government sponsored death squads and the conduct of extermination campaigns against hostile rural populations – common themes of civil conflicts in neighboring countries – are unknown in Nicaragua.[48]

The most serious human rights abuses committed by Sandinista forces grew out of a series of bloody contra attacks in the Atlantic coast region beginning in December 1981. During 1982 at least 20 Miskito Indians were murdered by government troops and another 70 disappeared and remain unaccounted for; 10,000 Indians were forcibly removed from their villages near the Honduran border and hundreds were subject to arbitrary arrest.

The Atlantic region is geographically isolated from the rest of the country and the indigenous peoples of the region are divided from most Nicaraguans by race, language, religion, and long-standing conflicts over local autonomy. As the Sandinistas now concede, their insensitive early administration of the area aggravated tensions growing out of these differences, which were then exploited by the contras and their American backers for their own purposes. The result was a Miskito contra movement, enjoying appreciable local support, and a war on the Atlantic coast.

By 1984, the Sandinistas were reversing their policies toward the region. The government openly recognized the legitimacy of many of the Indians' claims, curbed human rights abuses by the army, released most prisoners, issued a broad amnesty, allowed relocated villagers to return to their lands, and negotiated a regional autonomy plan with representatives of indigenous groups. Since 1985, the people of the Atlantic coast have lived a tense, but durable peace.[49]

By 1983, the covert war in Nicaragua had become a matter of open debate in the United States. Public and congressional uneasiness was fed by the administration's inconsistent explanations of its policy. Forced to abandon the interdiction rationale – no arms bound for El Salvador were ever captured by contra patrols – administration spokesmen suggested that the contra "pressure" was designed to compel the Sandinistas to stop meddling in El Salvador, or to respect democratic freedoms at home, or simply to negotiate. Occasionally, senior officials implied that the objective was, in fact, the overthrow of the revolutionary government. President Reagan, who liked to describe the contras as "freedom fighters" or even "the moral equivalent of our founding fathers," acknowledged at a 1985 press conference that US policy aimed to "remove" the Sandinista government "in the sense of its present structure."[50]

While the administration's public explanations of its policy varied, CIA operatives consistently told contra leaders that the United States government wanted them to drive the Sandinistas out of Managua. The contras themselves were unambiguous about their objective; it was, in the words of Col. Bermúdez, "to overthrow the communists."[51]

In early 1984, a Congress already uneasy about the direction of American policy was stunned to learn that CIA commandos had mined three Nicaraguan ports in the name of the FDN. The mines sank several Nicaraguan boats, damaged at least five foreign vessels, and brought an avalanche of international condemnation down on the United States.[52] But from the administration's point of view, the mines did their worst damage on Capitol Hill.

Congress rejected administration requests to refund the contras. It was not restored for over a year, and then only in the form of a modest appropriation for "non-lethal" aid, excluding munitions. Not until mid-1986 did Congress vote $100 million in unrestricted military aid.

During the two-year hiatus in lethal aid, the contra movement maintained a surprisingly high level of military activity. The mystery of contra financing and logistics during this period was unraveled between October 1986, when a C-123 cargo plane carrying military supplies for the rebels was shot down over Nicaragua, and August 1987, when the congressional hearings into the Iran–Contra affair ended in Washington. Linking the two events was the hearings' flamboyant star witness, Oliver North, a Marine colonel dismissed from the staff of the National Security Council shortly after the crash. It was learned that North had coordinated a secret contra supply operation from his office in the basement of the White House, in legal defiance of existing legislation but with the support of senior administration officials. The C-123 and its largely American crew were part of the colonel's logistics network.

North had also been deeply involved in shaping contra military and political strategy and in off-the-books schemes to pay for the supply flights and the munitions they carried. In the absence of Congressional appropriations, donations were gathered from private individuals and profits were diverted from the secret sales of arms to Iran. But the most significant unofficial funding for the contras came in the form of secret payments from conservative Third World governments solicited by senior American officials. Saudi Arabia alone contributed $32 million.[53]

## The Strains of War

The contra army sustained by the administration's creative financing was no closer to defeating the Sandinistas in 1988 than it had been in 1982, but the war did impose enormous social and economic costs on the revolution. Over 20,000 had died in the fighting; thousands of others had been left maimed or crippled. By 1985, the war had generated 7,000 orphans.[54]

Disruption of the economy was one of the FDN's main objectives.[55] By mid-1987, the war's direct costs in destruction of capital and lost production had reached $676 million, according to a government estimate.[56] The Reagan administration exacerbated the economic strain by imposing a trade embargo and blocking Nicaragua's access to international development credits from sources such as the World Bank. Government economists calculated the full economic cost of American hostility over six years of war at $3.7 billion, a prodigious sum for a very small economy.[57]

The social programs which were the hallmark of the early years of the revolution inevitably suffered as the war expanded. The FDN singled out health facilities, schools, and agrarian reform farms – along with the health workers, educators, agronomists, and peasants associated with them – as prime targets for their attacks.[58] Defense costs absorbed a growing proportion of the national budget, cutting into the resources available for social programs. In the early years of the revolution, education and health alone had absorbed 50 percent of the budget, and defense under 20 per cent. By 1987, these proportions had been reversed.[59] Wartime austerity budgets eliminated food subsidies and halted most construction of new schools, hospitals, housing, and utilities. Dozens of schools and health centers have been abandoned in conflict zones. The retreat of health care threatened previous gains in the control of epidemic diseases. Polio, eliminated by vaccination campaigns, began to reappear in 1984.[60]

The economic difficulties imposed by the war (and by some of the Sandinistas' own policies) along with the scaling down of social programs cut into Sandinista political support. The war also transformed political relations between the FSLN and the bourgeois opposition. The opposition (including the church hierarchy) lost interest in finding a *modus vivendi* with the Sandinistas. The FSLN came increasingly to see the bourgeois opposition as the political wing of the contra movement.

The 1984 elections offered a chance to break out of this political stalemate, but the opposition Democratic Coordinator proved more interested in delegitimating the electoral process in the eyes of foreign observers than in presenting its ideas to the Nicaraguan electorate. The United States was both directly and indirectly responsible for the Coordinator's decision to abstain from participation – indirectly, because the US-supported war suggested another route to power for the bourgeoisie and, directly, because the Reagan administration actively lobbied against participation. Late in the campaign, US embassy representatives visited leaders of the registered moderate parties and pressured them to withdraw. Some party leaders charged that American officials bribed or attempted to bribe Nicaraguan politicians. A senior administration official told the *New York Times*, "The administration never contemplated letting [Coordinator candidate Arturo] Cruz stay in the race because then the Sandinistas could justifiably claim that the elections were legitimate."[61]

## Nicaragua and the United States: The Dimensions of Conflict

The Reagan administration justified its hostile policies toward the Sandinista revolution with four claims: (1) that Nicaragua's military build-up jeopardized the security of its neighbors, (2) that the political regime the Sandinistas were creating in Nicaragua was undemocratic, (3) that Nicaragua was an ally of Cuba and the Soviet Union and therefore a threat to the United States, and (4) that Nicaragua was actively supporting revolutionary movements in neighbouring countries.

The first two were clearly pseudo-issues, after-the-fact rationalizations for American policy. The Sandinista military, initially modest, grew in direct response to contra attacks and remained, in the words of a classified CIA report, "primarily defense-oriented."[62] Nicaragua has minimal capacity to project force outside its own borders. Whatever might be said about the emerging Sandinista political system, the US attitude toward the 1984 Nicaraguan elections suggested that the administration was more interested in defeating the Sandinistas than in building democracy. The third and fourth issues form the real core of American concerns in Nicaragua and deserve closer examination.

The Sandinistas have had warm relations with Cuba and the Soviet Union since the beginning of the revolution. But the contra policy and American efforts to isolate Nicaragua economically have pushed the country into greater dependence on Soviet-bloc military and economic aid. Initially, the Soviet Union and its East European allies became Nicaragua's arms suppliers because the United States pressured its own allies not to sell arms to the Sandinistas. Pentagon data indicate that Soviet-bloc deliveries were relatively small through 1981, but surged as the covert war escalated in 1982 and thereafter. In 1984, the Soviet bloc supplied $250 million in munitions to Nicaragua, up from only $5 million in 1979 and $7 million in 1980.[63] There were 300 to 500 Soviet and Cuban military advisors in the country in 1987, along with 700 non-military advisors.[64] As Western development credits were cut off, Soviet-bloc financing of the Nicaraguan economy expanded from 25 percent of external financing in 1981 to 85 percent in 1984.[65]

Since the beginning of the revolution, the Cubans have generously supported Sandinista social programs. Cuba sent over 1,000 educators to help with the 1980 Literacy Crusade, modeled on the 1961 Cuban experience. By 1982, there were about 2,000 Cuban teachers in Nicaragua, many of them working in remote areas, and nearly 1,000 doctors, nurses, and other medical personnel, but these numbers probably declined as a new generation of teachers and doctors completed their training in expanded Nicaraguan schools. Cuba built a 150-bed hospital in Managua and provided advanced training on the island for Nicaraguan doctors in such areas as public health. The Cubans also provided economic and technical aid in areas they knew, including road construction, fishing, mining, poultry rearing, and sugar production.[66]

But if the Cubans and Soviets have been providing vital economic and military support to Nicaragua, there are apparent limits to their willingness to back the Sandinistas and thereby confront the United States in its own sphere of influence. The Soviets have given no indication that they intend to underwrite Nicaragua's economy as they have Cuba's. In the mid-1980s,

Soviet-bloc financing ran at $150 to $400 million annually – in bilateral trade credits rather than hard currency loans and far short of Nicaragua's needs. The Soviet Union was also meeting Nicaragua's full petroleum requirements, but in 1987 it abruptly decided to reduce shipments, and although that decision was later reversed, it left the Sandinistas insecure about the future of Soviet aid. During this period, Soviet-bloc purchases were absorbing a tiny and declining proportion of Nicaragua's exports.[67]

Soviet commentaries cautiously resist placing Nicaragua among the Third World's "socialist-oriented states," a label that would imply faith in the direction of the Sandinista revolution and a commitment to its survival.[68] The USSR has not given the Sandinistas sophisticated offensive weapons of the sort it has supplied to its closest allies – including the Syrians, whom the Soviets have armed with advanced MiGs and M-72 tanks.[69] Moreover, both the Soviets and the Cubans have made clear that they would not come to Nicaragua's defense in the event of an American invasion. This is another strategic fact of life that is understood by all parties.[70]

US complaints about the growth of the Sandinista military and the Soviet-bloc presence in Nicaragua are perhaps secondary to the US concern about the Sandinistas' alleged "export" of revolution to neighboring countries. The Sandinistas have not been coy about their sympathy for revolutionary movements like their own, which attack the regimes that defend privileged minorities against poor majorities. At an "international solidarity" conference, held in Managua in early 1981 while intense fighting raged in nearby El Salvador, Bayardo Arce declared, "We will never renounce our duty of solidarity with El Salvador." Tomás Borge told the same audience, "[A] revolution that turns inwards ceases to be a revolution. A true revolution reaches outward to grasp the hands of other peoples who struggle."[71] Two years earlier, in the "72 Hours Document," the National Directorate had called for a foreign policy that would "contribute to and promote the struggle for the peoples of Latin America against fascist dictatorships, for democracy and national liberation."[72]

But it is not clear from such statements how far revolutionary solidarity is to go. The "72 Hours Document" defines the central objective of Sandinista foreign policy – and its contribution to regional and world revolution – as the "consolidation of the Nicaraguan revolution."[73] This early statement implies some reluctance to sacrifice the interests of the Nicaraguan revolution to the needs of revolutions elsewhere.

The National Directorate's decision to support the Salvadoran rebels' ill-fated January 1981 offensive was, in fact, taken reluctantly and under extraordinary conditions. The Salvadorans approached the Sandinista leadership for help in mid-1980, when the military and associated death squads in their country were murdering hundreds of people, of quite varied political complexions, every month. In March, Archbishop Oscar

Romero of San Salvador, who had denounced the killings, was gunned down as he was saying the mass. In desperation, political moderates were joining the armed resistance, and El Salvador seemed to be heading for the sort of popular insurrection that had finally topped the Somoza dictatorship.[74] The Sandinistas had received help from moderate governments in Costa Rica and Venezuela under similar circumstances, but now the Nicaraguans were worried about compromising their relations with the United States if they helped the Salvadoran insurrection.

The Salvadoran rebel representatives found the FSLN "very conservative" and preoccupied with "protect[ing] the Nicaraguan revolution."[75] After some hesitation, the National Directorate agreed to help, but several months passed before arms began to flow from Nicaragua to El Salvador in significant quantities. The change came with the election of Ronald Reagan in November on a platform that suggested rolling back revolutions in Nicaragua and elsewhere. At this point the Sandinistas apparently felt that they had little to lose and might enhance their own imperiled security by helping to bring a friendly regime to power.[76]

Despite the early, brave talk of revolutionary solidarity, the Sandinistas have not adopted a policy of actively "exporting revolution" as the Cubans did (without success) in the late 1960s. The Sandinistas had nothing to do with the genesis of the Salvadoran insurgency. The Salvadoran oligarchy and its officer allies can take credit for that. In an especially candid 1981 speech to Sandinista army officers, Humberto Ortega remarked that Nicaragua had no intention of "meddling" in the affairs of its "bourgeois democratic" southern neighbor Costa Rica: "We can't because we are neighboring countries and we have to respect [the conditions] that each society imposes. Nor should they meddle in the type of society we propose to construct here."[77] After contras began to attack Nicaragua from bases in Honduras and Costa Rica, the Nicaraguans had good defensive reasons to foment political resistance in these countries. There is evidence they did, briefly and unsuccessfully, attempt to do so in Honduras.[78]

After the collapse of the January 1981 offensive in El Salvador, Nicaraguan assistance was apparently halted (when the Sandinistas thought they had an understanding with the Reagan administration about restarting US aid). The flow of arms may have later resumed at low levels – the public evidence is sparse. But news dispatches from the region based on interviews with unnamed US military and intelligence officials indicate that outside supplies are no longer extensive or vital for the Salvadoran guerrillas. Instead, the rebels rely largely on munitions captured or illegally purchased from Salvadoran government sources.[79] Under external attack supported by the United States, the Sandinistas have good reason to continue aiding the Salvadoran insurgency, if only to hang on to a bargaining chip that is obviously very important to Washington.

## Peace Initiatives

As the conflict between Nicaragua and the United States deepened, the search for a peaceful resolution to their differences quickened. Beginning in 1982, Nicaragua made repeated private and public attempts to open negotiations with the United States. Parallel to these overtures, a series of mediation proposals was put forward by Latin American governments concerned with the growing violence and the broadening scale of US involvement in Central America.[80] After US support for the contras became public knowledge, Mexico, Venezuela, Colombia and Panama – the Contadora Group, as they were collectively known, for the site of their first meeting on Panama's Contadora Island – embarked on a sustained diplomatic effort to build a Central American consensus for a comprehensive peace plan.

US responses to the overtures from Nicaragua and the initiatives of the regional powers soon fell into a predictable pattern: proposals from the Sandinistas needed to be backed by big concessions *before* negotiations could begin. The mediation proposals required "study" or were "constructive" but failed to address some critical concern; there the matter rested. Off the record, the Reagan administration was more candid.[81] In fact, the administration had no immediate interest in a negotiated settlement and regarded any pressure in that direction as a public relations problem.[82]

On September 7, 1984, the Contadora talks culminated in a revised draft treaty, covering the major regional security issues, that had the tentative approval of Washington's Central American allies. Two weeks later, Nicaragua caught its enemies off guard by announcing that it was ready to sign the treaty. The Reagan administration was stunned by what it regarded as a Sandinista propaganda victory. Soon US allies were raising new objections to the draft. A secret National Security Council background paper later explained how the the Reagan administration had "effectively blocked" the treaty by persuading El Salvador, Honduras, and Costa Rica to withdraw earlier support and raise new barriers to ratification.[83] The Contadora process did not die from this blow, nor did it every fully recover.

The search for a bilateral settlement of differences between the United States and Nicaragua was no more successful. The United States seemed indifferent to the increasingly explicit and conciliatory negotiating positions that Sandinistas elaborated in public statements and private exchanges with US officials.[84] Two interviews conducted by the author in late 1986 – one with a ranking Sandinista foreign-policy strategist and the other with a State Department official responsible for relations with Nicaragua – reveal the fate of these Nicaraguan overtures.

In response to questions about the major issues dividing the United States and Nicaragua, the Sandinista official indicated that Nicaragua was willing to respond to what he described as the "legitimate security concerns of the United States." Nicaragua, he said, would agree (1) to remove Cuban and Soviet military advisors from Nicaragua, (2) to prohibit foreign military bases on Nicaraguan soil, (3) to prevent the shipment of arms to rebel movements in neighboring countries, (4) to limit Nicaraguan arms, and (5) to provide for reasonable verification procedures. In return, Nicaragua would expect an end to American support for the contras and formal agreements with the United States and its Central American allies guaranteeing Nicaraguan security.

But Nicaragua was not, he added, willing to negotiate over its domestic political arrangements with a foreign power. No sovereign state could do so and remain sovereign. US demands that Nicaragua agree to conform to Washington's idea of "democracy" were unacceptable.

The substance of the Sandinista strategist's remarks was later described to the American official. Was this the Sandinistas' negotiating posture as he understood it? Yes. Were they sincere? Yes: probably. Had they officially conveyed their position to the United States? Yes, most explicitly at the 1984 talks in Manzanillo, Mexico. What about the issue of democracy? The United States, replied the American official, made democracy the condition of any agreement because "the right wing within the administration" (his words) did not want an agreement and knew that the Sandinistas would not sign anything that imposed on their internal politics.

The Manzanillo talks were the last high-level contacts between the United States and Nicaragua. Both informants agreed that the Nicaraguan side was forthcoming and conciliatory at Manzanillo while the US negotiators barely responded to their proposals. The State Department official explained what happened as follows: the White House agreed to the talks under the pressure of an impending presidential election, but the "right wing within administration " operating through the National Security Council tied the American representative's hands with detailed instructions that made any serious negotiations impossible. One month after the elections, the United States withdrew from the talks.

The State Department official was interviewed shortly before the central role of the National Security Council in Nicaraguan affairs was revealed by the Iran–Contra investigations. He would not have been surprised by a National Security Council memorandum, written as the Manzanillo talks continued, that came to light during the Congressional hearings. Under the title "Central America," National Security Advisor John Poindexter wrote: "Continue active negotiations but agree on nothing and try to work some way to support the contras, either directly or indirectly. Withhold true objectives from staff.[85]

## Arias

In August 1987, the five Central American presidents meeting in Guatemala accepted a regional peace plan authored by Costa Rican president Oscar Arias. The plan required the five governments to pursue a process of national reconciliation and democratization, to prohibit the use of their territory to insurgent movements fighting in neighboring countries, and to cease all aid to such movements. The willingness of the presidents to sign such an agreement reflected their sense of the waning strength of the Reagan administration, entering its last months, wounded by the recent Iran-Contra revelations, and unlikely to obtain new funding for the contras. While the provisions of the Arias plan were schematic at best, they provided a framework to break out of the diplomatic and political stalemate that US policy had helped to maintain since 1982.[86]

The Sandinistas seized the opportunity to escape the war that was bleeding the country and destroying their revolution. By January, the Nicaraguan government had lifted the state of emergency that had existed since the beginning of the war, published an amnesty law, opened a dialogue with the domestic political opposition, removed restrictions on opposition media, and closed down the special tribunals that had judged those suspected of collaboration with the contras. Going beyond the requirements of the peace accord and stretching their own revolutionary principles, the Sandinistas accepted direct negotiations with contra leaders.

In February, Sandinista concessions achieved their first objective, influencing Congress to reject new funding for the contras. The following month, Humberto Ortega and contra leader Adolfo Calero signed a cease-fire agreement. "Is Peace Breaking Out?" asked the next day's headline in *El Nuevo Diario*. "Nicaragua Triumphs," proclaimed *La Prensa*[87] In Washington, a "senior administration official" characterized the White House reaction to the accord as "discomfort".[88]

## Yankees and Sandinistas: Living History

Americans know little of their country's past involvement in Nicaraguan affairs and tend to forget what they do know. Their leaders debate US policy toward Nicaragua as if the country did not exist before 1979. But for Sandinistas, the looming Yankee presence in their nation's history is a living part of the present. Jaime Wheelock was thinking of the past when he discussed United States–Nicaraguan relations with a US reporter in 1983. "What guides Sandinism," he said, "is the conviction that our country, Nicaragua, has never been a country with real sovereignty or national independence. Nicaragua has been an appendage of the United States. Sandinism represents the possibility that Nicaragua could exist for Nicaraguans . . .

Finally it is a group of Nicaraguans who are deciding where Nicaragua goes and what it does." Because of the past, Wheelock concluded, "we have to be against the United States in order to reaffirm ourselves as a nation."[89]

Sandinistas have little trouble finding the past in recent US policy. The Marines and National Guard of the 1930s spring to life as the US-supported contras, led by former National Guard officers. Sandino's "Army for the Defense of National Sovereignty" returns as the "Sandinista Popular Army." Again there is disingenuous talk in Washington of defending democracy in Nicaragua.

As in the past, American intervention is only the backdrop against which the real drama of Sandinista history – the tale of betrayal and redemption – is played out. The betrayers, from Díaz to Somoza and Calero, are as easy to spot as bad guys in black hats. They are rich – and popular with Washington. The redeemers, men such as Sandino and Fonseca, side with the poor and are ready to give their lives to redeem the nation's honor.

The Sandinistas' identification with the redeemers is proclaimed in the slogans they have adopted from Sandino: "A Sandinista is not for sale, he does not surrender . . . The sovereignty of a people is not to be debated but to be defended with arms in hand . . . A free fatherland or die." The power of these slogans (which lose the force of their Spanish cadences in translation) is magnified by the sacrifices of Sandinista "martyrs" who have died for them.

It is the Sandinistas' sense of duty to a nation abused and betrayed, of their debt to its patriot-martyrs, and of their own place in living history that forms the emotional core of Sandinismo. Sandinistas may formally subscribe to Lenin's sophisticated, economic theory of imperialism. But when they say "imperialism" they mean Yankee interventionism from William Walker to Ronald Reagan.

The passionate nationalism of these "sons of Sandino" sustained them through a two-decade struggle against Somoza and equipped them to withstand a powerful counterrevolutionary challenge. It also exposed their leaders to wrenching emotions and painful questions from the ranks as they moved toward negotiations with the contras in late 1987 and early 1988. Four years earlier, the bishops' Easter message suggesting such talks had evoked an unprecedented torrent of Sandinista invective. As late as November 1987, a Sandinista Assembly declaration (read by Bayardo Arce) insisted that the party would "never" accept political talks with the contras.[90] The only appropriate negoiating partners were the contras' Yankee creators. Yet, on March 24, Sandinista representatives signed a truce agreement that implicity recognized the "Nicaraguan Resistance" as a legitimate force and opened the way for further political negotiations. For the Sandinista leadership this was a radical step, reflecting national war-weariness, calculations about US congressional opinion, and the essential pragmatism of the FSLN.

# Conclusion: The Vanguard and the Revolution

Nothing is so central to the Sandinistas' conception of themselves and their place in history as their definition of the FSLN as a revolutionary vanguard. They owe this powerful but problematic idea to Lenin, who conceived of an elite party of professional revolutionaries – capable of guiding a politically immature people through a process of radical social transformation. Lenin echoes in the Sandinista description of the vanguard as the "leader in the class struggle." But there is something more heroic and passionate – echos of Sandino – in the Sandinista vision of "a few men and women who at a given moment in history seem to contain within themselves the dignity of all the people."

The vanguard was the Sandinista solution to the political quandary posed by Nicaragua's backwardness, dependency, and political stagnation. The last decades of the old regime saw rapid economic growth, absurdly combined with spreading malnutrition, landlessness, and unemployment, under the rule of an anachronistic family dictatorship. For the Sandinistas, deposing the Somozas would only be a first step toward change. Behind the Somozas lay the power of the United States. The FSLN could read the lessons of Latin American history: from Guatemala (1954) to Chile (1973), the US, in collaboration with local reactionary elites, had demonstrated its capacity to defeat revolutions. Only the Cuban revolution had escaped.

The conclusion seemed obvious to the leaders of the FSLN. To survive, a Nicaraguan revolution would have to remain armed. It would have to organize mass support. The revolutionary transformation would be a lengthy process. Only a vanguard organization could provide the military and political leadership and the continuity that a revolution requires.

The ideology of the FSLN envisioned a Sandinista vanguard that would lead a broad-based insurrection against the dictatorship; shake the country loose from imperial domination; preside over an era of economic development, social reform, and political mobilization of the masses; and finally, guide the country to socialism. The Sandinistas wanted to do more than modernize the economy of an underdeveloped country; they expected to transform the social consciousness of its people. The complexity and gradual character of this undertaking reinforced the need for vanguard leadership.

The vanguard is the concept that links Sandinista theory and organization. To implement their program and extend the influence of their ideas, the Sandinistas have built an elaborate organizational system. At its center is the vanguard party – selective, hierarchical, and disciplined. The party controls a network of affiliated mass organizations. Its partisan structures reach deep into the state and the military. At the center of this system of power is the National Directorate of the FSLN, the vanguard within the vanguard.

## The FSLN in Action

The formal outlines of Sandinista organization and theory suggest a monolithic force driven by a rigid ideology – a Leninist organization imposing its Marxist vision of history on Nicaraguan society. But this stark image is clouded by contradictions when the Sandinistas are examined in action. Socialists, they promote petty capitalism in the countryside and preside over a mixed economy in which about half of production remains in private hands. Marxist materialists, they accept believers into their ranks, even into the leadership of the party, and preside over a national religious revival. Anti-Yankee nationalists, they seek an accommodation with Washington and negotiate with people whom they previously described as Washington's mercenaries.

A second image begins to emerge: a party of pragmatists sometimes stubborn but finally open to compromise. There is support for this conception of the FSLN in the Sandinistas' iconoclastic approach to Marxism. From the days when Fonseca, Borge, and Mayorga broke with the Moscow-line PSN to form the FSLN, the party has refused to be bound by dogma and insisted that Marxism must be adapted to Nicaraguan conditions. Fonseca, the party's chief ideologist, was suspicious of abstract theory ("pseudo-Marxist gobbledygook") and repeatedly warned against ideological rigidity. The ideological openness of the FSLN allowed its thinking to evolve over time. The Sandinistas learned from experience that Christians can be good revolutionaries, that state farms are problematic, and that the commerce of thousands of small grain producers cannot be controlled by the state.

The Sandinistas are neither unbending ideologues nor progmatists without principles. They came to power determined to free their country of foreign domination and build a just, socialist society, but willing to adjust their immediate course to practical circumstances. One result has been a growing tension between the ideology of the party and its current policies. The tension is evident in intra-party conflicts, such as the long debate over agrarian policy. It is reflected in divergent Sandinista conceptions of socialism.

Sandinista ideology, with its gradualist, two-stage approach to revolution, always assumed a gap between early policies and ultimate goals. Certain positions were understood to be "temporary and tactical." But some recent policies are hard to see in that light. Are individual land grants a tactical concession or a *fait accompli* with decisive implications for the future? Inaugurating a constitutional system may be a tactic in the minds of some Sandinistas, but it risks changing the character of national politics. It is now doubtful that Sandinistas agree about what is and what is not temporary and tactical.

## The Future of the Revolution

Prophecy is a risky enterprise and the Sandinistas have repeatedly confounded seers. What follows can be no more than informed speculation.

The end of the war, which, as this conclusion is written in May 1988, seems imminent, will compel Nicaraguans to turn their attention inward. Within the Sandinista Front, there will be a reexamination of goals and strategy. The war allowed, even required the Sandinistas to ignore their differences, to avoid debate over fundamental questions, to focus all energies on the immediate crisis. Given the disciplined and centralized organization of the FSLN, the Sandinista debate is, for the moment, unlikely to erupt into the public arena.

An early challenge to the leadership of Daniel Ortega and his supporters on the National Directorate is equally improbable. But if the foreign policy initiatives and moderate domestic policies of recent months prove unsuccessful, a realignment among the comandantes is at least conceivable. Given the collegial character of the Directorate, a shift in attitude by as few as two members could produce dramatic results. If, on the other hand, he is reasonably successful, Ortega will continue to consolidate his control of the party and to strengthen the independent power of the constitutional presidency.

Judging from past performance and current mood, the Sandinistas will be flexible and conciliatory in developing post-war policies. But they will be very reluctant to compromise about power – that is, they will want to safeguard their vanguard role.

The central challenge facing the Sandinista Front is the reconstruction of a devastated economy. Everything else they may hope to achieve – including lifting the living standards of the poor majority, revitalizing social programs, restoring flaging political support, and maintaining a defense capability – will depend on success in this realm.

Post-war economic policy, like recent agrarian policy, is likely to emphasize market incentives and support for small private producers. But the Sandinistas will also need the collaboration of the bourgeoisie to restore export earnings, which are crucial for the health of the entire economy, and to reestablish access to Western development credits. The representatives of the bourgeoisie will demand more than economic concessions – they will want a share in political power, which the Sandinistas will be reluctant to concede. The Sandinista formula "producers without power" will be problematic in the future as it was in the past.

The Sandinistas will not escape the economic dilemmas they face by turning East. The Soviets show little interest in increasing the current level of aid. Further economic integration with Eastern Europe seems equally improbable. The proportion of exports destined to the Soviet bloc has been declining. Full membership in the Soviet economic community would assume rapid socialization of the Nicaraguan economy, a step most Sandinista leaders know to be unworkable.

Continuing hostility from the United States (expressed in the maintenance of trade and credit sanctions, if not more violently) could retard economic recovery and exacerbate domestic political tensions. The Sandinistas will, as in the past, be prepared to make concessions to American security concerns, but unlikely to make domestic political concessions in negotiations with the United States. There is little in the history of relations between the two states to suggest that the United States might allow Nicaraguans to determine their own national destiny. But there are also good, practical reasons for a new administration in Washington to seek an understanding with Nicaragua.

The promised reopening of domestic politics will challenge the Nicaraguan opponents of Sandinismo as much as it does the FSLN. A decade of revolution and war had cut into the Sandinistas' popular following, but, to date, no sector of the opposition has demonstrated a capacity to attract those who have abandoned the FSLN. The bourgeois opposition has much less popular political significance than *La Prensa* and the international press attribute to it. The contras are ideologically divided and lacking in political finesse. (Unlike the FSLN of the 1970s, the FDN never learned how to be a *political*-military organization). Two key questions for the future are these: Will the domestic political opposition unite against the FSLN? Can the opposition reach beyond the naturally anti-Sandinista, upper and middle classes to a mass constituency?

For their part, the Sandinistas will want to allow the greatest political openness consistent with the preservation of their vanguard position. *La Prensa* will be permitted to publish, and COSEP, the bishops, and the political right will use its columns to register their complaints.

But the Sandinista Front will be less tolerant of encroachments on its chosen terrain of popular organizing. This could mean more freedom for the Conservatives than the independent labor unions or the Popular Christian Party. The opposition will not easily breach such Sandinista monopolies as the military or national television. But the opposition parties might expand their representation in the National Assembly and initiate the FSLN into the art of parliamentary politics.

The Sandinistas' redeeming qualities are their commitment to Nicaragua's impoverished majority, their willingness to acknowledge their own errors, and their preference, finally, for rule by persuasion rather than coercion. In the midst of the contra war, Daniel Ortega explained, for a visitor, the main challenge facing his government: ". . . so many children without shoes, children who have to quit school to work on farms . . .."[1] For a brief historical moment in the early 1980s, between two wars, Ortega's party was putting shoes on children's feet and expanding school enrollments. It will take all the commitment, all the wisdom, and all the luck that the Sandinistas can summon to recapture that moment and make it endure.

# Epilogue: Afloat on a Sea of Troubles

The 10th anniversary of the Sandinista revolution on July 19, 1989, unleashed a carnival in Managua. Three hundred thousand supporters of the Sandinista Front jammed the city's main plaza to scream, cheer, cry, and sing; to dance to roving bands; to listen to patriotic speeches; to wave Sandinista flags from atop human pyramids; and hoot at a giant papier-mâché Uncle Sam. They had gathered to celebrate the end (*de facto* if not formal) of the contra war and the survival of their embattled revolution. As one of the party's current slogans reminded them: "Reagan is gone. The revolution remains."

The revelers were also in the plaza to forget the daily desperation of Nicaraguan life. *Barricada*, the Sandinista newspaper, suggested as much with the next morning's four-inch headline, a forlorn phrase taken from President Daniel Ortega's address: "BETTER DAYS WILL COME!"

Nothing revealed the country's terrible state so clearly as the condition of its children. Visitors who had known Nicaragua in the early years of the revolution, when the government was able to devote large sums to their nutrition, education, and health, were affected by the unfamiliar sight of young Nicaraguans begging or peddling cigarettes in the streets. Children were the purpose of the Sandinista revolution. Now, teachers in a working-class barrio reported that hungry second-graders were fainting in class. Health-care workers noted that the infant mortality rate, which had fallen radically in the early years, was climbing again.

These developments reflected the deeply depressed state of the national economy and the government's own shrinking resources. In the plaza, Ortega conceded that output *per capita* had sunk to about half of what it had been in 1977. He might have added that the inflation rate had reached an unimaginable 36,000 percent, that workers' salaries had lost at least 70 percent of their purchasing power since the early 1980s, and that Nicaragua was, by some calculations, about to displace Haiti as the poorest country in the hemisphere. None of this would have surprised his listeners.[1]

Nicaragua's economic catastrophe embodied the cumulative effects of the US-sponsored contra war, a decade of hostile relations between capitalists and comandantes, and the Sandinistas' often incoherent economic policies. As if the man-made damage were not sufficient, a hurricane swept across the country at the end of 1988 doing damage equivalent to a half year's GNP and in 1989 a long drought depressed food production.

Since the beginning of 1988, the government had responded to the crisis with stern corrective measures, stemming its own spending, eliminating most consumer subsidies, repeatedly devaluing the national currency, raising interest rates to reflect inflation, and freeing business to hire, fire, and set wages and prices. This market-oriented austerity program was precisely what the US had been prescribing for troubled Third World economies — the triumph of Reaganism in revolutionary Nicaragua! But as Ortega spoke, there was no indication that such policies were producing the desired economic results or that they were likely to mollify Reagan's successors in Washington.

One reason for the failure was that the material base of the Nicaraguan economy had been worn away by 10 years of war and revolution. The economy was struggling with exhausted machinery, depleted cattle herds, run-down coffee estates, failing power grids, and crumbling roads. Nicaragua had also lost critical elements of its human capital, as trained professionals fled the country for opportunities elsewhere.

The problem facing the Sandinistas was not "getting the economy going again" but rebuilding it almost from scratch, and that would require substantial external funding. But the United States continued to block aid to Nicaragua from such international sources as the World Bank and the International Monetary Fund and from most Western governments. (President Bush had gone so far as to call Western heads of state urging them to withhold development aid from Nicaragua.)[2] Sandinista efforts to obtain foreign aid and revive the economy were further stymied by continuing conflict with the bourgeoisie — notwithstanding the government's well-publicized campaign to build a more cooperative relationship with the private sector, a policy the Sandinistas called *concertacion*.

Ortega's speech was notably conciliatory toward the revolution's foreign and domestic opponents, even offering praise for Cardinal Obando, Violeta de Chamorro and Alfonso Robelo. But in a passage obviously directed at party members and close supporters, he characterized the Sandinista revolution as "10 years of no to Somocismo, capitalism, and imperialism." A year earlier, on the ninth anniversary, Ortega had gone further, proclaiming that Nicaragua was *"socialist" and had been since 1979*. This remarkable declaration, coming just when the government was reorienting the economy toward the capitalist market, was allowed to fall silently like the philosopher's unattended tree in the forest. Nicaragua became officially socialist without the campaign of editorials, posters, slogans, and rallies that herald important departures in Sandinista policy. Clearly, the old tension between ideology and policy was not about to be resolved.[3]

But the FSLN's biggest political concerns lay elsewhere. The economic problems confronting the Sandinistas were eroding their political base. Popular support inevitably waned with rising unemployment, hyper-inflation, and austerity budgets for the social programs which had been the hallmark of Sandinista rule. A series of opinion surveys taken in the year preceding the 10th anniversary suggested that the broad following enjoyed by the Sandinista Front at the beginning of the decade had shrunk to about one-third of the potential electorate. At the same time, the opposition parties — small, divided, ideologically muddled, and disconnected from the masses of Nicaraguans — did not appear to be absorbing the support the Sandinistas were losing, leaving the outcome of any electoral contest uncertain.[4]

The government was preparing for elections in February 1990. By lifting press censorship and restrictions on political activity, arranging for opposition access to broadcast media, and other, similar measures, the Sandinistas were creating something approaching a level playing field for the elections. This process of political liberalization was part of a sustained diplomatic offensive through which the Sandinistas had already succeeded in undermining support for the contras, both in Washington and among the Central American presidents joined in the Esquipulas peace process. By the time George Bush took his oath of office, he appeared to have little chance of reviving Ronald Reagan's war against Nicaragua.

As they recalled the victory over Anastasio Somoza, the Sandinistas could savor some recent military and diplomatic triumphs, knowing, at the same time, that the revolution was trapped by economic failure. Worse still, American officials and Nicaragua businessmen unsympathetic to Sandinista rule held the keys to economic revival. The morning after the 10th anniversary of their revolution, the Sandinistas would awake to find themselves afloat – on a sea of troubles.

# Notes

*Preface*

1 FSLN National Directorate [DN], *On the General Political-Military Platform of the Struggle of the Sandinista Front for National Liberation* (Oakland, CA: Resistance Publications, 1977); [hereafter FSLN-DN, *General Platform*]; Daniel Ortega, "Interview," *Latin American Perspectives*, 6 (Winter 1979), pp. 117–18; Oleg Ignatiev and Genrykh Borovik, *The Agony of a Dictatorship: Nicaraguan Chronicle* (Moscow: Progress Publishers, 1979) pp. 46–8; Humberto Ortega, *Sobre la insurrección* (Havana: Editoral de Ciencias Sociales, 1981), pp. 25–36.


*Historical Introduction: From Sandino to the Sandinistas*

1 *New York Times*, Dec. 23. 1972.
2 Bernard Diederich, *Somoza and the Legacy of U.S. Involvement in Central America* (New York: Dutton, 1981), p. 93.
3 *Time*, Jan. 8, 1973.
4 Diederich, *Somoza*, pp. 94–5; Richard Millett, *Guardians of the Dynasty* (Maryknoll, NY, 1977), p. 237.
5 John Booth, *The End and the Beginning: The Nicaraguan Revolution*, 2nd edn (Boulder, Colo.: Westview, 1985), pp. 76–7.
6 Diederich, *Somoza*, p. 54.
7 Ibid., p. 100.
8 Ibid., pp. 96, 100.
9 Inter-American Development Bank, *Social Progress in Latin America; 1978 Report* (Washington, DC: IDB, 1979), pp.135–41; Charles Teller, "The demography of malnutrition in Latin America," *Intercom*, 9 (1981), p. 10; Harvey Williams, "The social impact in Nicaragua," in Thomas Walker (ed.), *Reagan versus the Sandinistas: The Undeclared War on Nicaragua* (Boulder, Colo.: Westview, 1987), pp. 245, 261; Booth, *The End and the Beginning*, p. 86.
10 Booth, *The End and the Beginning*, p. 85; Carmen Diana Deere, Peter Marchetti, and Nola Reinhardt, "The peasantry and the development of

Sandinista agrarian policy, 1979–1984," *Latin American Research Review*, 20 (1985), p. 79.

11   Booth, *The End and the Beginning*, pp.84–5; James Rudolph (ed.), *Nicaragua: A Country Study* (Washington, DC: USGPO 1982), p. 234; and Inter-American Development Bank, *Economic and Social Progress in Latin America: 1978 Report*, pp. 135–41.

12   Diederich, *Somoza*, p. 79.

13   Tomás Borge, *Carlos, el amanecer ya no es una tentación* (Managua: Sindicato Nicaragua Machinery Company, n.d.), p. 22.

14   Ibid., p. 23.

15   Michael Dodson and T. S. Montgomery, "The churches in the Nicaraguan revolution," in Thomas Walker (ed.), *Nicaragua in Revolution* (New York: Praeger, 1982), p. 186.

16   Diederich, *Somoza*, pp. 124–30; Amnesty International, *Republic of Nicaragua* (London, 1977); *Latin America Political Report*, Aug. 11, 1978; *New York Times*, Mar. 2, 1977.

17   Chamorro's death was later attributed to Somoza's son and a business partner, whose blood export enterprise had been the subject of an exposé in Chamorro's paper.

18   Booth, *The End and the Beginning*, pp. 160–1.

19   *El País*, June 8, 1978, quoted in Claribel Alegría and D. J. Flakoll, *Nicaragua: la revolución sandinista: una crónica política: 1855–1979* (Mexico: Ed. Era, 1982), p. 403.

20   FSLN-DN, "Documentos de Unificación" in Empar Pineda (ed.), *La revolución nicaragüense* (Madrid: Ed. Revolución, 1980).

21   Algería and Flakoll, *Nicaragua*, p. 346; Shirley Christian, *Nicaragua: Revolution in the Family* (New York: Random House, 1985), pp. 79–81, 89–90, 95–6; and James Goodsell, "Nicaragua," in Robert Wesson (ed.), *Communism in Central America and the Caribbean* (Stanford, CA: Hoover Institution Press, 1982), p. 58; Diederich, *Somoza*, pp. 146–7.

22   Booth, *The End and the Beginning*, p. 173.

23   Ibid, p. 183; and Diederich, *Somoza*, p. 327.

24   Deborah Barndt, "Popular education," in Thomas Walker (ed.), *Nicaragua: The First Five Years* (New York: Praeger, 1985), p. 331; and Williams, "Social impact."

25   *New York Times*, July 20, 1987.

26   *Washington Post*, Aug. 18, 1987; *Journal of Commerce*, Aug. 3, 1987.

*Chapter 1 The Ideology of the FSLN*

1   "Borge discusses his life," *Juventud Rebelde*, Feb. 10, 1980 (Joint Publications Research Service 75341, p. 173). Borge and Fonseca also read Bukharin's classic Bolshevik primer, *ABC of Communism* (see Alegría and Flakoll, *Nicaragua*, p. 138). In this the Sandinistas were ahead of the Soviets, who did not rehabilitate Bukharin, one of Stalin's most prominent victims, until 1988.

2  Anastasio Somoza, *El vadadero Sandino o el calvario de las segovias* (Managua: Tipografía Robelo, 1936).

3  Alan Wald, "Some perspectives on the FSLN," *Against the Current*, Jan.–Feb. 1987, p. 6.

4  On Sandino see Neil Macaulay, *The Sandino Affair* (Chicago: Quadrangle Books, 1967); Gregorio Selser, *Sandino* (New York: Monthly Review Press, 1981); and Carlos Fonseca, *Obras* (2 vols; Managua: Ed. Nueva Nicaragua, 1982); David Nolan, *FSLN: The Ideology of the Sandinistas* (Miami: Institute of Inter-American Studies, University of Miami, 1984), pp. 16–18; Donald Hodges, *Intellectual Foundations of the Nicaraguan Revolution* (Austin: University of Texas Press, 1987); and other sources cited below. Sandino's writings have been collected in Sergio Ramírez, *El pensamiento vivo de Sandino* (San José; Ed. Universitaria Centroamericana, 1974). For an interpretation of Sandino and his relationship to the FSLN at odds with the one advanced here see Hodges's book.

5  Borge, *Carlos*, p. 28; Diederich, *Somoza*, p. 68.

6  Victor Tirado López, "Karl Marx: the international workers' movement's greatest fighter and thinker," in Bruce Marcus (ed.), *Nicaragua: The Sandinista People's Revolution* (New York: Pathfinder, 1985), p. 105. Omar Cabezas observed in his memoir of the insurrection, "I know and came to Sandino through Ché" (*Fire from the Mountain: The Making of Sandinista* (New York: Crown, 1985), p. 12).

7  Fonseca, *Obras*, vol.1, p. 377 and vol. 2, pp. 192–7.

8  Ramón de Belausteguigoitia, *Con Sandino en la hora de la paz* (Madrid: Espasa-Calpe, 1934), p. 181.

9  Fonseca, *Obras*, vol. 2, p. 177.

10  Belausteguigoitia, *Con Sandino*, pp. 174–6, 193.

11  Ramírez, *Pensamiento*, p. 205.

12  Ibid., pp. 183–4.

13  Humberto Ortega, *Cincuenta años de lucha sandinista* (Mexico: Editoral Diogenes, 1979), p. 68.

14  The red and black of the flag stand for liberty or death. The FSLN transformed Sandino's *patria y libertad* ("fatherland and freedom") into the more active, though slightly awkward, *patria libre o morir* ("a free fatherland or die").

15  Victor Tirado López, "Las enseñanzas de Carlos Marx en Nicaragua," *Barricada*, Apr. 25, 1983; Tomás Borge, "Interview," *Le Monde Diplomatique* (Spanish edn.), Sept. 1984 (Foreign Broadcasting Information Service-LAM 84-78); Humberto Ortega, *Discurso del Ministro de Defensa . . . en la clausura de la reunión de especialistas* (Managua: Ejército Popular Sandinista, 1981), p. 8. See also FSLN-DN, *General Platform*, p. 14. Ortega, *Cincuenta años*, p. 104; René Núñez, "Vencer es nuestra responsibilidad con la historia y con América," *Barricada*, Apr. 25, 1983; Bayardo Arce, *Discurso secreto del Comandante Bayardo Arce ante el Partido Socialista Nicaragüense (PSN)* (Washington, DC: US Department of State, 1985), p. 7; Fonseca, *Obras*, vol. 1, p. 227.

16  For example, Tomás Borge, "Large scale aggression is being prepared," in Marcus (ed.), *Nicaragua*, p. 69; Bayardo Arce, "Bayardo on FSLN political,

ideological views," *Radio Sandino*, Sept. 19, 1985 (Foreign Broadcasting Information Service, Sept. 24, 1985, p. P18).

17    Gabriele Invernizzi, Francis Pisani, and Jesus Ceberio, *Sandinistas: Entrevistas a Humberto Ortega Saavedra, Jaime Wheelock Román y Bayardo Arce Castraño* (Managua: Vanguardia, 1986), pp. 11–12.

18    Fonseca, *Obras*, vol.1, pp. 110, 128.

19    Quoted in Marcel Liebman, *Leninism under Lenin* (London: Jonathan Cape, 1975), p. 26.

20    Isaac Deutscher, *The Prophet Armed: Trotsky 1879–1921* (New York: Oxford University Press, 1954), p. 90.

21    V. I. Lenin, *Collected Works* (Moscow: Progress Publishers, 1966), vol. 31, p. 150.

22    Tony Cliff, *Lenin* (London: Pluto Press, 1976), vol. 3, p. 97.

23    V. I. Lenin, *Selected Works: One Volume Edition* (New York: International Publishers, 1971), p. 320. Sandinista leader Dora María Tellez indicated in an interview that *State and Revolution* was one of the books that Sandinistas read in the 1970s. See Margaret Randall, *Sandino's Daughters: Testimonies of Nicaraguan Women in Struggle* (Vancouver: New Star Books, 1981), p. 52.

24    Ibid., p. 281.

25    Fonseca, *Obras*, vol. 1, p. 69.

26    ATC, *Pequeño vocabulario de la reforma agraria* (MIDINRA, Dec. 1980), p. 7.

27    *Barricada*, May 2, 1982. See also FSLN-DN, *General Platform*, pp. 13–14 and Victor Tirado López, "El pensamiento político de Carlos Fonseca Amador," in Fernando Carmona (ed.), *Nicaragua: estrategia de la victoria* (Mexico: Ed. Nuestro Tiempo, 1980), p. 127.

28    See, for examples, FSLN-Secretaria Nacional de Propaganda y Educación Política del FSLN, "El Sandinismo no es democratismo," *Barricada*, Mar. 14, 1980; H. Ortega, *Discurso*, p. 8.

29    FSLN-DN, *Análisis de la coyuntura y tareas de la revolución sandinista* (Managua: FSLN, 1979) [hereafter cited as the "72 hours document'], pp. 31,11. For a similar statement see FSLN, *Plan de lucha del FSLN* (Managua: FSLN, 1984), p. 2.

30    For examples, see FSLN, "Programa del FSLN aprobado en 1969" in Manlio Tirado, *La revolución sandinista* (Mexico: Ed. Nuestro Tiempo, 1983); FSLN, *General Platform*, pp. 15–19; H. Ortega, *Discurso*, p. 7; Tomás Borge, *Los primeros pasos la revolución popular sandinista* (Mexico: Siglo XXI, 1984), pp. 281–2; FSLN, *Plan de lucha*, p. 2.

31    FSLN, *General Platform*, pp. 17,13.

32    ATC, *Pequeño vocabulario*, p. 19.

33    Stephen Kinzer, "Nicaragua: the beleaguered revolution," *New York Times Magazine*, Aug. 28, 1983.

34    Jaime Wheelock, "Solo queremos la soberania," *El Nuevo Diario*, Dec. 10, 1981; Bayardo Arce, *Romper la dependencia: tarea estrategica de la revolución* (Managua: FSLN, 1980); FSLN-DN, *General Platform*,

pp. 15–16; Victor Tirado López, "Improvement in the situation of the workers is the task of the workers themselves," in Marcus (ed.), *Nicaragua*, pp. 99–100.

35 Jaime Wheelock and Luis Carrión, *Apuntes sobre el desarrollo económico y social de Nicaragua* (Managua: FSLN, n.d.).

36 Carmona, *Nicaragua.*, p. 178.

37 Wheelock and Carrión, *Apuntes*, pp. 13–14; Carlos Fonseca, "Hora zero" in *Obras*, vol. 1, pp. 75–77; Sergio Ramírez, "Los sobrevivientes del naufragio," in *Estado y clases sociales en Nicaragua* (Managua: Associación Nicaraguense de Cientificos Sociales, 1982), p. 70.

38 On this period see chapter 7.

39 FSLN-DN, *General Platform*, p. 16. See also Fonseca, "Hora zero," p. 82; Wheelock and Carrión, *Apuntes*, p. 14; and FSLN-DN, "72 hours document," p. 6.

40 Tirado López, "El pensamiento político de Fonseca," p. 127. See also Orlando Núñez Soto, "The third social force in national liberation movements," *Latin American Perspectives*, 8 (Spring 1981), pp. 5–21.

41 On the Marxist-Leninist background of the worker–peasant alliance see chapter 4 and FSLN, "Programa . . . 1969"; Tirado López, "El pensamiento político de Fonseca," p. 127; FSLN-DN, *General Platform*, p. 20; FSLN-DN, "Documentos de unificación" in Pineda (ed.), *La revolución nicaragüense*, 1980), p. 107. (This version of the unification agreement is more complete than the one generally available to foreign readers.)

42 FSLN-Tendencia Proletaria, *La crisis interna y las tendencias* (Los Angeles, CA: Sandinistas por el socialismo en Nicaragua, 1978), p. 14.

43 FSLN, *General Platform*, pp. 19–20.

44 Ibid., p. 21. For a theoretical analysis of the role of the petite bourgeoisie in the insurrection see O. Nuñez, "The third force," Nuñez, a Sandinista sociologist, places particular emphasis on the role of youth.

45 FSLN, *General Platform*, pp. 27–8.

46 "Interview with Daniel Ortega," *Latin American Perspectives*, 6 (Winter 1979), pp. 117–18. See also FSLN-DN, "72 hours document". pp. 9–10.

47 See, for example, FSLN-DN, "72 hours document," p. 8; *Barricada*, Apr. 30 and Aug. 8, 1986; FSLN-Secretaria Nacional de Propaganda y Educación Politica, "El Sandinismo no es democratismo."

48 Borge, *Primeros pasos*, pp. 224, 232, 281–2; FSLN, *Plan de lucha*, p. 2.

49 O. Núñez, "The third force," for example, leaves the post-revolutionary role of the petite bourgeoisie an open question.

50 Randall, *Sandino's Daughters* p. 53.

51 FSLN-DN, "72 hours document", pp. 29–30.

52 ATC, *Pequeño vocabulario*, p. 37.

53 FSLN-DN, "72 hours document," p. 10.

54 Jaime Wheelock, "The Sandinista Front is the organization of the working people," in Marcus (ed.), *Nicaragua*, p. 274.

55 O. Núñez, "The third force."

56    Jaime Wheelock, *El futuro es del pueblo* (Managua: FSLN, 1980).
57    Borge, *Primeros pasos*, p. 66. See also Carlos Fonseca, "Sintesis de algunos problemas actuales," *Obras*, vol. 1, p. 113.
58    FSLN-Secretaria Nacional de Propaganda y Educación Política, "El Sandinismo no es democratismo."
59    FSLN-DN, "Pronunciamiento del FSLN sobre las elecciones," *Patria Libre*, 6 (August 1980). See also Marefeli Perez-Stable, "Pluralismo y poder popular: entrevista con Sergio Ramírez," *Areito*, 9 (1983), pp. 4–7.
60    Perez-Stable, "Pluralismo," p. 20.
61    *Barricada*, Aug. 16, 1980. See also Victor Tirado López, Omar Cabezas, and Carlos Núñez, *Primer seminario Miguel Bonilla: la universidad y la revolución* (Managua: Universidad Nacional Autoriona de Nicaragua, 1980), pp. 19–20, 36–7.
62    FSLN-DN, *"Pronunciamiento,"* p. 20. See also H. Ortega, *Discurso*, p. 16; Bayardo Arce, "Extracto de la charla ofredica ... en el Ministerio de Educación," in FSLN-DN, *La revolución a traves de nuestra Dirección Nacional* p. 87; "Borge Discusses His Life," p. 7; FSLN-DN, "72 hours document," p. 14; Ramírez, "Los sobrevivientes," p. 67.
63    Quoted in Sonia Suarez, "Elecciones y garantias," *Patria Libre*, 28 (Nov. 1983), p. 48. The same article quotes the 1980 pronouncement on elections at length.
64    Fonseca, *Obras*, vol. 1, pp. 168–9.
65    FSLN-DN, *General Platform*, pp. 14–15. Wheelock used very similar language in 1983 when he declared to a union audience, "We have to fight for two objectives ... national liberation and socialism. These are our two basic tasks, and that is why we are ... our people's vanguard," "Speech to National Council of the CST," *Radio Sandino* (Managua, 1983; Joint Publications Research Service 83215, p. 162); see also FSLN-DN, "Documentos de unificación," pp. 106, 108; FSLN-DN, "72 hours document," pp. 6, 11, 18, 30; Tirado et al., *Primer seminario Miguel Bonilla*, pp. 33–4, 64–5; H. Ortega, *Discurso*, p. 12; ATC, *Pequeño vocabulario*, p. 21; and references to socialism below.
66    FSLN, "Análisis histórico de la lucha del pueblo de Nicaragua [Feb. 1979]," in Pineda (ed.), *La revolución nicaragüense*, p. 76.
67    Fonseca, "Hora zero," pp. 93–4; Humberto Ortega, "La estrategia de la victoria," in Carmona (ed.), *Nicaragua*, p. 34; FSLN-DN, "72 hours document"; D. Ortega, "Interview," p. 11.
68    FSLN-DN, "Documentos de unificación," p. 108.
69    FSLN, "Programa ... 1969"; FSLN-DN, *General Platform*; FSLN-DN, "Documentos de unificación"; FSLN-DN, "72 hours document."
70    *Barricada*, Aug. 3, 1979.
71    FSLN-Secretaria Nacional de Propaganda y Educación Politica, "El Sandinismo no es Democratismo."
72    H. Ortega, *Discurso*, p. 19.
73    FSLN-DN, *General Platform*, p. 17; see also FSLN-DN, "Documentos de unificación," p. 108; FSLN-DN, "72 hours document," pp. 6–8.
74    See, for example, Jaime Wheelock, "El FSLN conduce al estado y jamás

lo sustituye" and Humberto Ortega, "Un solo ejército" in FSLN-DN, *Habla la dirección de la vanguardia* (Managua: FSLN, 1981), pp. 52, 54, 89.

75   Fonseca, "Hora zero," p. 93. See also FSLN, "Mensaje no.12" (1974), in Carmona (ed.), *Nicaragua*, p. 171.

76   *El Nuevo Diario*, June 9, 1980; Bayardo Arce, "Entrevista," *Patria Libre*, 21 (May 1982); Lucio Jimenez, "Defense can only be assured by increasing production," in Marcus (ed.), *Nicaragua*, pp. 18–22.

77   Wheelock, "Speech to National Council of the CST"; Tirado López, "Improvement in the situation of the workers," pp. 99–100; Arce, *Discurso secreto*; Victor Tirado López, "Nuestro Socialismo," *Revista nicaragüense de ciencias sociales*, 1 (Sept. 1986).

78   FSLN-Secretaria Nacional de Propaganda y Educación Politica, "El Sandinismo no es democratismo."

79   Carlos Tunnermann, *Hacia una nueva educación en Nicaragua* (Managua: Distribudora Cultural, 1983), p. 19.

80   Some writers have portrayed liberation theology as a basic influence on Sandinista thought. Conor Cruise O'Brien pushes this view to its logical limites in an otherwise insightful article that defines the Sandinista revolution as a radical Christian undertaking ("God and man in Nicaragua," *Atlantic Monthly*, Aug. 1986). It would seem more reasonable to say that some Sandinista militants like Tunnermann (and many more supporters of the party) regard their involvement with the revolution as the logical outgrowth of their Christian commitment. *Their* revolution *is* a Christian revolution. But the party documents examined in this chapter do not indicate that they have had a significant effect on the overall ideology of the FSLN. There is one crucial exception to this generalization. The revolutionary commitment of radical Christians convinced the Sandinista leadership that believers could be true revolutionaries and therefore should be accepted into the party without reservation – a sharp break with Marxist-Leninist orthodoxy. The party's attitudes toward Christianity and its relations with Christians are explored in chapter 6.

81   Borge, *Primeros pasos*, pp. 192–3 and Bayardo Arce, "El dificil terreno de la lucha: la lucha," in FSLN–DN, *Habla la Dirección de la vanguardia*, p. 157.

82   Junta de Gobierno de Reconstruccion Nacional, "Fines, Objectivos y Principios de la Nueva Educacion," *Barricada*, March 1, 1983.

83   On Marxist revolution and the New Man see Paul Hollander, "Research on Marxist societies," *Annual Review of Sociology*, 8 (1982), pp. 340–3.
Daniel Ortega raises the question of incentives in a couple of understated paragraphs of a 1980 speech. See D. Ortega, "La revolución y la Iglesia Católica en Nicaragua" in FSLN-DN, *Habla la Dirección de la vanguardia*, p. 289. For recent Cuban views see Fidel Castro, "Address to Young Communist League," *Grandma* (English edn), Apr. 18, 1982 and *New York Times*, Feb. 8, 1987.

84   H. Ortega, *Discurso*, p. 21.

85   Tirado López, "Improvement in the situation of the workers," p. 99. Tirado delivered the same message in a second speech to a similar audience three years later, in 1986. See "Nuestro socialismo."

*Chapter 2 The Party*

1   Aug. 3, 1979.
2   Carlos Núñez, "La consigna es: organización, organización, y más organización," *Barricada*, Dec. 11, 1979.
3   FSLN-DN, "Comunicado," *Barricada*, Sept. 10, 1980.
4   Junta de Gobierno de Reconstrucción Nacional, "Comunicado," *Barricada*, Sept. 16, 1980. Among the indicated signatories of this statement was junta member Arturo Cruz, later a contra political leader.
5   Marcus (ed.), *Nicaragua*, p. 204.
6   FSLN-Secretaria de la Dirección Nacional, "Comunicado," *Barricada*, Aug. 4, 1985.
7   Some second-ranking Sandinista leaders received the title Comandante guerrillero. Unless otherwise specified, the term comandante is used in this book to refer to Directorate members.
8   By this rough classification, the families of Borge, Arce, and the Ortegas were middle class; those of Ruíz, Tirado, and Núñez were working class. Material on backgrounds of the comandantes was drawn from interviews and the following sources: Consejo de Estado, *Primera Legislature 1980 ... Instauración del Consejo de Estado* (Managua, 1980); Pilar Arias, *Nicaragua: revolución: relatos de combatientes del frente sandinista* (Mexico: Siglo veinteuno, 1980), pp. 215–21; *Patria Libre*, 20–3 (Mar.–Sept. 1982); Nolan, *FSLN*, pp. 18–22, 137–54; Stephen Kinzer, "Portrait of a powerful Sandinista," *New York Times*, Sept. 3, 1985; "The Man Behind the Designer Glasses," *Time*, Mar. 31, 1986; "Low-Key First Day for Daniel Ortega," *Latin America Weekly Report*, Jan. 18, 1985; Diederich, *Somoza*, pp. 85–86; "Borge discusses his life".
9   Cabezas, *Fire from the Mountain*, p. 132.
10  Material on Borge drawn from author's interviews and Kinzer, "Portrait of a powerful Sandinista"; Arias, *Nicaragua*, p. 216; Nolan, *FSLN*, p. 139; and Andrew Reding's introduction to Tomás Borge, *Christianity and Revolution: Tomás Borge's Theology of Life* (Maryknoll, NY: Orbis Books, 1987).
11  See, for example, Americas Watch, *Human Rights in Nicaragua 1985–1986* (New York: Americas Watch, 1986).
12  "Playboy Interview: the Sandinistas," *Playboy* (Sept. 1983), p. 63.
13  Material on Ortega drawn from interviews and *Patria Libre*, 23 (Sept. 1982); Nolan, *FSLN*, p. 148; Diederich, *Somoza*, pp. 85–6; "Low-key first day"; "The man behind the designer glasses."
14  Jaime Wheelock, *El gran desafío* (Managua: Ed. Nueva Nicaragua, 1983), p. 17. See also Booth, *The End and the Beginning*, p. 199; and Invernizzi et al., *Sandinistas*, pp. 36–46.
15  Booth, *The End and the Beginning*, pp. 187–8; Christian, *Nicaragua*, p. 101.
16  Bayardo Arce, "Estructuras de la vanguardia y tareas de la revolución," *Barricada*, Sept. 17, 1980; Invernizzi et al., *Sandinistas*, pp. 39–41.

17 FSLN-[SDN] Secretaria de la Dirección Nacional, "Comunicado," *Barricada*, Aug. 4, 1985.

18 Ibid. The new body, consisting of the Ortegas, Wheelock, Arce, and Borge, replaced a smaller "Political Committee," created in 1980.

19 Ruiz, who was not included in the new Executive Committee of the Directorate, seems to have been the biggest loser in the restructuring of party and state, confirming the nice-guys-finish-last assessment of him quoted earlier.

20 Invernizzi et al., *Sandinistas*, p. 66; FSLN-SDN, "Comunicado," *Barricada*, Aug. 4, 1985.

21 FSLN-SDN, "Comunicado," *Barricada*, Aug. 4, 1985. See also FSLN-DN, "Comunicado," *Barricada*, September 16, 1980; Invernizzi et al., *Sandinistas*, pp. 64–5.

22 Emphasis added. FSLN-DN, "Comunicado," *Barricada*, May 6 and 9, 1986.

23 FSLN-SDN, "Comunicado," *Barricada*, Aug. 4, 1985. See also FSLN-DN, "Comunicado," *Barricada*, Sept. 16, 1980;

24 Invernizzi et al., *Sandinistas*, p. 44.

25 "Dora María Téllez," *NACLA*, Sept.–Dec. 1986, p. 24.

26 Invernizzi et al., *Sandinistas*, pp. 63–6; Arce, "Estructuras de la vanguardia"; Fonseca, *Obras*, vol. 1, p. 110; Borge, *Primeros pasos, pp. 60–2; FSLN-DN, General Platform*, p. 23.

27 Arce, "Estructuras de la vanguardia."

28 FSLN-DN, "72 hours document", pp. 34–5, also p. 33; C. Núñez, "La consigna es: organización.

29 Borge, *Primeros pasos*, p. 61; C. Núñez, "La consigna es: organización." See also Rafael Solis cited in *Los Angeles Times*, Apr. 18, 1985.

30 Arce, "Estructuras de la vanguardia."

31 FSLN-DN, "72 hours document," p. 31.

32 Ibid., p. 31. See also Fonseca, *Obras*, vol.1, pp. 109–10.

33 Borge, *Primeros pasos*, p. 60.

34 Estimates of membership are from Dan Williams, "The Sandinista Front: dogma and discipline," *Los Angeles Times*, Apr. 18, 1985; *Financial Times*, Aug 21, 1985; *Miami Herald*, Aug. 4, 1985; Wald, "Some perspectives on the FSLN," p. 6.

35 Ricardo Morales Aviles, *Obras: No paremos de andar jamás* (Managua: Ed. Nueva Nicaragua, 1981), p. 126.

36 *Barricada*, June 1, 1981.

37 *Barricada Internacional*, Mar. 26, 1987.

38 Wald, "Some perspectives on the FSLN," p. 6.

39 Disappointed candidates may reapply for membership at a later date and, if accepted, restart the probationary process.

40 Carlos Fonseca et al., *Qué es un sandinista?* (Managua: FSLN, 1980), pp. 7–11; FSLN, *Propaganda de la producción* (Managua, 1980), p. 22. See also Borge, *Primeros pasos*, pp. 64–7 and Daniel Ortega, "The Sandinista People's Revolution is an irreversible political reality," in Marcus (ed.), *Nicaragua*, p. 204.

41 Fonseca, *Obras*, vol. 1, p. 112.

42   The phrase about "vacillating men" echoes the language of Sandino fifty years earlier.
43   Cabezas, *Fire from the Mountain*, p. 34. Emphasis added.
44   Tirado López et al., *Primer seminario Miguel Bonilla*, p. 53.
45   "Exitosa Tercera Asamblea de Cuadros y Militantes del FSLN," *Patria Libre*, 7 (1980), p. 54.
46   Cabezas, *Fire from the Mountain*, pp. 86–7.
47   Fonseca et al., *Qué es un Sandinista?*, p. 10.
48   Randall, *Sandino's Daughters*, p. 54.
49   FSLN-Secretaria de la Dirección Nacional, "Comunicado," *Barricada*, Aug. 4, 1985.
50   Bayardo Arce, "Arce stresses process of Sandinista reaffirmation," *Sistema Sandinista Television Network*, July 18, 1985 (Foreign Broadcasting Information Service, July 23, 1985, p.P22); "Montealegre expelled from FSLN for Somocista links," *Radio Sandino Network*, Mar. 1, 1985 (Foreign Broadcasting Information Service, Mar. 5, 1985, p. 13). See also Bayardo Arce, "Arce on FSLN 'Purges, Friendly separations,'" *Managua Radio Sandino*, July 17, 1985 (Foreign Broadcasting Information Service, July 19, 1985, p.P22).

*Chapter 3 The Party in the State and Mass Organizations*

1   *Barricada*, Jan. 8, 1985.
2   See FSLN-Secretaria Nacional de Propaganda y Educación Política, "El Sandinismo no es democratismo"; Junta de Gobierno de Reconstrucción Nacional, "Comunicado," *Barricada*, Sept. 16, 1980; FSLN-DN, *General Platform*, pp. 16–17. The 1977 Platform anticipates a "popular democratic" government under the "hegemony" of the FSLN.
3   Jaime Wheelock, "El FSLN conduce al estado y jamos lo sustituye" in FSLN-DN, *Habla la Dirección de la Vanguardia*, pp. 54–5.
4   Invernizzi et al, *Sandinistas*, pp. 38, 42. Emphasis added.
5   *Barricada*, Jan. 8, June 1, 1981; Aug. 4, 1985.
6   FSLN-DN, Nacional, "Comunicado," *Barricada*, Aug. 4, 1985; Luis Carrión, "'Oidos abiertos para recoger el sentir y la opinón del pueblo,'" "*Barricada*, July 10, 1985; "Herrera on Sandinista Assembly Reorganization," *Radio Sandino*, Aug. 15, 1985 (Foreign Broadcasting Information Service, Aug. 16, 1985, p. P18.
7   FSLN, "Programa del FSLN aprobado en 1969," pp. 184–5.
8   FSLN-DN, "72 Hours Document," p. 28.
9   Humberto Ortega, "Un solo ejército" in FSLN-DN, *Habla la Dirección de la Vanguardia*, p. 77; Stephen Gorman and Thomas Walker, "The armed forces" in Thomas Walker (ed.) *Nicaragua: The First Five Years* (New York: Praeger, 1985), p. 91.
10   FSLN-DN, "Comunicado," *Barricada*, Aug. 4, 1985.
11   CIA, *Directory of the Republic of Nicaragua: A Reference Aid* (CR 86-11702, May 1986).
12   Omar Cabezas, "En el MINT ha sido el FSLN lo que el pueblo

esperaba?" and Raul Valdivia, "A discusión tareas del futuro," *Bocay: Organo de la Dirección Política del Ministerio del Interior*, 6 (Mar. 1986), pp. 26, 21.

13  Captain Rodrigo Castillo, "El ejército: una gran escrula," *Revista Segovia: Organo de la Dirección Politica del E.P.S.*, 8 (Apr. 1986), pp. 30–2.

14  Many upper- and middle-class men have fled the country to avoid conscription.

15  These themes, especially the latter, are emphasized in *Revista Segovia*, which is apparently designed for broad distribution in the army.

16  *Barricada*, Feb. 17, 1984.

17  This section is based on four months of field work in Matagalpa in 1984 and brief follow-up visit in 1986. Research included extensive interviews with barrio and city-wide CDS leaders and barrio residents, in addition to observation of CDS meetings.

18  In the midst of a conversation about possible dialogue between the Sandinista government and the contras, a woman in a nearby barrio recalled a similar experience: "There was a man named Salomon Rio – a Somocista. When he wanted me off his land, he just knocked down our house. That's how I lost my little girl. We had to leave in the rain. How can we dialogue with those people and be traitors to the blood of our children?"

19  My reaction to Barrio Sandino, as a former member of the Peace Corps elsewhere in Latin America, was this: "The CDS is doing exactly what we were trying to do. And succeeding, where we usually failed. The reason is simple. The governments we worked with were corrupt and indifferent. This government cares."

20  Bayardo Arce, "Letter to the leaders of the Sandinista Defense Committees" in Marcus (ed.), *Nicaragua*, pp. 61–3 and *Barricada*, Feb. 17, 1984.

21  "One cannot rule with the masses," a member of the Peruvian oligarchy once told the author. "The problem is to find a way to neutralize them."

22  Carlos Núñez, *El papel de las organizaciones de masas en el proceso revolucionario* (Managua: FSLN, 1980).

23  Ibid., pp. 20–2.

24  CST, *Principios de la CST* (Managua:CST, 1985), p. 6; Gary Ruchwarger, "The Sandinista mass organizations and the revolutionary process," in Richard Harris and Carlos Vilas (eds), *Nicaragua: A Revolution Under Siege* (Totowa: Zed Books, 1985), p. 117; ATC, "Declaración de principios," *Asamblea Nacional Constitutiva* (1979), p. 54; UNAG, *La Unión Nacional de Agricultores y Ganaderos de Nicaragua = La Organización de los Productores del Campo Nicaragüense* (Managua: UNAG, 1984), p. 24, cited by Ilja Luciak, "Popular Democracy in the New Nicaragua: The Case of a Rural Mass Organization," *Comparative Politics*, 1 (Oct. 1987), p. 39; Luis Serra, "The grassroots organizations," in Walker (ed), *Nicaragua: The First Five Years*, p. 77.

25  FSLN-SDN, "Comunicado," *Barricada*, Aug. 4, 1985.

26  Inquiries at the national offices of UNAG, two regional CDS offices, and a zonal CDS office revealed that all the members of their respective

committees were Sandinista militants. Similarly, Ruchwarger found that most of the regional CDS committee and the regional CDS committee in Estelí were militants. See his "Sandinista mass organizations," p. 98.

27 For example, in 1984, Daniel Núñez, a regional agriculture ministry official, became head of UNAG. In 1985 Fernando Cardenal left Sandinista Youth to become Education Minister. Ivan Garcia, the first head of CST, subsequently became leader of the CDS network, and still later moved into a government position. Earlier it was noted that the entire zonal CDS committee in Matagalpa was recruited from the Sandinista labor movement.

28 Serra, "The grass-roots organizations," p. 79.

29 Ruchwarger, "Sandinista mass organizations," pp. 95–6.

30 Ibid., p. 96.

31 Joseph Collins, *Nicaragua. What Difference Could a Revolution Make?* 3rd edn (New York: Grove Press, 1986), pp. 81–2; Carlos Vilas, "Democracía popular y participación obrera en la Revolución Sandinista," *Estudios Sociales Centroamericanos*, 35 (1983), pp. 131–4.

32 Maxine Molyneux, "Women," in Walker (ed.), *Nicaragua: The First Five Years*, pp. 149–50.

33 Luciak, "Popular democracy," In an interview conducted some months after Luciak completed his research, a member of UNAG's national board denied that the organization favored direct representation. By then, the party's position had been incorporated into a draft constitution.

34 On the unions see Carlos Vilas, "The workers' movement in the Sandinista revolution," in Harris and Vilas, *Nicaragua*; George Black, *The Triumph of the People: The Sandinista Revolution in Nicaragua* (London: Zed, 1981), pp. 272–87; Maria Florez-Estrada and José Lobo, "La consigna es sobrevivir," *Pensamiento Propio*, 33 (May–June 1986).

35 Jimenez, "Defense can be assured only by increasing production," in Marcus (ed.), *Nicaragua*, p. 18.

36 CST, "Resolutions of the Assembly" in Marcus (ed.), *Nicaragua*, p. 346; for a similar statement from the National Directorate see Victor Tirado López,*La primera gran conquista: la toma de poder político* (Managua: CST, 1985), p. 133.

37 For Sandinista union priorities see relevant pieces in Marcus (ed.), *Nicaragua*; CST, *Funciones generales y contenido de trabajo de los sindicatos y sus juntas directivas* (Managua: CST, n.d.) and *Principios de la CST*; ATC, "Declaración de principles"; FSLN-Secretaria Nacional de Propaganda y Educación Política, "El Sandinismo no es democratismo,"; *Barricada*, Mar. 14, 1980; Vilas, "The workers' movement."

38 Henri Weber, *Nicaragua: The Sandinist Revolution* (London: Verso, 1981), pp. 107–8; James Petras, "Nicaragua in transition," *Latin American Perspectives*, 2 (Spring 1981), pp. 86–9; Americas Watch, *Human Rights in Nicaragua 1985–1986*, pp. 18–25 and *Human Rights in Nicaragua* (New York: Americas Watch, 1984), p. 24; Amnesty International, *Nicaragua: The Human Rights Record* (New York, 1986), p. 12; The International League for Human Rights, *Report on Human Rights in Nicaragua* (New York, 1986), pp. 103–21.

39 FSLN-Secretaria Nacional de Propaganda y Educación Politica, "El Sandinismo no es democratismo."

40 Luciak, "Popular democracy" and interviews with UNAG national board member. On rural politics see chapter 4.

41 See Serra, "The grassroots organizations," p. 78 and Ruchwarger, "Sandinista mass organizations," p. 114.

42 The most complete account to date is Gary Ruchwager, *People in Power: Forging Grassroots Democracy in Nicaragua* (S. Hadley, MA: Bergin and Gerney, 1987), published after this book went into production.

*Chapter 4 Peasants: Sandinista Agrarian Policy*

1 From 1950 until 1977, GDP was growing at about 6 percent per year. See Rudolph (ed.), *Nicaragua*, p. 234. For data on nutrition see Inter-American Development Bank, *Economic and Social Progress in Latin America: 1978 Report* (Washington, DC: IDB, 1979), pp. 135–41 and Collins, *Nicaragua: What Difference Could a Revolution Make?*, p. 270.

2 On agro-export development in Nicaragua see Jaime Wheelock, *Nicaragua: imperialismo y dictadura* (Havana: Ed. de Ciencias Sociales, 1980); Orlando Núñez, *El Somocismo y el modelo capitalista agro-exportador* (Managua: Universidad Nacional Autonoma de Nicaragua, n.d.); Robert Williams, *Export Agriculture and the Crisis in Central America* (Chapel Hill: University of North Carolina Press, 1986); Jaime Biderman, "Class structure, the state and capitalist development in Nicaraguan agriculture" (Unpublished Ph.D. thesis, University of California, Berkeley, 1982); Peter Dorner and Rodolfo Quiros, "Institutional dualism in Central America's agricultural development" *Journal of Latin American Studies*, 5 (1973), pp. 220–32.

3 Williams, *Export Agriculture*, pp. 106, 110; Wheelock, *Nicaragua: imperialismo*, pp. 163–75.

4 The notable exceptions to this generalization are the small and medium producers of coffee and the large rice producers. The former make a significant contribution to total production; the latter, who have received substantial government aid, dominate the domestic rice market.

5 Collins, *Nicaragua*, pp. 274–5; and Biderman, "Nicaraguan agriculture," p. 174.

6 The land- tenure data presented in table 4.1 do not take into account the quality of land or use to which it is put. A well-cultivated 200-acre coffee plantation could be the basis for a considerable personal fortune. A cattle ranch of similar size (but probably lower land quality) might provide a modest living for a peasant family. To make the table easier for readers, data have been converted to acres and rounded off; categories appear to overlap by 1 acre. These procedures are not inconsistent with the rough estimates on which the table is based.

7 David Browning, *El Salvador: Landscape and Society* (Oxford: Oxford University Press, 1971), pp. 237–8; Dorner and Quiros, "Institutional dualism."

8 Maxine Molyneux, "Women," in Thomas Walker (ed.), *Nicaragua: The*

*First Five Years*, p. 154; Williams, *Export Agriculture*, p. 71.

9   Collins, *Nicaragua*, p. 107.

10   Wheelock, *Imperialismo*, p. 77.

11   Booth, *The End and the Beginning*, pp. 62, 177–21; Williams, *Export Agriculture*, pp. 129–34.

12   Sergio Ramírez (ed.), *El pensamiento vivo de Sandino* (San José: Ed. Universitaria Centroamericana, 1974), p. 254; Jorge Eduardo Arellano, *Lecciones de Sandino* (Managua: Ed. Distribudora Cultural, 1983), p. 75; and Macaulay, *The Sandino Affair*, pp. 248, 254.

13   Karl Marx, *The Eighteenth Brumaire of Louis Bonaparte* (New York: International Publishers, 1969), p. 128, see also pp. 123–31. The phrase "idiocy of rural life" is taken from the *Communist Manifesto*, published during the same era.

14   Carmen Diana Deere, "Agrarian reform, peasant participation, and the organization of production in the transition to socialism," in Richard Fagen, C. D. Deere, and José Luis Coraggio (eds), *Transition and Development: Problems of Third World Socialism* (New York: Monthly Review, 1986).

15   Deere, in a letter to the author, questions this characterization of Marx's attitude toward the worker–peasant alliance. Not an "afterthought," she insists, but something that "grew out of the confrontation of theory with reality." True, but the notion was never well assimilated to Marx's theory.

16   Wheelock, *Imperialismo*; and O. Núñez, *El modelo capitalista agro-exportador*.

17   Junta de Gobierno de Reconstrucción Nacional, "Programa de la Junta de Gobierno de Reconstrucción Nacional de Nicaragua," *Comercio Exterior* (Mexico), 29 (August 1979), p. 898.

18   On the reasoning behind this early decision see Joseph Thome and David Kaimowitz, "Nicaragua's agrarian reform: the first year (1979–1980)," in Walker, *Nicaragua: The First Five Years*, pp. 4–5; Carmen Diana Deere et al., "The peasantry and the development of Sandinista agrarian policy, 1979–1984," pp. 77–80; Collins, *Nicaragua*, pp. 59–63.

19   *Barricada*, Sept. 14, 1979.

20   Salvador Mayorga, quoted in *Barricada*, Feb. 12, 1980.

21   Carlos Pineiro, "Jaime Wheelock interviewed," *Bohemia* (Havana), Oct. 19, 1979 (Joint Publications Research Service 74650, p. 106).

22   FSLN-DN, *General Platform*, p. 19.

23   Collins, *Nicaragua*, p. 80.

24   Valerie Miller, "The Nicaraguan literacy crusade," in Thomas Walker (ed.), *Nicaragua in Revolution* (New York: Praeger, 1982), p. 245. For a Sandinista guerrilla's experience of rural life, see Cabezas, *Fire from the Mountain*. For crop statistics, see FAO, *Production Yearbook* vols 31, 37 (Rome: FAO, 1978–4).

25   Collins, *Nicaragua*, pp. 31, 39.

26   Thome and Kaimowitz, "Agrarian reform," p. 300; David Kaimowitz and Joseph Thome, "Nicaragua's agrarian reform: the first year (1979–1980)," in Walker, *Nicaragua in Revolution*, pp. 228–9.

27  *Barricada*, Mar. 6, 1980.
28  Collins, *Nicaragua*, p. 81.
29  *Barricada*, Feb. 26, 1980.
30  *Barricada*, July 20, July 24, Aug. 3, 1980.
31  Deere et al., "The peasantry," pp. 83–4; Collins, *Nicaragua*, pp. 87–8.
32  The ministry is officially the Ministry of Agricultural–Livestock Development and Agrarian reform (MIDINRA).
33  Deere et al., "The peasantry," pp. 83, 85; Forrest Colburn, *Post-Revolutionary Nicaragua: State Class and the Dilemmas of Agrarian Policy* (Berkeley: University of California Press, 1986), pp. 87–8.
34  Colburn, *Post-Revolutionary Nicaragua*, p. 90.
35  Collins, *Nicaragua*, pp. 51–8.
36  *Barricada*, July 20, 1981.
37  Collins, *Nicaragua*, pp. 48–50; David Kaimowitz and David Stanfield, "The organization of production units in the Nicaraguan agrarian reform," paper presented at International Studies Association Meetings (Mar. 1985), p. 11.
38  Junta de Gobierno de Reconstrucción Nacional, "Decreto No. 782," July 19, 1981; "Comentarios y aclaraciones a las partes importantes de la ley," *Consejo de Estado*, No. 2 (1981), pp. 25–9; Deere et al., "The peasantry," pp. 91–3.
39  This figure refers to the aggregate holdings of nuclear families.
40  "Comentarios, " *Consejo de Estado*, p. 28.
41  *Lunes socio-económico de Barricada* (Managua: Barrricada and CIERA, 1984, p. 227.
42  Collins, *Nicaragua*, p. 187; and *Lunes socio-económico*, pp. 77–83.
43  Ilja A. Luciak, "National Unity and Popular Hegemony: the Dialectics of Sandinista Agrarian Reform Policies, 1979–1986," *Journal of Latin American Studies*, 1 (May 1987). Calculated from tables 2 and 3. These figures refer to 404,187 manzanas titled to individuals and cooperatives, excluding the legalization of squatter claims under the special titling program and the recognition of land rights extended to indigenous communities.
44  Jaime Wheelock, "Primer Congreso Nacional Campesino. Balance y perspectivas de la reforma agraria," *Informaciones Agropecuarias* (MIDINRA) Documento Especial, Apr. 26, 1986.
45  Luciak, "Sandinista agrarian reform"; "The Nicaraguan peasantry gives new direction to agrarian reform," "*Envio*, 4: 51 (Sept. 1985), pp. 1c–19c; Collins, *Nicaragua*; Deere el al., "The peasantry,"
46  There is no definitive set of Nicaraguan grain-production statistics. Statistics issued by different government departments vary significantly. A series produced by the private-sector farmers' organization UPANIC, a COSEP affiliate, agrees with some government estimates, but not others. Some published series do not reflect a significant decline in per capita production; they are so at variance with the daily preoccupations of most Nicaraguans as to be simply unbelievable. The series in table 4.2 is an average of four sets of statistics, three from government agencies

and one from UPANIC, which were included in Colburn, "Nicaragua's agrarian reform." It probably underestimates the drop in production.

47  Informal evidence suggests that there may have been a postinsurrection baby boom, but population growth for revolutionary Nicaragua must be estimated from available data on the growth rates of the early seventies. The figure given here is based on the assumption that the 3.4 annual rate of increase recorded in that period continued into the 1980s. See United Nations, *1978 Statistical Yearbook* (New York, 1979), p. 70.

48  *Lunes socio-económico*, p. 158.

49  Michael Zalkin, "Agrarian policies and the marketing of corn and beans in Nicaragua, 1979–1984," paper delivered at the 1985 meetings of the Latin American Studies Association; Zalkin, "Peasant response to state grain policy in revolutionary Nicaragua," paper at the 1986 meetings of the Latin American Studies Association; Collins, *Nicaragua*, pp. 193–240.

50  This was explicitly suggested by Wheelock in FSLN-DN, *La Dirección National en el Primer Encuentro International de Solidaridad con Nicaragua* (Managua: FSLN, 1981), p. 70.

51  Collins, *Nicaragua*, pp. 39–51, 167–74; Colburn, *Post-Revolutionary Nicaragua*, pp. 45–85; author's interviews.

52  David Kaimowitz, "Nicaraguan debates on agrarian structure and their implications for agricultural policy and the rural poor," *Journal of Peasant Studies*, 14 (Oct. 1986), p. 111; and Collins, *Nicaragua*, pp. 64–7, 248.

53  *New York Times*, Mar. 19 and 24, Apr.23, 1985; *Washington Post*, Nov. 27, 1985; *Miami Herald*, Jan. 27, 1985.

54  Luciak, "Popular Democracy in the New Nicaragua"; "Entrevista con el Comandante Jaime Wheelock," *Barricada*, Jan. 13, 1987.

55  Collins, *Nicaragua*, p. 151.

56  *El Nuevo Diario*, July 19, 1983.

57  "Nicaraguan peasantry gives new direction"; Colburn, *Post-Revolutionary Nicaragua*, pp. 95–120; *Barricada Internacional*, Jan. 30, 1986; *Miami Herald*, Sept. 16, 1984, Jan. 27, 1985.

58  An agriculture ministry report on cooperatives in the León–Chindega region notes weak presence of the party and UNAG "in the cooperatives and the countryside in general." MIDINRA, *Evaluación–Investigación del Modelo "CAS" de Reforma Agraria*, Dec. 1985 (typescript). See also, *Barricada*, Sept. 16, 1983.

59  Luis Serra, "The grassroots organizations," in Walker, *Nicaragua: The First Five Years*, pp. 66–7.

60  Daniel Núñez, "Reforma agraria en Nicaragua: talar los grandes arboles (Entrevista a Daniel Núñez)," *Pensamiento Propio*, 30 (Jan.–Feb. 1986), pp. 31–3.

61  Jaime Wheelock, *Entre la crisis y la agressión: la reforma agraria sandinista* (Managua: MIDINRA, 1984), p. 25.

62  Luciak, "Sandinista agrarian reform"; Kaimowitz and Stanfield, "Organization . . . of agrarian reform," p. 32.

63  UNAG National Executive Committee, *Main Report: National Farmers'*

*and Cattleraisers' Union (UNAG), Fifth Anniversary, First National Congress* (Managua, Apr. 18, 1986).

64 D. Núñez, "Reforma agraria," p. 32.

65 Eduardo Baumeister and Oscar Neira, "Economía y politica en las relaciones entre el estado y el sector privado en el proceso nicaragüense," Paper prepared for Seminar on "Los Problemas de la Transición en Pequeñas Economías Perifericas," Managua Sept. 3–8, 1984; *Lunes socio-económico*, pp. 60–71, 84–9.

66 D. Núñez, "Reforma agraria," p. 33.

67 Luciak, "Popular democracy"; UNAG National Executive Council, *Main Report*; author's interviews.

68 On developments in Masaya see "Nicaraguan peasantry gives new direction"; Luciak, "Sandinista agrarian reform"; Collins, *Nicaragua*, pp. 241–6.

69 "Nicaraguan peasantry gives new direction," p. 9c.

70 Luciak, "Sandinista agrarian reform," calculated from table 3. These figures refer to land distributed to cooperatives and individuals.

71 Collins, *Nicaragua*, p. 246.

72 On the 1986 law and its political context, see Luciak, "Sandinista agrarian reform"; "Agrarian reform undergoes changes in Nicaragua," *Update*, 5 (Feb. 7, 1986); *Barricada*, Jan. 13, 1986.

73 Wheelock, "Primer Congreso Nacional Campesino."

74 *Barricada*, Apr. 26, 1986.

75 Wheelock, "Primer Congreso Nacional Compesino," p.8.

76 "Nicaragua: Factores políticos condicionan reforma agraria," *Infopress Centroamericana*, Apr. 9, 1987.

77 Collins, *Nicaragua*; "Slow motion toward a survival economy," *Envio*, 63 (Sept. 1986), pp. 20–1; Zalkin, "Peasant Response," pp. 3–4; Luciak, "Popular democracy."

78 *Latin America Weekly Report*, May 21 and June 25, 1987.

79 "Reforming the agrarian reform," *Nicaragua Through Our Eyes*, 1:4, pp. 11–12.

80 Luciak, "Sandinista agrarian reform," table 2; "Agrarian reform undergoes changes," p. 4.

81 *Barricada Internacional*, Aug. 1986; "Porque reforma agraria," *Pensamiento Propio*, 30 (Jan.–Feb. 1986), p. 34.

*Chapter 5 The Bourgeoisie and the Revolution*

1 Invernizzi et al., *Sandinistas*, p. 180.

2 This conceptualization of the private sector ignores foreign holdings that were, in fact, relatively insignificant in the Nicaraguan economy. On American holdings, see Jorge Castañeda, *Contradicciones en la revolución* (Mexico: Extra, 1980), pp. 20–4.

3 Wheelock, *Imperialismo*, pp. 163–76; and Black, *The Triumph of the People*, p. 34.

4 Booth, *The End and the Beginning*, p. 98.

5   Diederich, *Somoza*, p.33.
6   Ibid., p. 58.
7   Arias, *Nicaragua*, p. 21.
8   Enrique Bolaños, "Discurso ... clausurando la Asamblea Anual de INDE ... el 13 de marzo de 1986" (Managua: COSEP, 1986; xerox typescript); Booth, *The End and the Beginning*, pp. 81, 102–3. For simplicity, organizational history has been collapsed here. COSEP (reorganized 1978) was originally COSIP (founded 1972) and grew out of INDE (founded 1963), which remains a member organization of COSEP. Both the INDE and COSEP statutes, according to Bolaños's speech, contained the phrases quoted here.
9   See, for example, Fonseca, "Hora zero," pp. 93–4 and H. Ortega, "La estrategia de la victoria" in Carmona (ed.), *Nicaragua, passim.*
10  FSLN-DN, *General Platform*, pp. 16, 6.
11  Junta de Gobierno de Reconstrucción Nacional, "Programa," pp. 893–901.
12  Chamorro's remarks at Cornell University, Apr. 16, 1987.
13  FSLN-DN, "72 hours document," p. 7.
14  FSLN-DN, "Documentos de unificación," p. 108.
15  FSLN-DN, "72 hours document," pp. 18,11.
16  FSLN-DN, *General Platform*.
17  "Interview with Daniel Ortega," p. 117.
18  Stephen Gorman, "Power and consolidation in the Nicaraguan revolution," *Journal of Latin American Studies*, 13 (1981), pp. 133–49.
19  These concerns surface repeatedly in speeches and party documents. For example, FSLN-DN, "72 hours document", pp. 25–6; Wheelock's remarks in *Barricada*, Feb. 26, 1980.
20  John Nichols, "The news media in the Sandinista revolution" in Walker (ed.), *Nicaragua in Revolution*; Black, *The Triumph of the People*, pp. 343–5.
21  Tirado, *La Revolución sandinista*, pp. 85–9.
22  The document refers specifically to the FSLN-DN's August 1980 "Pronunciamiento sobre las elecciones," quoted in chapter 1.
23  COSEP, *Análisis sobre la ejecución del Programa de Gobierno de Reconstrucción Nacional* (Managua, 1980).
24  The fullest account of the Salazar conspiracy is in Christian, *Nicaragua: Revolution in the Family*, pp. 170–85.
25  *El Nuevo Diario*, Nov. 13, 1980.
26  *Barricada*, July 30, 1981.
27  Collins, *Nicaragua: What Difference Could a Revolution Make?*, p. 44.
28  Richard Sholk, "The national bourgeoisie in post-revolutionary Nicaragua," *Comparative Politics*, 16 (Apr. 1984), p. 260.
29  Ibid., p. 262; Colburn, *Post-Revolutionary Nicaragua, pp. 56–9;* Anthony Wilson, "Nicaragua's private sector and the Sandinista revolution," *Studies in Political Economy*, 17 (Summer 1985), pp. 94–7; author's interviews. Evidence comes from farmers, private sector organizations, and government officials.
30  *Barricada*, July 30, 1981.
31  *El Nuevo Diario*, June 13, 1981; see also Collins, *What Difference*, p. 42.
32  Borge et al., *Sandinistas Speak*, p. 134.

33   H. Ortega, *Discurso*, p. 8.

34   "FSLN confirma dialogo," *La Prensa*, Oct. 17, 1981.

35   *Barricada*, Oct. 22, 1981.

36   Wheelock, *El gran desafio*, p. 35. Emphasis added.

37   *Barricada*, Feb. 1, 1982.

38   *New York Times*, June 19, 1983; on political use of expropriation, see Wheelock, *El gran desafio*, p. 35.

39   Arce, *Discurso secreto*, p. 4. Emphasis added.

40   FSLN-DN, "Pronunciamiento del FSLN sobre las elecciones," p. 20.

41   Daniel Ortega, *Texto integro del discurso pronunciado . . . en ocasión del cuarto aniversario*, July 19, 1983 (Managua: Casa de Gobierno, 1983), p. 11. The notion of the "irreversibility" of the revolution appeared regularly in Sandinista texts before and after the 1984 elections. See, for example, H. Ortega, *Discurso*, pp. 15–16 and Victor Tirado, *La primera gran conquista* (1985), p. 124.

42   *New York Times*, November 16, 1983; Arce, *Discurso secreto*.

43   This conclusion is based on interviews with Coordinator leaders. See also *New York Times*, Nov. 16, 1983; Robert J. McCartney, "Sandinista foes always intended to boycott vote," *Washington Post*, July 30, 1984; Enrique Bolaños, *Linea directa: entrevista radial* (Managua: n.p., 1984).

44   *La Prensa*, Dec. 28, 1983.

45   *La Prensa*, July 24, Aug. 24, 1983; *Financial Times*, Aug. 1, 1984.

46   *Los Angeles Times*, Oct. 9, 1984; *Washington Post*, Oct. 1, 3, 4, 1984; *Miami Herald*, Oct. 3, 1984; author's interviews.

47   Names have been changed and minor details altered to disguise the identity of these families.

48   The implications of the 1986 Agrarian Reform Act are, of course, double-edged for the bourgeoisie since the act clearly threatens large landowners in some areas, but more generally the law strengthens the mixed economy.

49   "Nicaragua: Continued Decline in 1987," *Latin America Economic Report*, Dec. 31, 1986.

*Chapter 6 Christians: The Church and the Revolution*

1   Margaret Randall, *Christians in the Nicaraguan Revolution* (Vancouver: New Star Books, 1983), pp. 174–5.

2   "Contribution to Hegel's *Philosophy of Right*" in Robert C. Tucker (ed.), *The Marx–Engels Reader*, 2nd edn (New York: Norton, 1978), p. 54.

3   See, for example, Marx's "On the Jewish question" and "Theses on Feuerbach" in Tucker (ed.), *The Marx–Engels Reader* and similar collections, and "The fetishism of commodities," *Capital* (I, 1, 4).

4   V. I. Lenin, "Socialism and religion," in *Collected Works* (Moscow: Progress Publishers, 1966), vol. 10, p. 83.

5   V. I. Lenin, "The attitude of the Workers' Party to religion," *Collected Works*, vol. 15, p. 402.

6　Ibid., p. 409.

7　Borge, "Discusses His Life"; and Alegría and Flakoll, *Nicaragua: la revolución sandinista*, p. 138.

8　Friedrich Engels, *Herr Eugen Dühring's Revolution in Science (Anti-Dühring)*. (New York: International Publishers, 1939), pp. 344–6. Emphasis added.

9　N. I. Bukharin and E. Preobrazhensky, *The ABC of Communism: A Popular Explanation of the Program of the Communist Party of Russia* (Ann Arbor: University of Michigan Press, 1966), pp. 247–57. Humberto Belli, a former party member, recalls this book in widespread use by Sandinista study circles in the late 1960s. During the same period, Omar Cabezas led study groups, using Marta Harnecker's *Los conceptos elementales del materialismo histórico* (numerous editions), a work similar in theory to Engels and Bukharin, but devoid of political advice on religion. See Humberto Belli, *Breaking Faith: The Sandinista Revolution and its Impact on Freedom and Christian Faith in Nicaragua* (Westchester, IL: Cross Way Books, 1985), p. 9; and Cabezas, *Fire from the Mountain, p. 19*.

10　Fonseca, *Obras*, vol. 1, p. 69; Morales Aviles, *Obras*, pp. 89, 121–2; Giulio Girardi, *Sandinismo, Marxismo, Cristianismo en la nueva Nicaragua* (Mexico: Ed. Nuevomar, 1986), pp. 263–7.

11　Fonseca, *Obras*, vol. 1, p. 69.

12　Morales Aviles, *Obras*, p. 161.

13　There have been notable exceptions to this general pattern, such as the colonial bishop Antonio Valdivieso, who lost his life defending Indian rights, and Bishop Octavio Calderón y Padilla of Matagalpa who – unlike his fellow bishops – consistently refused to have anything to do with the Somozas, going so far as to boycott the old man's funeral in 1956.

14　On the pre-1970 history of the Nicaraguan church see J. E. Arellano, "Nicaragua," in E. Dussel et al. (eds.), *Historia general de la Iglesia en América Latina*, vol. 6 (Salamanca: Ed. Sigueme, 1985); and Phillip Williams, "The Catholic hierarchy in the Nicaraguan revolution," *Journal of Latin American Studies*, 17 (1985), pp. 341–69.

15　Arellano, "Nicaragua," pp. 409–10.

16　From a joint pastoral letter of the Central American bishops. See Arellano, "Nicaragua," p. 496.

17　Ibid., p. 352.

18　Williams, "Catholic hierarchy," p. 352.

19　On Liberation theology and related changes in the Latin American church see Robert McAfee Brown, *Theology in a New Key; Responding to Liberation Themes* (Philadelphia: Westminster, 1978); Edward Cleary, *Crisis and Change: The Church in Latin America Today* (Maryknoll, NY: Orbis Books, 1985); Phillip Berryman, *Liberation Theology* (New York: Pantheon, 1987); and Michael Dodson and Laura O'Shaughnessy, *The Other Revolution: The Church and Popular Struggle in Nicaragua* (forthcoming); Girardi, *Sandinismo*.

20　Gustavo Gutiérrez, *A Theology of Liberation* (Maryknoll, NY: Orbis, 1971), p. 295; cited in Cleary, *Crisis and Change*, p. 89.

21 On Christian base communities see Phillip Berryman, "Basic Christian Communities and the future of Latin America," *Monthly Review*, 36 (July/Aug. 1984), pp. 27–40; and Cleary, *Crisis and Change.*

22 On these years see also Arellano, "Nicaragua"; Phillip Berryman, *The Religious Roots of Rebellion: Christians in the Central American Revolutions* (Maryknoll, NY: Orbis, 1984); Randall, *Christians*; and Michael Dodson and T. S. Montgomery, "The churches in the Nicaraguan revolution" in Walker (ed.), *Nicaragua in Revolution.*

23 Williams, "Catholic hierarchy." p. 350.

24 Kate Pravera, "The base Christian community of San Pablo: an oral history of Nicaragua's first CEB," *Brethren Life and Thought*, 29 (Autumn 1984), pp. 206–15.

25 Sandy Darlington, "The Bible, the Frente and the Revolution," *Christianity and Crisis*, 45 (July 22, 1985), pp. 299–302.

26 Randall, *Christians*, pp. 127–8.

27 Ibid., p. 166.

28 Williams, "The Catholic hierarchy"; Laura O'Shaughnessy, "The conflicts of class and world view: theology in post-revolutionary Nicaragua" paper delivered at the Annual Meeting of the Southeastern Council of Latin American Studies, San Juan, Puerto Rico, April 1983; Dodson and Montgomery, "The churches in the Nicaraguan revolution."

29 *Fe Cristiana y Revolución Sandinista en Nicaragua* (Managua: Instituto Histórico Centroamericano, 1980), p.94.

30 Williams, "Catholic hierarchy," p. 361.

31 Dodson and Montgomery, "The churches in the Nicaraguan revolution," p. 161.

32 "Popular church" was a term occasionally used by those to whom it referred (see, for example, references in *Fe Cristiana*). But once Catholic conservatives began to use it in attacks on what they saw as a breakaway tendency in the church, revolutionary Catholics abandoned it in favor of "church of the poor" – stressing, at the same time, that they were not separate from the Catholic church.

33 This attitude is evident in two documents from late 1979: FSLN-DN, "72 hours document", p. 21; and *Fe Cristiana, passim.*

34 Conferencia Episcopal de Nicaragua, "Mensaje de la Conferencia Episcopal al pueblo Católico y a todos los Nicaragüenses" (Managua, July 31, 1979; mimeo).

35 Conferencia Episcopal de Nicaragua, "Carta pastoral del episcopado nicaragüense [Nov. 17, 1980]," *Cuadernos DEI*, 2 (n.d.), pp. 15–31. Emphasis added.

36 *La Prensa*, Sept. 16, 1980.

37 Belli, *Breaking Faith*, p. 184.

38 FSLN-DN, "Communicado Oficial de la Dirección Nacional del FSLN sobre la religión" *Barricada*, Oct. 7, 1980. Emphasis added.

39 Cuban attitudes in this area may be shifting under the influence of the Nicaraguan revolution.

40   Conferencia Episcopal de Nicaragua, "A la Dirección Nacional del Frente Sandinista" (Managua, Oct. 17, 1980; mimeo).
41   "Teaching authority of the Church (Magisterium)," *New Catholic Encyclopedia*, vol. 13 (New York: McGraw-Hill, 1967), pp. 959–65.
42   *La Prensa*, Dec. 6–9, 11, 14, 16, 1981 and Jan. 6, 1982; *Barricada*, Dec. 9, 1981; *El Nuevo Diario*, Dec. 10, 1981 and Jan. 4–5, 1982.
43   "La Iglesia Católica en Nicaragua despues de la revolución," *Envio: Informes* (Dec. 1983), p. 11b; Christian, *Nicaragua: Revolution in the Family*, p. 204; *La Prensa*, Nov. 4, 28, Dec. 11, 28, 1982.
44   This attitude is illustrated by a publication of the archdiocese from the 1980s: Comisión Catequística Arquidiocesana, *Principles dificultades en la lectura de la Biblia (punto de vista católico)* (Managua: Archdiocese of Managua, n.d.).
45   Belli, *Breaking Faith*, p. 234.
46   "La Iglesia Católica en Nicaragua," p. 15b.
47   Stephen Kinzer, "Nicaragua's combative archbishop," *New York Times Magazine*, Nov. 18, 1984, p. 90. On Obando see also Andrew Reding, "Getting to know Managua's new Cardinal," *Christianity and Crisis*, July 22, 1985; "La Iglesia Católica en Nicaragua"; and Ana Maria Ezcurra, *Ideological Aggression Against the Sandinista Revolution: The Political Opposition Church in Nicaragua* (New York: Circus Publications, 1984).
48   Patty Edmonds, "Obando talk with U.S. Executive told in memo," *National Catholic Reporter*, July 20, 1984; Ezcurra, *Ideological Aggression* pp. 43–50, 70–5.
49   "La Iglesia Católica en Nicaragua," pp. 17b–18; Belli, *Breaking Faith*, p. 207. The importance of this issue to the church was emphasized by the Pope, who devoted one of two homilies during his March 1983 visit to thinly veiled criticism of Sandinista education policies.
50   "Church and politics: internal upheaval and state confrontation in Nicaragua," *Update*, 5. Central American Historical Institute (Jan. 21, 1986); *Los Angeles Times*, Jan. 17, 1983 and May 21, 1986.
51   "La participación de sacerdotes en cargos de gobierno: cronologia de hechos," *Centro Regional de Informaciones Económicas*, 76–7 (July 1981); and *Los Angeles Times*, Jan 17, 1983 and May 21, 1986. One priest was finally forced to renounce his priesthood. Another was expelled from the Jesuit order, but remains a priest.
52   Christian, *Nicaragua*, p. 234.
53   On these events see "La Iglesia Católica en Nicaragua"; Christian, *Nicaragua*, pp. 228–9; *Miami Herald*, Aug. 19, 1982; *New York Times*, Aug. 18, 21, 1982; and *La Prensa*, *El Nuevo Diario*, and *Barricada*, July 21 to Aug. 20, 1982.
54   "La Iglesia Católica en Nicaragua," p. 15b.
55   Complete text also published in *La Nación Internacional* (San José), Aug. 12–18, 1982. For English excerpts see *New York Times*, Aug. 21, 1982.
56   Aug. 13, 1982.

57 A priest with close government connections reports that Borge did not deny the involvement of his ministry, but claimed he did not know exactly who was responsible.

58 FSLN-DN, "Comunicado," *Barricada*, Aug. 19, 1982.

59 FSLN-DN, "Second Official Communiqué on Religion" in Ezcurra, *Ideological Aggression*; Christian, *Nicaragua*, pp. 228–9.

60 On the Pope's visit see *El Papa en Nicaragua: Análisis de su vista* (Madrid: IEPLA, 1983; Conor Cruise O'Brien, "God and Man in Nicaragua," *Atlantic Monthly* (Aug. 1986); *New York Times*, Mar. 5, 1983; *Washington Post*, Mar. 5, 1983; and June Erlick, "If Reagan backs off Cardinal will leave post," *National Catholic Reporter*, Mar. 2, 1984.

61 The Spanish text of the homily is in *El Papa en Nicaragua*; English in Belli, *Nicaragua: Christians under Fire* (San José: Instituto Puebla, n.d.).

62 "La Iglesia Católica en Nicaragua," p. 20b.

63 Belli, *Breaking Faith*, p. 234; FSLN-DN, *Proclama de la Dirección Nacional del FSLN de noviembre de 1986* (Managua: FSLN, 1986), p. 31; Betsy Cohen and Patricia Hynds, "The manipulation of the religion issue," in Walker (ed.), *Reagan versus the Sandinistas, p. 101*.

64 Conferencia Episcopal de Nicaragua, "Carta pastoral del Episcopado Nicaragüense sobre la reconciliación," Managua, Apr. 22, 1984.

65 *Barricada*, Apr. 24, 1984; *Washington Post*, May 22, 1984.

66 O'Brien, "God and Man in Nicaragua," p. 50; Reding, "Getting to know Managua's new Cardinal," p. 310; "Church and politics," p. 6.

67 Quoted in "The church of the poor in Nicaragua," *Envio*, 5 (Apr. 1985), p. 17.

68 *National Catholic Reporter*, July 18, 1986; *Los Angeles Times*, July 5, 1984.

69 "The church of the poor in Nicaragua," p. 15.

70 O'Brien, "God and Man in Nicaragua," p. 53; *Washington Post*, Nov. 14, 1983; *Miami Herald*, Nov. 13, 1983; interviews.

71 Miguel D'Escoto, "Palabras del Padre D'Escoto al finalizar el Viacrucis," *Amanecer*, 40–2 (Jan.–May), p. 31; see also "The church of the poor in Nicaragua," pp. 25–8 and O'Brien, "God and Man in Nicaragua," pp. 62–6.

72 On the spectrum of attitudes toward religion within the FSLN see especially César Jerez, *The Church and the Nicaraguan Revolution*, Justice Papers No. 5 (London: Catholic Institute for International Relations, 1984), pp. 15–17; also, "Nicaragua en la encrucijada," *Envio*, Monogra pk 9 (June 1983), pp. 30–1; and Francois Houtart's observations in *El papa en Nicaragua*, p. 83. For the attitudes of individual Sandinista leaders, see Randall, *Christians* and Teofilo Cabestrero, *Revolucionarios por el Evangelio: Testimonio de 15 Cristianos en el Gobierno Revolucionario de Nicaragua* (Bilbao: Ed. Descleede Brouwer, 1983).

73 "Nicaragua en la encrucijada," pp. 30–1.

74 Randall, *Christians*; Cabestrero, *Revolucionarios*; FSLN-SDN, "Comunicado," *Barrricada*, Aug. 4, 1985; CIA, *Directory of the Republic of Nicaragua*.

75 *Fe Cristiana*, pp. 356–7.

76 See Borge, *Christianity and Revolution*.

77   Wheelock, "The Sandinista Front is the organization of the working people," in Marcus (ed.), *Nicaragua*, pp. 286–7.
78   H. Ortega, *Discurso*, p. 24; see also scattered remarks on religion in his *Cincuenta años*, pp. 31, 70, 103.
79   FSLN-DN, *General Platform*; "72 hours document"; "Documentos de unificacion," in Pineda (ed.), *La revolución nicaragüense.*
80   St Paul quoted by John Paul II, in his 1982 "Carta del Papa a los Obispos de Nicaragua"; FSLN-DN, "72 hours document," p. 31.
81   *Christian Science Monitor*, July 7, 1986; see also *Washington Post*, Nov. 29, 1986.

*Chapter 7 Yankees and Sandinistas*

1   The same label was applied to the first Somoza, before the dictatorship became a dynasty.
2   Karl Bermann,*Under the Big Stick: Nicaragua and the United States Since 1848* (Boston: South End Press, 1986), pp. 65, 70.
3   Ibid., p. 158.
4   Booth, *The End and the Beginning*, p. 40.
5   On this period see Macaulay, *The Sandino Affair.*
6   Diederich, *Somoza*, p. 13.
7   Ramírez (ed.), *Augusto C. Sandino: El pensamiento vivo*, vol. 1, p. 111. Emphasis in original. See also pp. 94–110 for Sandino's account of this period.
8   The Tipitapa Pact is known in Nicaragua as the Espino Negro Pact, for the blackthorn tree under which Moncada and Stimson negotiated at Tipitapa. For Sandinista interpretations of its significance, see Fonseca, *Obras*, vol. 2, pp. 46–7; Introduction to Ramírez *Augusto C. Sandino*, vol. 1, especially p. 42; H. Ortega, *Cincuenta años, pp. 20–4; FSLN-DN, pp. 3–5.*
9   There are other nationalist heroes recognized by Sandinista historians, such as Benjamin Zeledon, a Liberal general who died resisting the US intervention of 1912. But Sandino was apparently the only one who made a difference.
10   Ramírez, *Augusto C. Sandino*, vol. 1, p. 97.
11   FSLN-DN, *General Platform*, p. 16.
12   On Sandino's tactics see Macaulay, *The Sandino Affair.*
13   Ibid., pp. 84, 225.
14   Diederich, *Somoza* and Richard Millett, *Guardians of the Dynasty* (Maryknoll, NY, 1977) are the best political accounts of the dynasty.
15   For example, Fonseca, *Obras*, vol. 1, pp. 81–2 and Ramírez, *Augusto C. Sandino*, vol. 1, p. 62.
16   Millett, *Guardians of the Dynasty*, pp. 145–68; Bermann, *Under the Big Stick*, p. 222.
17   Millett, *Guardians of the Dynasty*, p. 182.
18   Ibid., p. 184.
19   Sometimes a Somoza held the dual titles of President of Nicaragua and *Jefe Director* of the Guard. After the sons grew to adulthood, there was

often one Somoza in each post. In 1974, Anastasio Somoza Debayle puffed up his title to *Jefe Supremo*, which he described as a civilian position, so that he could satisfy a constitutional requirement and run for the presidency as a civilian, without relinquishing control of the Guard's daily affairs. See Millett, *Guardians of the Dynasty*, p. 240.

20  Ibid., pp. 251–2, 198, 239–40, 254; and Diederich, *Somoza*, pp. 34, 79, 86–7, 117–18, 124–6.

21  Bermann, *Under the Big Stick*, p. 242.

22  Millett, *Guardians of the Dynasty*, p. 230; Bermann, *Under the Big Stick*, p. 242.

23  Diederich, *Somoza*, pp. 88–95, 105, 115–16; Millett, *Guardians of the Dynasty*, pp. 235–7; Bermann, *Under the Big Stick*, pp. 254–5.

24  Millett, *Guardians of the Dynasty*, pp. 203–13; Bermann, *Under the Big Stick*, pp. 234–7; Diederich, *Somoza*, pp. 27–30.

25  Bermann, *Under the Big Stick*, pp. 240–1, 246; and Diederich, *Somoza*, pp. 45, 64–7, 255.

26  Bermann, *Under the Big Stick*, p. 240.

27  Carmona (ed.), *Nicaragua*, pp. 34–5, 243.

28  Booth, *The End and the Beginning*, p. 129. Formally, Somoza declined further military aid, rather than submit to an evaluation of Nicaragua's human rights performance as a condition of aid.

29  William LeoGrande, "The United States and the Nicaraguan Revolution," in Walker (ed.), *Nicaragua in Revolution*, p. 66.

30  Ibid., p. 69.

31  FSLN-DN, "72 hours document," p. 17.

32  FSLN-DN, "Documentos de unificación," p. 105.

33  LeoGrande, "The United States," pp. 73–5.

34  Alejandro Bendaña, "The Foreign policy of the Nicaragua revolution," in Walker (ed.), *Nicaragua in Revolution*, pp. 319–28.

35  Shirley Christian, *Nicaragua: Revolution in the Family* (New York: Random House, 1985), p. 195; Christopher Dickey, *With the Contras: A Reporter in the Wilds of Nicaragua* (New York: Simon and Schuster, 1983), p. 105.

36  Dickey, *With the Contras*, p. 106.

37  Roy Gutman, "America's Diplomatic Charade", *Foreign Policy*, Fall 1984, pp. 4–10; Smith, "Lies About Nicaragua", pp. 94–6.

38  Peter Kornbluh, "The Covert War" in Thomas Walker (ed.) *Reagan versus the Sandinistas*, p. 24. On the history of the contra movement see also Dickey, *With the Contras*.

39  *New York Times* and *Washington Post*, Mar. 16, 1982.

40  *New York Times*, Nov. 11, 1984; *Wall Street Journal*, Mar. 6, 1985.

41  *Miami Herald*, Mar. 15, 1987.

42  Dickey, *With the Contras*; See also James LeMoyne, "Can the Contras Survive?" *New York Times Magazine*, Oct. 4, 1987; *Newsweek*, June 1, 1987; *New York Times*, Mar. 19 and 24, Apr. 23, 1985; *New York Post*, Nov. 27, 1984; *Miami Herald*, Jan. 27, 1985.

43  Letter to *New York Times*, Jan. 9, 1986.

44   Americas Watch, *Violations of the Laws of War by Both Sides in Nicaragua, 1981–1985* (New York: Americas Watch, 1985). See also Americas Watch, *Human Rights in Nicaragua* (New York: Americas Watch, 1986); *New York Times*, Nov. 25, 1984, Jan. 15, Mar. 7, Apr. 9, 1985, Mar. 10, 1987; *Washington Post*, Sept. 30, 1984, Mar. 7, 1987; *Miami Herald*, January 27, 1985.

45   Americas Watch, *Human Rights in Nicaragua 1985–1986*, p. 101.

46   Kornbluh, "The covert War," in Walken (ed.) *Reagan versus the Sandinistas*, p. 28.

47   *The CIA's Nicaraguan Manual: Psychological Operations in Guerrilla Warfare* (New York: Vintage Books, 1985).

48   Contra use of terror is described in the sources cited earlier in this section, including the Americas Watch reports and reports of journalists who have spent time with contra fighters or visited areas attacked by them. Sandinista violations of human rights, *off the battlefield*, have been systematic, though not bloody. Civil rights were suspended under the 1982 emergency decree. Under the decree, recined in 1987, *habeas corpus* was not respected. Many political suspects were held for long periods, incomunicado, often subject to severe forms of psychological torture, and tried in special courts unregulated by the procedural guarantees that still hold in ordinary courts. On the Sandinistas see the Americas Watch reports and *New York Times*, Feb. 10 and June 28, 1987.

49   Americas Watch, *The Miskitos in Nicaragua: 1981–1984* (New York: Americas Watch, 1984); Martin Diskin, et al., "Peace and Autonomy on the Atlantic of Nicaragua," *LASA Forum* 16 (Spring 1986), pp. 6–7; Martin Diskin, "The Manipulation of Indigenous Struggles," in Walker (ed.), *Reagan Versus the Sandinistas*; David Close, *Nicaragua: Politics, Economics and Society* (New York: Pinter, 1988) pp. 47–60.

50   *New York Times*, Feb. 22, Mar. 2, 1985; See also statements by the President and Secretary Schultz in *New York Times*, May 25, 1983 and Feb. 28, 1985; *Washington Post*, Aug. 8, 1983.

51   *Washington Post*, Nov. 27, 1984; *Los Angeles Times*, Mar. 3, 1985 *New York Times*, Dec. 9, 1983; *Washington Post*, Apr. 3, 1983.

52   *Los Angeles Times*, Mar. 4 and 5, 1985; *Wall Street Journal*, Mar. 6, 1985.

53   Joel Brinkley and Stephen Engleberg, (eds), *Report of the Congressional Committee Investigating the Iran–Contra Affair* (New York: Times Books, 1988), p. 55.

54   Booth, "Nicaragua"; "A balance sheet of contra aid," *Update*, Oct. 26, 1987; *San Francisco Chronicle*, April 24, 1985.

55   Americas Watch, *Violations of the Laws*.

56   "A balance sheet of contra aid"; Booth, "Nicaragua."

57   "A balance sheet of contra aid"; Booth, "Nicaragua"; E.V.K. Fitzgerald, "Una evalucion del costa economico de la agresion del gobierno estadounidense contra el pueblo de Nicaragua" (paper presented before the National Meeting of the Latin American Studies Association, Albuquerque, NM, Apr. 18–20, 1985.

58   Americas Watch, *Violations of the Laws*.

59   *Los Angeles Times*, July 20, 1987; *New York Times*, Mar. 10, 1987.

60 Fitzgerald, "Una evaluacion del costo." For a local perspective see *Los Angeles Times*, July 19, 1987.

61 *New York Times*, Oct. 21, *Washington Post*. Nov. 9, 1984.

62 *Wall Street Journal*, Apr. 3, 1985. The defensive intent of the Sandinista military is also reflected in early Sandinista plans for the armed forces – see FSLN-DN, "The 72 Hours Document", in a 1982 report by a retired US Marine officer (US Congress, House Subcommittee on Foreign Affairs, *Prepared Statement delivered by John H. Buchannan*, 97th Congress, 2nd Session, Sept. 21, 1982 (mimeographed) – and in Sandinista plans for the 1990s described in a secret government document brought from Nicaragua by Major Roger Miranda, a Sandinista defector. The Miranda document assumes that "direct invasion by American troops" is the main danger Nicaragua faces in the future and that the purpose of the military is to discourage such an attack. The document projects rapid expansion of neighborhood militia, which are to be equiped with little more than rifles. It indicates that the Sandinistas hope to obtain weapons such as anti-aircraft guns and mine-sweepers. Even the MIG jets which they apparently requested from the Soviets (but have very little chance of obtaining) would be equiped as interceptors to confront invading aircraft. See *Principles lineamientos para el perfaccionamiento organico, fortalecimiento y equipamiento del Ejercito Popular Sandinista para el periodo 1988–1990, y lineamientos preliminares para el quinguenio 1991–1995 (Dirigen I – Dirigen II)*, Oct 1987 (photocopy of typescript provided by US Department of Defense); *New York Times*, Mar. 10,1985, Dec. 13, 16–18, 20, 1987; *Washington Post*, Dec. 13, 1987; *Los Angeles Times*, Mar. 4, 1985.

63 *Wall Street Journal*, Apr. 3, 1985; US Departments of State and Defense, *The Soviet–Cuban Connection in Central America and the Caribbean* (Washington, DC: Departments of State and Defense, Mar. 1985), p. 25.

64 The lower figure for military advisors was given to the *New York Times* by Daniel Ortega. The upper figure is based on Sandinista defector Miranda's observation that there were under 500 Cuban and no more than 12 Soviet military advisors. See *New York Times*, Oct. 8 and Dec. 14, 1987.

65 Richard Stahler-Sholk, "Foreign debt and economic stabilization," in Rose Spalding (ed.), *The Political Economy of Revolutionary Nicaragua* (Boston: Allen and Unwin, 1987), p. 162.

66 Theodore Schwab and Harold Sims, "Relations with the communist states," in Walker ed., *Nicaragua: the First Five Years*, pp. 448–9.

67 *Wall Street Journal*, Apr. 3, 1985; Fitzgerald, "Una evaluación del costo," p. 28; *New York Times*, Aug. 20, 1987; *Latin America Weekly Review*, June 11, 1987.

68 Marc Edelman, "The other super power: the USSR and Latin America, 1917–1987," *NACLA*, 23 (Jan./Feb. 1987), p. 27.

69 *New York Times*, Oct. 5, 1983.

70 Robert Leiken, "Fantasies and facts: the Soviet Union and Nicaragua," *Current History*, Oct. 1984; Schwab and Sims, "Relations with the communist states," p. 461.

71 FSLN-DN, *La Dirección Nacional en el Primer Encuentro Internacional*

*de Solidaridad con Nicaragua*. Managua: FSLN, 1981, pp. 14, 98.

72  FSLN-DN, "72 hours document," p. 25.

73  FSLN-DN, "72 hours document."

74  Martin Diskin and Kenneth Sharpe, "El Salvador" in Morris Blachmann, William LeoGrande, and Kenneth Sharpe (eds.), *Confronting Revolution: Security Through Diplomacy in Central America* (New York: Pantheon, 1986), pp. 55–60.

75  Dickey, *With the Contras*, p. 72.

76  Ibid., pp.72–5, 280–2. Dickey finds support for this version of events in both interviews with participants and documents captured from the Salvadoran rebels and later released by the Reagan administration. His conclusions are supported by Robert Pastor, Latin American expert on Carter's National Security Council, in *Condemned to Repetition: The United States and Nicaragua* (Princeton: Princeton University Press, 1987), pp. 223–9.

77  Ortega, *Discurso*, pp. 15–16.

78  Dickey, *With the Contras*, p. 269.

79  *New York Times*, Feb. 12, 1981, Mar. 5, 1983, Apr. 25, 1983, July 30, 1983; *Washington Post*, Feb. 21, 1983.

80  On these diplomatic initiatives see William LeoGrande, "Rollback or containment? The United States, Nicaragua, and the search for peace in Central America," *International Security*, 2 (Fall 1986); Dennis Gilbert, "Nicaragua," in Blachmann et al., *Confronting Revolution*; Roy Gutman, "America's diplomatic charade," *Foreign Policy*, 56 (Fall 1984).

81  *Washington Post*, Apr. 17, 1982; *New York Times*, Oct. 7, 1982; *New York Times*, July 25, 1983.

82  This conclusion is supported by a 1982 National Security Council strategy document, later leaked to the press. See *New York Times*, Apr. 7, 1983.

83  *Washington Post*, Nov. 6, 1984; *New York Times*, Nov. 2, 1984; *Los Angeles Times*, Oct. 6, 1984.

84  On the public definition of Sandinista positions see Gilbert, "Nicaragua," pp. 118–22.

85  *New York Times*, Sept. 12, 1987.

86  For the text of the agreement see US Department of State, *Negotiations in Central America (Revised Edition) 1981–1987*. Washington, DC: Department of State, 1987.

87  Mar. 24, 1988.

88  *New York Times*, Mar. 25, 1988.

89  Kinzer, "Nicaragua: the Beleagured Revolution."

90  *Miami Herold*, Dec. 26, 1988.

## Conclusion

1  Peter Davis, *Where is Nicaragua?* (New York: Simon & Schuster, 1988), p. 251.

*Epilogue*

1   *Nicaragua through Our Eyes*, July 1989; *New York Times*, July 26, 1989; *Wall Street Journal*, March 31, 1989; *Financial Times*, February 13, 1989; Marc Cooper, "Soaring Prices, Plunging Hopes," *The Village Voice*, July 25, 1989.
2   *Los Angeles Times*, May 23, 1989.
3   Daniel Ortega, *Discurso, July 19, 1988* (Managua: Oficina de Prensa, 1989) and "Esta Revolucion es Irreversible," *Barricada*, July 20, 1989.
4   Nicaraguan Institute of Public Opinion, *Nicaragua Public Opinion* Interamerican's Public Opinion Series No. 7 (Los Angeles: Interamerican Research Center, 1988): *Washington Post*, March 3, 1989; *Los Angeles Times*, March 6, 1989.

# Bibliography

## Newspapers

*Barricada* (Managua)
*Barricada International* (Managua)
*Christian Science Monitor*
*Financial Times*
*Juventud Rebelde*
*Latin America Weekly Report*
*Los Angeles Times*
*Miami Herald*
*La Nación Internacional* (San José)
*National Catholic Reporter*
*New York Times*
*El Nuevo Diario* (Managua)
*El País*
*Parade Magazine*
*La Prensa* (Managua)
*Wall Street Journal*
*Washington Post*

## Sandinista Sources

Arce, Bayardo. "Arce on FSLN 'Purges, friendly separations.'" *Managua Radio Sandino*, July 17, 1985 (Foreign Broadcasting Information Service, July 19, 1985, p. P22).

Arce, Bayardo. "Arce stresses process of Sandinista reaffirmation." *Sistema Sandinista Televisión Network*, July 18, 1985 (Foreign Broadcasting Information Service, July 23, 1985, p. P22).

Arce, Bayardo. "Bayardo on FSLN Political, Ideological Views." *Radio Sandino*, Sept. 19, 1985 (Foreign Broadcasting Information Service, Sept. 24, 1985, p. P18).

Arce, Bayardo. *Discurso secreto del Comandante Bayardo Arce ante el Partido Socialista Nicaragüense (PSN)*. Washington, DC: US Department of State, 1985. [translation: *Secret Speech Before the Nicaraguan Socialist Party (PSN)*. Ibid.]

Arce, Bayardo. "El difícil terreno de la lucha: el ideologico," in FSLN-DN, *Habla la Dirección de la vanguardia*. Managua: FSLN, 1981.

Arce, Bayardo. "Entrevista." *Patria Libre*, 21 (May 1982), pp. 39–41.

Arce, Bayardo. "Estructuras de la vanguardia y tareas de la revolución." *Barricada*, Sept. 17, 1980.

Arce, Bayardo. "Extracto de la charla ofredica . . . en el Ministerio de Educación," in FSLN-DN, *La revolución a través de nuestra Dirección Nacional*. Managua: FSLN, 1980.

Arce, Bayardo. "Letter to the leaders of the Sandinista Defense Committees," in Bruce Marcus (ed.), *Nicaragua: The Sandinista People's Revolution*. New York: Pathfinder, 1985.

Arce, Bayardo. *Romper la dependencia: tarea estrategica de la revolución*. Managua: FSLN, 1980.

ATC. "Declaración de principios." *Asamblea Nacional Constitutiva* (1979).

ATC. *Pequeño vocabulario de la reforma agraria*. MIDA-INRA, Dec. 1980.

Baumeister, Eduardo, and Neira, Oscar. "Economía y political en las relaciones entre el estado y el sector privado en el proceso Nicaragüense." Paper prepared for Seminar on "Los problemas de la transición en pequeñas economías periféricas," Managua, Sept. 3–8, 1984.

Borge, Tomás. *Carlos, el amanecer ya no es una tentación*. Managua: Sindicato Nicaragua Machinery Company, n.d. [translation: *Carlos, the Dawn Is no Longer Beyond Our Reach*. Vancouver: New Star Books, 1984.]

Borge, Tomás. *Christianity and Revolution: Tomas Borge's Theology of Life*. (Introduction by Andrew Reading.) Maryknoll, NY: Orbis Books, 1987.

Borge, "Discusses His Life," *Juventud Rebelde* (Havana), Feb. 10, 1980 (Joint Publications Research Service 75341, p. 173).

Borge, Tomás. "Interview." *Le Monde Diplomatique* (Spanish edn), Sept. 1984 (Foreign Broadcasting Information Service-LAM 84–78).

Borge, Tomás. "Large scale aggression is being prepared," in Bruce Marcus (ed.), *Nicaragua; the Sandinista People's Revolution: Speeches by Sandinista Leaders*. New York: Pathfinder, 1985.

Borge, Tomás. *Los primeros pasos la revolución popular sandinista*. Mexico: Siglo XXI, 1984.

Borge, Tomás, et al. *Sandinistas Speak*. New York: Pathfinder, 1982.

Cabezas, Omar. "En el MINT ha sido el FSLN lo que el pueblo esperaba?" *Bocay: Organo de la Dirección Política del Ministerio del Interior*, 6 (Mar. 1986), pp. 24–31.

Cabezas, Omar. *Fire from the Mountain: The Making of a Sandinista*. New York: Crown, 1985.

Carrión, Luis. "'Oidos abiertos para recoger el sentir y la opinión del pueblo.'" *Barricada*, July 10, 1985.

CST. *Funciones generales y contenido de trabajo de los sindicatos y sus juntas directivas*. Managua: CST, n.d.

CST. *Principios de la CST*. Managua: CST, 1985.

CST. "Resolutions of the Assembly," in Bruce Marcus (ed.), *Nicaragua: The Sandinista People's Revolution*. New York: Pathfinder, 1985.

"Documentos de unificación," in Pineda (ed.). *La revolución Nicaragüense*. Madrid: Ed. Revolución, 1980.

"Dora María Téllez." *NACLA* (Sept.–Dec. 1986).

"Exitosa Tercera Asamblea de Cuadros y Militantes del FSLN." *Patria Libre*, 7 (1980), pp. 52–5.

Fonseca, Carlos. "Hora Zero," in *Obras*, vol. 1. [translation: "Nicaragua: Zero Hour," in Marcus (ed.). *Sandinistas Speak*.]

Fonseca, Carlos. *Obras* (2 vols). Managua: Ed. Nueva Nicaragua, 1982.

Fonseca, Carlos, "Sintesis de algunos problemas actuales," in *Obras*, vol. 1.

Fonseca, Carlos, et al. *Qué es un Sandinista?* Managua: FSLN, 1980.

FSLN. "Análisis historico de la lucha del pueblo de Nicaragua [Feb. 1979]," in Empar Pineda (ed.). *La revolución nicaragüense*. Madrid: Ed. Revolución, 1980.

"FSLN claims progress in anti-contra propaganda campaign." *Barricada*, Sept. 16, 1983 (Joint Publications Research Service 84728, p. 84).

"FSLN confirma dialogo." *La Prensa*, Oct. 17, 1981.

FSLN. "Mensaje no. 12," (1974), in Fernando Carmona (ed.), *Nicaragua: estrategia de la victoria*. Mexico: Ed. Nuestro Tiempo, 1980.

FSLN. *Plan de lucha del FSLN*. Managua: FSLN, 1984.

FSLN. "Programa del FSLN aprobado en 1969," in Manlio Tirado, *La revolución sandinista*. Mexico: Ed. Nuestro Tiempo, 1983. [translation: "The Historic Program of the FSLN," in Marcus (ed.), *Sandinistas Speak*.]

FSLN. *Propaganda de la producción*. Managua, 1980.

FSLN-DN. *Análisis de la coyuntura y tareas de la revolución popular sandinista: asamblea de cuadros Rigoberto Lopez Perez, 21, 22, y 23 de septiembre de 1979*. Managua: FSLN, 1979 (Spanish text cited as "72 Hours Document"). [translation: "The 72-hours document: the Sandinista blueprint for constructing communism in Nicaragua." Washington, DC: US Department of State, 1986.]

FSLN-DN. "Comunicado." *Barricada*, May 6, 1986.

FSLN-DN. "Comunicado." *Barricada*, May 9, 1986.

FSLN-DN. "Comunicado." *Barricada*, Sept. 16, 1980.

FSLN-DN. "Comunicado." *Barricada*, Aug. 19, 1982.

FSLN-DN. "Comunicado Oficial de la dirección nacional del FSLN sobre la religión." *Barricada*, Oct. 7, 1980. [translation: "The Role of Religion in the New Nicaragua" in Marcus (ed.), *Sandinistas Speak*.]

FSLN-DN. *La dirección nacional en el primer encuentro international de solidaridad con Nicaragua*. Managua: FSLN, 1981.

FSLN-DN. "Documentos de unificación," in Empar Pineda (ed.), *La revolución nicaragüense*. Madrid: Ed. Revolución, 1980.

FSLN-DN. *Habla la dirección de la vanguardia*. Managua: FSLN, 1981.

FSLN-DN. *On the General Political-Military Platform of the Struggle of the Sandinista Front for National Liberation*. Oakland, CA.: Resistance Publications, 1977.

FSLN-DN. *Proclama de la Dirección Nacional del FSLN de noviembre de 1986*. Managua: FSLN, 1986.

FSLN-DN. "Pronunciamiento del FSLN sobre las elecciones." *Patria Libre*, 6 (Aug. 1980). [translation: "FSLN: Statement on the Electoral Process," in Robert Leiken and Barry Rubin. *The Central American Crisis Reader*. New York: Summit Books, 1987.]

FSLN-DN. *La Revolución a traves de nuestra Dirección Nacional*. Managua: FSLN, 1980.

FSLN-DN. "Second Official Communiqué on Religion" in Ana Maria Ezcurra, *Ideological Aggression Against the Sandinista Revolution*. New York: Circus Publications, 1986.

FSLN-Secretaria de la Dirección Nacional. "Comunicado." *Barricada*, Aug. 4, 1985.

FSLN-Secretaria Nacional de Propaganda y Educatión Política del FSLN. "El Sandinismo no es democratismo." *Barricada*, Mar. 14, 1980. [Translation: "Sandinism is not 'Democratism,'" in Richard Fagen, *The Nicaraguan Revolution: A Personal Report*. Washington, DC: Institute for Policy Studies, 1981.]

FSLN-Tendencia Proletaria. *La crisis interna y las tendencias*. Los Angeles, CA: Sandinistas por el Socialismo en Nicaragua, 1978.

"Herrera on Sandinista Assembly reorganization." *Radio Sandino*, Aug. 15, 1985 (Foreign Broadcasting Information Service, Aug. 16, 1985, p. P12).

Ignatiev, Oleg, and Borovik, Genrykh. *The Agony of a Dictatorship: Nicaraguan Chronicle*. Moscow: Progress Publishers, 1979.

"Interview with Daniel Ortega." *Latin American Perspectives*, 6 (Winter 1979).

Invernizzi, Gabriele, Pisani, Francis, and Ceberio, Jesus. *Sandinistas: Entrevistas a Humberto Ortega Saavedra, Jaime Wheelock Román y Bayardo Arce Castraño.* Managua: Vanguardia, 1986.

Jimenez, Lucio. "Defense can only be assured by increasing production," in Bruce Marcus (ed.), *Nicaragua: the Sandinista People's Revolution.* New York: Pathfinder, 1985.

*Lunes socio-económico de Barricada.* Managua: Barricada and Centro de Investigaciones y Estudios para la Reforma Agraria, 1984.

Marcus, Bruce (ed.). *Nicaragua: the Sandinista People's Revolution: Speeches by Sandinista Leaders.* New York, Pathfinder, 1985.

Marcus, Bruce (ed.). *Sandinistas Speak.* New York: Pathfinder, 1982.

"Montealegre expelled from FSLN for Somocista links." *Radio Sandino Network.* Mar. 1, 1985 (Foreign Broadcasting Information Service, Mar. 5, 1985, p. P13).

Morales Aviles, Ricardo. *Obras; No paremos de andar jamás.* Managua: Editorial Nueva Nicaragua, 1981.

Núñez, Carlos. *El papel de las organizaciones de masas en el proceso revolucionario.* Managua: FSLN, 1980.

Núñez, Carlos. "La consigna es: organización, organización, y más organización." *Barricada,* Dec. 11, 1979.

Núñez, Daniel. "Reforma agraria en Nicaragua: talar los grandes arboles (Entrevista a Daniel Núñez)." *Pensamiento Propio,* 30 (Jan.–Feb. 1986), pp. 31–3.

Núñez, Orlando. *El Somocismo y el modelo capitalista agro-exportador.* Managua: Universidad Nacional Autonoma de Nicaragua, n.d..

Núñez Soto, Orlando. "The third social force in national liberation movements." *Latin American Perspectives,* 8 (Spring 1981).

Núñez, René. "Vencer es nuestra responsibilidad con la historia y con América." *Barricada,* Apr. 25, 1983.

Ortega, Daniel. "Interview." *Latin American Perspectives,* 6 (Winter 1979), pp. 117–18.

Ortega, Daniel. "La revolución y la Iglesia Católica en Nicaragua" in *Habla la Dirección de la Vanguardia.* Managua: FSLN, 1981.

Ortega, Daniel. "The Sandinista people's revolution is an irreversible political reality," in Bruce Marcus (ed.), *Nicaragua: The Sandinista People's Revolution.* New York: Pathfinder, 1985.

Ortega, Daniel. *Texto integro del discurso pronunciado ... en ocasión del cuarto aniversario, July 19, 1983.* Managua: Casa de Gobierno, 1983.

Ortega, Humberto. *Cincuenta años de lucha sandinista.* Mexico: Editorial Diogenes, 1979.

Ortega, Humberto. *Discurso del Ministro de Defensa ... en la clausura de la reunión de especialistas.* Managua: Ejército Popular Sandinista, 1981.

Ortega, Humberto. "La estrategia de la victoria," in Fernando Carmona (ed.), *Nicaragua: estrategia de la victoria*. Mexico: Ed. Nuestro Tiempo, 1980. [translation: "Nicaragua – the strategy of victory," in Marcus (ed.), *Sandinistas Speak*.]

Ortega, Humberto. *Sobre la insurrección*. Havana: Ed. de Ciencias Sociales, 1981.

Ortega, Humberto. "Un solo ejército," in FSLN-DN. *Habla la Dirección National de la vanguardia*. Managua: FSLN, 1981.

*Patria Libre*, 20–3 (Mar.–Sept. 1982).

Pineda, Empar (ed.). *La revolución nicaragüense*. Madrid: Ed. Revolución, 1980.

Pineiro, Carlos. "Jaime Wheelock interviewed." *Bohemia* (Havana), Oct. 19, 1979 (Joint Publications Research Service 74650, p. 106).

"Porque reforma agraria." *Pensamiento Propio*, 30 (Jan.–Feb. 1986), p. 34.

Ramírez, Sergio (ed.). *Augusto C. Sandino: El pensamiento vivo*, vol. 1. Managua: Ed. Nueva Nicaragua, 1984.

Ramírez, Sergio (ed.). *El pensamiento vivo de Sandino*. San José: Ed. Universitaria Centroamericana, 1974.

Ramírez, Sergio. "Los sobrevivientes del naufragio," in *Estado y clases sociales en Nicaragua*. Managua: Asociación Nicaragüense de Científicos Sociales, 1982.

Suárez, Sonia. "Elecciones y garantías." *Patria Libre*, 28 (Nov. 1983).

Tirado López, Victor. "Las enseñanzas de Carlos Marx en Nicaragua." *Barricada*, Apr. 25, 1983.

Tirado López, Victor. "Improvement in the situation of the workers is the task of the workers themselves," in Bruce Marcus (ed.), *Nicaragua: The Sandinista People's Revolution*. New York: Pathfinder. 1985.

Tirado López, Victor. "Karl Marx: The international workers' movement's greatest fighter and thinker," in Bruce Marcus (ed.), *Nicaragua: The Sandinista People's Revolution*. New York: Pathfinder, 1985.

Tirado López, Victor. "Nuestro socialismo." *Revista nicaragüense de ciencias sociales*, 1 (Sept. 1986).

Tirado López, Victor. "El pensamiento político de Carlos Fonseca Amador," in Fernando Carmona (ed.), *Nicaragua: estrategia de la victoria*. Mexico: Ed. Nuestro Tiempo, 1980.

Tirado López, Victor. *La primera gran conquista: la toma de poder político*. Managua: CST, 1985.

Tirado López, Victor, Cabezas, Omar, and Núñez, Carlos. *Primer seminario Miguel Bonilla: la universidad y la revolución*. Managua: Universidad Nacional Autonoma de Nicaragua, 1980.

Tunnerman, Carlos. *Hacia una nueva educación en Nicaragua*. Managua: Distribudora Cultural, 1983.

UNAG. *La Unión Nacional de Agricultores y Ganaderos de Nicaragua = La Organización de los Productores del Campo Nicaragüense.* Managua: UNAG, 1984.

UNAG National Executive Committee. *Main Report: National Farmers' and Cattleraisers' Union (UNAG), Fifth Anniversary, First National Congress.* Managua, Apr. 18, 1986.

Valdivia, Raul. "A discusión tareas del futuro." *Bocay: Organo de la Dirección Política del Ministerio del Interior,* 6 (March 1986), pp. 20–1.

Wheelock, Jaime. "Balance y perspectivas de la reforma agraria." Speech before the First National Congress of UNAG, Apr. 26, 1986. *Informaciones agropecuarias. Documento especial.* Managua: MIDINRA, 1986.

Wheelock, Jaime. *Entre la crisis y la agresión: la reforma agraria sandinista.* Managua: MIDINRA, 1984.

Wheelock, Jaime. "Entrevista con el Comandante Jaime Wheelock." *Barricada,* Jan. 13, 1987.

Wheelock, Jaime. "El FSLN conduce al estado y jamás lo sustituye," in FSLN-DN, *Habla la dirección de la vanguardia.* Managua: FSLN, 1981.

Wheelock, Jaime. *El futuro es del pueblo.* Managua: FSLN, 1980.

Wheelock, Jaime. *El gran desafio.* Managua: Ed. Nueva Nicaragua, 1983. [translation: "The Great Challenge," in Marcus (ed.), *Nicaragua.*]

Wheelock, Jaime. *Nicaragua: imperialismo y dictadura.* Havana: Editorial de Ciencias Sociales, 1980.

Wheelock, Jaime. "Primer Congreso Nacional Campesino. Balance y perspecitvas de la reforma agraria." *Informaciones Agropecuarias.* (MIDINRA). Documento Especial, Apr. 26, 1986.

Wheelock, Jaime. "The Sandinista Front is the organization of the working people," in Marcus (ed.), *Nicaragua.*

Wheelock, Jaime. "Solo queremos la soberania." *El Nuevo Diario,* Dec. 10, 1981.

Wheelock, Jaime. "Speech to National Council of the CST." *Radio Sandino* (Managua, 1983; Joint Publications Research Service 83215).

Wheelock, Jaime, and Carrión, Luis. *Apuntes sobre el desarrollo económico y social de Nicaragua.* Managua: FSLN, n.d.

**Other Sources**

"Agrarian reform undergoes changes in Nicaragua." *Update,* 5 (Feb. 7, 1986).

Alaniz Pinell, Jorge. *Nicaragua: una revolución reaccionaria*. Costa Rica: Kosmos, 1985.

Alegría, Claribel and Flakoll, D.J. *Nicaragua: la revolución sandinista: una crónica política, 1855–1979*. Mexico: Ed. Era, 1982.

Americas Watch. *Human Rights in Nicaragua*. New York, Americas Watch, 1984.

Americas Watch. *Human Rights in Nicaragua, 1985–1986*. New York: Americas Watch, 1986.

Americas Watch. *Violations of the Laws of War by Both Sides in Nicaragua, 1981–1985*. New York: Americas Watch, 1985.

Amnesty International. *Nicaragua: The Human Rights Record*. New York: 1986.

Amnesty International. *Republic of Nicaragua*. London: 1977.

Arellano, Jorge Eduardo. *Lecciones de Sandino*. Managua: Ed. Distribudora Cultural, 1983.

Arellano, Jorge Eduardo. "Nicaragua," in E. Dussel, et al (eds.). *Historia general de la Iglesia en América Latina*, vol. 6. Salamanca: Ed. Sigueme, 1985.

Arias, Pilar. *Nicaragua: revolución: relatos de combatientes del frente sandinista*. Mexico: Siglo veinteuno, 1980.

"A Balance Sheet of Contra Aid." *Update*, Oct. 26, 1987.

Barndt, Deborah. "Popular education," in Thomas Walker (ed.). *Nicaragua: The First Five Years*. New York: Praeger, 1985.

Belausteguigoitia, Ramón de. *Con Sandino en la hora de la paz*. Madrid: Espasa-Calpe, 1934.

Belli, Humberto. *Breaking Faith: The Sandinista Revolution and its Impact on Freedom and Christian Faith in Nicaragua*. Westchester, IL: Cross Way Books, 1985.

Belli, Humberto. *Nicaragua: Christians under Fire*. San José: Instituto Puebla, n.d.

Bendana, Alejandro. "The foreign policy of the Nicaraguan revolution," in Walker (ed.). *Nicaragua in Revolution*. New York: Praeger, 1982, pp. 319–28.

Bermann, Karl. *Under the Big Stick: Nicaragua and the United States since 1848*. Boston: South End Press, 1986.

Berryman, Phillip. "Basic Christian communities and the future of Latin America." *Monthly Review*, 36 (July/August 1984), pp. 27–40.

Berryman, Phillip. *Liberation Theology*. New York: Pantheon, 1987.

Berryman, Phillip. *The Religious Roots of Rebellion: Christians in the Central American Revolutions.*. Maryknoll, NY: Orbis, 1984.

Biderman, Jaime. "Class structure, the state and capitalist development in Nicaraguan agriculture. "Unpublished Ph.D. thesis, University of California, Berkeley, 1982.

Blachmann, Morris, LeoGrande, William, and Sharpe, Kenneth (eds.). *Confronting Revolution: Security Through Diplomacy in Central America*. New York: Pantheon, 1986.

Black, George. *The Triumph of the People: The Sandinista Revolution in Nicaragua*. London: Zed, 1981.

Bolaños, Enrique. "Discurso ... clausurando la Asamblea Anual de INDE ... el 13 de marzo de 1986." Managua: COSEP, 1986 (xerox typescript).

Bolaños, Enrique. *Linea directa: Entrevista radial*. Managua: no publisher, 1984.

Booth, John. *The End and the Beginning: The Nicaraguan Revolution*. 2nd edn. Boulder, Colo.: Westview, 1985.

Booth, John. "Nicaraguan," in *Latin and Caribbean Contemporary Record: 1987*. New York: Holmes and Meier, forthcoming.

Brinkley, Joel. "CIA primer tells Nicaraguans how to kill." *New York Times*, Oct. 17, 1984.

Brinkley, Joel and Stephen Engelberg (eds). *Report of the Congressional Committees Investigating the Iran–Contra Affair*. New York: Times Books, 1988.

Brown, Robert McAfee. *Theology in a New Key; Responding to Liberation Themes*. Philadelphia: Westminster, 1978.

Browning, David, *El Salvador: Landscape and Society*. Oxford: Oxford University Press, 1971.

Bukharin, N.I. and Preobrazhensky, E. *The ABC of Communism: A Popular Explanation of the Program of the Communist Party of Russia*. Ann Arbor: University of Michigan Press, 1966.

Cabestrero, Teofilo. *Revolucionarios por el Evangelio: Testimonio de 15 Cristianos en el Gobierno Revolucionario de Nicaragua*. Bilbao: Editorial Descleede Brouwer, 1983.

Carmona, Fernando (ed.). *Nicaragua: estrategia de la victoria*. Mexico: Ed. Nuestro Tiempo, 1980.

Castaneda, Jorge. *Contradicciones en la revolución*. Mexico: Extra, 1980.

Castillo, Captain Rodrigo. "El ejército: una gran escrula." *Revista Segovia: Organo de la Dirección Política del E.P.S.* 8 (April 1986).

Castro, Fidel. "Address to the Congress of the Young Communist League," *Grandma*, Apr. 18, 1982.

Chance, James. "The End of the Nicaraguan War?" *New York Review of Books*, Oct. 8, 1987, p. 30.

Christian, Shirley. *Nicaragua: Revolution in the Family*. New York: Random House, 1985.

"Church and politics: internal upheaval and state confrontation in Nicaragua." *Update*, 5. Central American Historical Institute (Jan. 21, 1986).

"The church of the poor in Nicaragua." *Envio*, 5 (Apr. 1985).

CIA. *Directory of the Republic of Nicaragua: A Reference Aid.* CR 86-11702, May 1986.

*The CIA's Nicaraguan Manual: Psychological Operations in Guerrilla Warfare.* New York: Vintage Books, 1985.

Cleary, Edward. *Crisis and Change: The Church in Latin America Today.* Maryknoll, NY: Orbis Books, 1985.

Cliff, Tony. *Lenin.* Vol. 3. London: Pluto Press, 1976.

Cohen, Betsy, and Hynds, Patricia. "The manipulation of the religion issue," in Thomas Walker (ed.). *Reagan versus the Sandinistas: The Undeclared War on Nicaragua.* Boulder, Colo.: Westview, 1987.

Colburn,, Forrest. "Nicaragua's Agrarian Reform." (Unpublished MS.)

Colburn, Forrest. *Post-Revolutionary Nicaragua: State Class and the Dilemmas of Agrarian Policy.* Berkeley: University of California Press, 1986.

Collins, Joseph. *Nicaragua: What Difference Could a Revolution Make?* 3rd edn. New York: Grove Press, 1986.

"Comentarios y aclaraciones a las partes importantes de la ley." *Consejo de Estado*, 2 (1981): pp. 25–9.

Comisión Catequística Arquidiocesana. *Principles dificultades en la lectura de la Biblia (punto de vista católico).* Managua: Archdiocese of Managua, n.d..

Conferencia Episcopal de Nicaragua. "A la Dirección Nacional del Frente Sandinista." Managua, Oct. 17, 1980 (mimeo).

Conferencia Episcopal de Nicaragua. "Carta pastoral del Episcopado Nicaragüense [Nov. 17, 1980]." *Cuadernos DEI*, 2(n.d.), pp. 15–31.

Conferencia Episcopal de Nicaragua. "Carta pastoral del Episcopado Nicaragüense sobre la reconciliación." Managua, Apr. 22, 1984.

Conferencia Episcopal de Nicaragua. "Mensaje de la Conferencia Episcopal al pueblo Católico y a todos los Nicaragüenses." Managua, July 31, 1979 (mimeo).

Consejo de Estado. *Primera Legislature 1980 ... Instauración del Consejo de Estado.* Managua, 1980.

"Contribution to Hegel's *Philosophy of Right.*" in Robert C. Tucker (ed.). *The Marx-Engels Reader.* 2nd edn. New York: Norton, 1978.

COSEP. *Análisis sobre la ejecución del programa de Gobierno de Reconstrucción Nacional.* Managua, 1980.

Darlington, Sandy. "The Bible, the Frente and the Revolution." *Christianity and Crisis*, 45 (July 22, 1985) pp. 299–302.

Deere, Carmen Diana. "Agrarian reform, peasant participation and the organization of production in the transition to socialism," in Richard Fagen, C. D. Deere, and José Luis Coraggio (eds). *Transition and Development: Problems of Third World Socialism.* New York: Monthly Review, 1986.

Deere, Carmen Diana, Marchetti, Peter, and Reinhardt, Nola, "The peasantry and the development of Sandinista agrarian policy, 1979–1984." *Latin American Research Review*, 20 (1985), pp. 75–109.

D'Escoto, Miguel. "Palabras del Padre D'Escoto al finalizar el Viacrucis." *Amanecer*, 40–2 (Jan.–May), p. 31.

Deutscher, Isaac. *The Prophet Armed: Trotsky 1879–1921*. New York: Oxford University Press, 1954.

Dickey, Christopher. *With the Contras: A Reporter in the Wilds of Nicaragua*. New York: Simon and Schuster, 1983.

Diederich, Bernard. *Somoza and the Legacy of U.S. Involvement in Central America*. New York: Dutton, 1981.

Diskin, Martin, and Sharpe, Kenneth. "El Salvador," in Morris Blachman, William LeoGrande, and Kenneth Sharpe (eds). *Confronting Revolution: Security Through Diplomacy in Central America*. New York Pantheon, 1986.

Diskin, Martin, et al. "Peace and autonomy on the Atlantic coast of Nicaragua: a report of the LASA Task Force on Human Rights and Academic Freedom." 2-part article. *LASA Forum*, 26 (Spring 1986) and 27 (Summer 1986).

Dodson, Michael, and Montgomery, T. S. "The Churches in the Nicaraguan Revolution," in Walker (ed.). *Nicaragua in Revolution*. New York: Praeger, 1982.

Dodson, Michael, and O'Shaughnessy, Laura. *The Other Revolution: The Church and the Popular Struggle in Nicaragua* (forthcoming).

Dorner, Peter, and Quiros, Rodolfo. "Institutional dualism in Central America's agricultural development." *Journal of Latin American Studies*, 5 (1973), pp. 220–32.

Draper, Theodore. "The rise of the American junta." *New York Review of Books*, Oct. 8, 1987, pp. 48–9.

Edelman, Marc. "The other super power: the USSR and Latin America, 1917–1987." *NACLA*, 23 (Jan./Feb. 1987), p. 27.

Edmonds, Patty. "Obando talk with U.S. Executive told in Memo." *National Catholic Reporter*, July 20, 1984.

Engels, Friedrich. *Herr Eugen Dühring's Revolution in Science (Anti-Dühring)*. New York: International Publishers, 1939.

Erlick, June. "If Reagan backs off Cardinal will leave post." *National Catholic Reporter*, Mar. 2, 1984.

Ezcurra, Ana Maria. *Ideological Aggression Against the Sandinista Revolution: The Political Opposition Church in Nicaragua*. New York: Circus Publications, 1984.

FAO (UN Food and Agriculture Organization), *Trade Yearbook*, vols. 31–9. Rome, 1977–85.

*Fe Cristiana y Revolución Sandinista en Nicaragua.* Managua: Instituto Histórico Centroamericano, 1980.

Fitzgerald, E.V.K. "Una evaluación del costo económico de la agresión del gobierno estadounidense contra el pueblo de Nicaragua." Paper presented before the National Meeting of the Latin American Studies Association, Albuquerque, NM, Apr. 18–20, 1985.

Florez-Estrada, Maria and Lobo, José. "La consigna es sobrevivir." *Pensamiento Propio*, 33 (May–June 1986): pp. 25–30.

Gilbert, Dennis. "Nicaragua," in Blachmann et al., *Confronting Revolution: Security Through Diplomacy in Central America.* New York: Pantheon, 1986.

Girardi, Giulio. *Sandinismo, Marxismo, Cristianismo en la nueva Nicaragua.* Mexico: Ed. Nuevomar, 1986.

Goodsell, James. "Nicaragua," in Robert Wesson (ed.). *Communism in Central America and the Caribbean.* Stanford, CA: Hoover Institution Press, 1982.

Gorman, Stephen. "Power and consolidation in the Nicaraguan revolution." *Journal of Latin American Studies*, 13 (1981).

Gorman, Stephen, and Walker, Thomas. "The armed forces," in Thomas Walker (ed.). *Nicaragua: The First Five Years.* New York: Praeger, 1985.

Gutiérrez, Gustavo. *A Theology of Liberation.* Maryknoll, NY: Orbis, 1971.

Gutman, Roy. "America's diplomatic charade." *Foreign Policy*, 56 (Fall 1984).

Harris, Richard, and Vilas, Carlos (eds). *Nicaragua: A revolution Under Siege.* Totowa: Zed Books, 1985.

Hodges, Donald. *Intellectual Foundations of the Nicaraguan Revolution.* Austin: University of Texas Press, 1987.

Hollander, Paul. "Research on Marxist Societies." *Annual Review of Sociology*, 8 (1982), pp. 340–3.

"La Iglesia Católica en Nicaragua despúes de la revolución." *Envio: Informes.* Dec. 1983.

Inter-American Development Bank. *Economic and Social Progress in Latin America: 1978 Report.* Washington, DC: IDB, 1979.

The International League for Human Rights. *Report on Human Rights in Nicaragua.* New York, 1986.

Jerez, César. *The Church and the Nicaraguan Revolution*, Justice Papers No. 5. London: Catholic Institute for International Relations, 1984.

John Paul II. "Carta del Papa a los Obispos de Nicaragua."

Junta de Gobierno de Reconstrucción Nacional. "Comunicado." *Barricada*, Sept. 16, 1980.

Junta de Gobierno de Reconstrucción Nacional. "Decreto No. 782." July 19, 1981.

Junta de Gobierno de Reconstrucción Nacional. "Programa de la Junta de Gobierno de Reconstrucción Nacional." *Comercio Exterior* (Mexico), 29 (August 1979), p. 898.

Kaimowitz, David. "Nicaraguan debates on agrarian structure and their implications for agricultural policy and the rural poor." *Journal of Peasant Studies*, 14 (Oct. 1986).

Kaimowitz, David, and Stanfield, David. "The organization of production units in the Nicaraguan Agrarian Reform." Paper presented at International Studies Association Meetings. Mar. 1985.

Kaimowitz, David, and Thome, Joseph. "Nicaragua's agrarian reform: the first year (1979–1980)," in Walker (ed.). *Nicaragua in evolution*, pp. 223–40.

Kinzer, Stephen. "Nicaragua: the Beleagured Revolution." *New York Times Magazine*, Aug. 28, 1983.

Kinzer, Stephen "Nicaraguas combative archbishop."

Kinzer, Stephen. "Portrait of a powerful Sandinista." *New York Times*, Sept. 3, 1985.

Kornbluh, "The covert war," in Thomas Walker (ed.). *Reagan versus the Sandinistas: The Undeclared War.* Boulder, Colo.: Westview, 1987?.

*Latin America Political Report*, Aug. 11, 1978.

Leiken, Robert. "Fantasies and facts: the Soviet Union and Nicaragua." *Current History* (October 1984).

Lemoyne, James. "Can the contras survive?' *New York Times Magazine*, Oct. 4, 1987.

Lenin, V. I. "The attitude of the Workers' Party to religion," in *Collected Works*, vol. 15.

Lenin, V.I. *Collected Works*. 45 vols. Moscow: Progress Publishers, 1960–70.

Lenin, V.I. *Selected Works: One Volume Edition.* New York: International Publishers, 1971.

Lenin, V.I. "Socialism and religion," in *Collected Works*,vol. 10.

LeoGrande, William. "Rollback or containment? The United States, Nicaragua, and the search for peace in Central America." *International Security*, 2 (Fall 1986).

LeoGrande, William. "The United States and the Nicaraguan Revolution," in Thomas Walker (ed.). *Nicaragua in Revolution.* New York: Praeger, 1982.

Liebman, Marcel. *Leninism under Lenin.* London: Jonathan Cape, 1975.

"Low-Key First Day for Daniel Ortega." *Latin America Weekly Report*, Jan. 18, 1985.

Luciak, Ilja A. "National unity and popular hegemony: the dialectics of Sandinista agrarian reform policies, 1979–1986." *Journal of Latin American Studies*, 1 (May 1987), pp. 113–40.

Luciak, Ilja A. "Popular democracy in the new Nicaragua: the case of rural mass organization." *Comparative Politics*, 1 (Oct. 1987), pp. 35–55.

Macaulay, Neil. *The Sandino Affair*. Chicago: Quadrangle Books, 1967.

"The man behind the designer glasses." *Time*, Mar. 31, 1986.

Marx, Karl. *Capital*, vol. 1. Many editions.

Marx, Karl. "Contribution to Hegel's *Philosophy of Right*," in Robert C. Tucker (ed.), *The Marx-Engels Reader*, 2nd edn. New York: Norton, 1978.

Marx, Karl. *The Eighteenth Brumaire of Louis Bonaparte*. New York: International Publishers, 1969.

Marx, Karl, "The Fetishism of Commodities," in *Capital* 1, 1, 4.

Marx, Karl. "On the Jewish question" and "Theses on Feuerbach," in Robert C. Tucker (ed.). *The Marx-Engels Reader*. 2nd edn. New York: Norton, 1978 and similar collections.

McCartney, Robert. "Sandinista foes always intended to boycott vote." *Washington Post*, July 30, 1984.

MIDINRA. *Evaluación–Investigación del modelo "CAS" de reforma agraria*, Dec. 1985 (typescript).

Miller, Valerie. "The Nicaraguan literacy crusade," in Thomas Walker (ed.). *Nicaragua in Revolution*. New York: Praeger, 1982.

Millett, Richard. *Guardians of the Dynasty*. Maryknoll, NY, 1977.

Molyneux, Maxine. "Women," in Thomas Walker (ed.). *Nicaragua: The First Five Years*. New York: Praeger, 1985.

"Nicaragua: continued decline in 1987." *Latin America Economic Report*, Dec. 31, 1986.

"Nicaragua en la encrucijada." *Envio*, Monografico No. 9 (June 1983), pp. 30–1.

"Nicaragua: Factores políticos conducionan reforma agraria." *Infopress Centroamericana*, Apr. 9, 1987.

"The Nicaraguan peasantry gives new direction to agrarian reform." *Envio*, 4: 51 (Sept. 1985), pp. 1c–19c.

Nichols, John. "The news media in the Sandinista revolution," in Thomas Walker (ed.). *Nicaragua in Revolution*. New York: Praeger, 1982.

Nolan, David. *FSLN: The Ideology of the Sandinistas and the Nicaraguan Revolution*. Miami: Institute of Inter-American Studies, University of Miami, 1984.

O'Brien, Conor Cruise. "God and Man in Nicaragua." *Atlantic Monthly* (Aug. 1986).

O'Shaughnessy, Laura. "The conflicts of class and world view: theology in the post-revolutionary Nicaragua." Paper delivered at the Annual Meeting of the Southeastern Council of Latin American Studies, San Juan, Puerto Rico, April 1983.

*El Papa en Nicaragua: analisis de su visita*. Madrid: IEPLA, 1983.

"La participación de sacerdotes en cargos de gobierno: cronología de hechos." *Centro Regional de Informaciones Económicas*, 76–7 (July 1981).

Pastor, Robert. *Condemned to Repetition*. Princeton: Princeton University Press, 1987.

Perez-Stable, Marefeli. "Pluralismo y poder popular: entrevista con Sergio Ramírez." *Areito*, 9 (1983).

Petras, James. "Nicaragua in transition." *Latin American Perspectives*, 2 (Spring 1981).

"Playboy Interview: The Sandinistas." *Playboy*, Sept. 1983, p. 63.

Pravera, Kate. "The base Christian community of San Pablo: an oral history of Nicaragua's first CEB." *Brethren Life and Thought*, 29 (Autumn 1984), pp. 206–15.

*Principales lineamientos para el perfaccionamiento organico, fortalecimiento y equipmento del Ejercito Popular Sandanista para el periodo 1988–1990, y lineamientos preliminares para el quinquenio 1991–1995 (Dirigen I-Dirigen II)*, Oct. 1987. Photocopy of typescript provided by US Department of Defense.

Randall, Margaret. *Christians in the Nicaraguan Revolution*. Vancouver: New Star Books, 1983.

Randall, Margaret. *Sandino's Daughters: Testimonies of Nicaraguan Women in Struggle*. Vancouver: New Star Books, 1981.

Reding, Andrew. "Getting to know Managua's new Cardinal." *Christianity and Crisis*, July 22, 1985.

Reding, Andrew. "Nicaragua's new constitution." *World Policy Journal*, 2 (Spring 1987), pp. 257–94.

"Reforming the agrarian reform." *Nicaragua Through Our Eyes*, 1:4, pp. 11–12.

Ruchwarger, Gary. "The Sandinista mass organizations and the revolutionary process," in Richard Harris and Carlos Vilas (eds.). *Nicaragua: A Revolution Under Siege*. Totowa: Zed Books, 1985.

Rudolph, James (ed.) *Nicaragua: A Country Study*. Washington, DC: USGPO, 1982.

Schwab, Theodore, and Harold Sims. "Relations with the Communist States" in Thomas Walker (ed.). *Nicaragua: The First Five Years*. New York: Praeger, 1985.

Selser, Gregorio. *Sandino*. New York: Monthly Review Press, 1981.

Serra, Luis. "The grassroots organizations" in Thomas Walker (ed.). *Nicaragua: The First Five Years*. New York: Praeger, 1985.

Sholk, Richard. "The national bourgeosie in post-revolutionary Nicaragua." *Comparative Politics*, 16 (Apr. 1984).

"Slow motion toward a survival economy." *Envio*, 63 (Sept. 1986).

Smith, Wayne. "Lies about Nicaragua." *Foreign Policy* (Summer 1987).

Somoza, Anastasio. *El vadadero Sandino o el calvario de las segovias.* Managua: Tipografía Robelo, 1936.

Stahler-Sholk, Richard. "Foreign debt and economic stabilization," in Rose Spalding (ed.). *The Political Economy of Revolutionary Nicaragua.* Boston: Allen and Unwin, 1987.

Teaching authority of the Church (Magisterium)." *New Catholic Encyclopedia,* vol. 13. New York: McGraw Hill, 1967, pp. 959–65.

Teller, Charles. "The demography of malnutrition in Latin America." *Intercom,* 9 (1981).

Thome, Joseph, and Kaimowitz, David. "Nicaragua's agrarian reform: the first year (1979–1980)," in Thomas Walker (ed.). *Nicaragua: The First Five Years.* New York: Praeger, 1985.

Tirado, Manlio. *La revolución sandinista.* Mexico: Ed. Nuestro Tiempo, 1983.

United Nations. *1978 Statistical Yearbook.* New York, 1979.

United States Congress. House Subcommittee on Foreign Affairs, prepared statement delivered by John H. Buchannan, 97th Congress, 2nd Session, Sept. 21, 1982.

United States Department of State. *Background Paper: Central America.* Washington, DC: Department of State, 1983.

United States Department of State. *Negotiations in Central America (Revised Edition) 1981–1987.* Washington, DC: Department of State, 1987.

United States Departments of State and Defense. *The Soviet–Cuban Connection in Central America and the Caribbean* (Washington, DC: Departments of State and Defense, Mar. 1985), p. 25.

Vilas, Carlos. "Democracía popular y participación obrera en la revolución Sandinista." *Estudios Sociales Centroamericanos,* 35 (1983), pp. 95–138.

Vilas, Carlos. "The Workers' movement in the Sandinista revolution," in Richard Harris and Carlos Vilas (eds.). *Nicaragua: A Revolution Under Siege.* Totowa, Zed Books, 1985.

Wald, Alan. "Some perspectives on the FSLN." *Against the Current,* Jan.–Feb. 1987, pp. 5–10.

Walker, Thomas (ed.). *Nicaragua in Revolution.* New York: Praeger, 1982.

Walker, Thomas (ed.). *Nicaragua: The First Five Years.* New York: Praeger, 1985.

Walker, Thomas (ed.). *Reagan versus the Sandinistas: The Undeclared War on Nicaragua.* Boulder, Colo.: Westview, 1987.

Weber, Henri. *Nicaragua: the Sandinista Revolution.* London: Verso, 1981.

Williams, Dan. "The Sandinista Front: dogma and discipline." *Los Angeles Times.* Apr. 18, 1985.

Williams, Harvey. "The social impact in Nicaragua," in Thomas Walker (ed.). *Reagan versus the Sandinistas: The Undeclared War on Nicaragua.* Boulder, Colo.: Westview, 1987.

Williams, Phillip. "The Catholic hierarchy in the Nicaraguan revolution." *Journal of Latin American Studies*, 17, pp. 341–69.

Williams, Robert. *Export Agriculture and the Crisis in Central America.* Chapel Hill: University of North Carolina Press, 1986.

Wilson, Anthony. "Nicaragua's private sector and the Sandinista revolution." *Studies in Political Economy*, 17 (Summer 1985).

Zalkin, Michael. "Agrarian policies and the marketing of corn and beans in Nicaragua, 1979–1984." Paper delivered at the 1985 meetings of the Latin American Studies Association.

Zalkin, Michael. "Peasant response to state grain policy in revolutionary Nicaragua." Paper at the 1986 meetings of the Latin American Studies Association.

# Index

*Index compiled by Meg Davies*